MIXED MEDIA

Moral Distinctions in Advertising, Public Relations, and Journalism

MIXED MEDIA

Moral Distinctions in Advertising, Public Relations, and Journalism

Thomas H. Bivins
University of Oregon

LEA LAWRENCE ERLBAUM ASSOCIATES, PUBLISHERS
2004 Mahwah, New Jersey London

Lawrence Erlbaum Associates, Inc., Publishers
10 Industrial Avenue
Mahwah, NJ 07430

Cover design by Kathryn Houghtaling Lacey

Library of Congress Cataloging-in-Publication Data

Mixed Media: Moral Distinctions in Advertising, Public Relations, and Journalism, by Thomas H. Bivins.

ISBN 0-8058-4257-8 (pbk: alk. paper).

Includes bibliographical references and index.

Copyright information for this volume can be obtained by contacting the Library of Congress.

Books published by Lawrence Erlbaum Associates are printed on acid-free paper, and their bindings are chosen for strength and durability.

Printed in the United States of America
10 9 8 7 6 5 4 3

Contents

INTRODUCTION **ix**

1 WHAT MAKES AN ETHICAL ISSUE? **1**

Ethics or Morals? *1*
Ethics and the Act of Communication *2*
The Media and Morality *3*
Are the Media Prone to Ethical Dilemmas? 3
The Media Are Not Us 4
Media Culture and the Clash of Priorities 5
The Effects of Organizational Structure on Moral Decision Making 7
Moral Excuses 9
Can Personal Ethics Become Professional Ethics? *10*
Media Similarities: The Common Threads *11*
Media Differences: A Coat of Many Colors *13*
Media Goals 13
Media Loyalties 16
Forming Ethical Standards for the Mass Media *17*
Values, Ideals, and Principles *18*
Professional Codes and the Law *20*
Can the Media Be Ethical? *22*
Exercises *23*
Case Study: *Newsweek* and the Death of a Story *23*
Case Study Questions *25*
Case Study: Patriotism in the Newsroom *26*
Case Study Questions *27*

2 MORAL CLAIMANTS, OBLIGATION, AND SOCIAL RESPONSIBILITY 28

The Linkage Concept *29*
The Importance of Consequences *32*
The Nature of Obligation *33*
Synthesizing the Approaches *37*
The Libertarian Approach *40*
The Social Responsibility Approach *41*
Exercises *44*
Hypothetical: Education for Sale *45*
Questions for Hypothetical 46
Case Study: Profits Versus Professional Obligation *46*
Case Study Questions *48*

3 THE MEDIA AND PROFESSIONALISM 49

Central Features *50*
Secondary Features *50*
Are the Media Professions? *51*
Service to Society *53*
The Public Journalism Debate *54*
Pro Bono Work *55*
The Professional–Client Relationship *57*
Journalism and the Paternalistic Model 58
Advocacy and Agency 60
The Fiduciary Model 61
Trust and the Professional–Client Relationship 62
Can the Fiduciary Model Work? 66
Codes *66*
Profession Versus Professionalism: If It Walks Like a Duck . . . *70*
Exercises *71*
Hypothetical: The Terrorist Manifesto *71*
Questions on Hypothetical *72*
Case Study: Defining a Journalist *72*
Case Study Questions *73*

4 ETHICAL THEORY 74

Why Can't We All Be Right? The Dilemma of Relativism *75*
Subjectivism *75*
The Test of Reason *76*
Why We Reason the Way We Do *77*
Social Contract Theory *78*
Plato 79

Aristotle 81
Thomas Hobbes 82
John Locke 83
Jean-Jacques Rousseau 84
The Argument Over Means and Ends *86*
Nonconsequential Ethical Theories *86*
Immanuel Kant 87
Nonconsequential Theory in Modern Practice *90*
Consequential Ethical Theories *91*
Egoism 92
Utilitarianism 93
Modern Utilitarianism 95
Virtue Ethics 98
History of Virtue Ethics 98
Virtue Ethics in Modern Practice 100
Free Speech Theories *102*
Benedict Spinoza 103
John Milton and the Marketplace of Ideas 103
The Marketplace of Ideas in Modern Times 104
The Liberty Theory *106*
Free Speech and the Individual Versus Society *108*
How to Choose Applicable Theories *112*
Exercises *114*
Hypothetical: Free Speech or Freedom From Fear *115*
Questions on Hypothetical *116*

5 TO TELL THE TRUTH 117

Truth as a Legal Concept *118*
Defamation 119
Invasion of Privacy 120
Truth and the Act of Communication *121*
Journalistic Truth *122*
Journalistic Deception *123*
Truth in Advertising and Public Relations *125*
Ethics and Persuasion *129*
The Art of Persuasion 131
The Strategies of Persuasion 131
Guidelines For Ethical Persuasion 134
Can We Tell the Truth From Fiction? *135*
Consumers: Victims or Informed Choosers? *137*
The Case for Withholding Information *138*
The Ultimate Truth *140*
Exercises *142*
Hypothetical: Deceptive Advertising *142*
Questions on Hypothetical *143*
Hypothetical: PR and the Gun Lobby *143*

Questions on Hypothetical *144*
Case Study: To Air or Not to Err *144*
Case Study Questions *146*

6 AVOIDING HARM **147**

Causal Harm *149*
Professional Responsibility *150*
Liberty-Limiting Principles *151*
The Harm Principle 151
The Offense Principle 152
The Principle of Legal Paternalism 153
The Principle of Legal Moralism 153
Mitigating Harm in Journalism *154*
Mitigating Harm in Advertising and Public Relations *156*
Caring and Harm *159*
Can the Media Care? 162
Persuasive Models and Care 163
The Right Thing to Do *166*
Exercises *167*
Case Study: Arthur Ashe and Invasion of Privacy 168
Case Study Questions *169*

7 A CHECKLIST FOR ETHICAL DECISION MAKING **172**

A Checklist for Moral Decision Making *174*
An Example *180*
Rules *183*
Summary *185*
Hypothetical: Sports Team Names *186*
Further Analysis *187*

APPENDIX: MEDIA CODES OF ETHICS **188**

REFERENCES **222**

AUTHOR INDEX **225**

SUBJECT INDEX **227**

Introduction

Media professionals spend a great deal of time talking about "doing the right thing." Why is it then that the consumers of mass media perennially find so much fault with the "ethics" of the disseminators of news, information, and entertainment? What has led the purveyors of mass communication to believe and act the way they do? Do they have a special obligation for ethical behavior that ordinary citizens do not; or do they, in fact, have a special waiver of the basic moral tenets that the rest of us must accept in order that we may have access to a "free marketplace of ideas"? These are the questions we must ask ourselves if we are to be moral agents of the mass media.

This book is designed to familiarize you with the tools needed to make moral decisions regarding the use of mass media, both as a consumer of the "products" of the media and as a potential or actual working member of the media. You should realize from the outset that there are no "right" answers in this book—only answers that are "most appropriate" in certain situations. To whom they are the most appropriate is a major concern of this book. Many questions will be asked, and many answers will be discussed. Ultimately, it will be up to you to draw your own conclusions about the rightness of the answers you choose to accept. It is to be hoped that you will come away with a greater appreciation for the complexities of making a moral decision. At the very least, you will be forced to develop a personal yardstick by which to measure your decisions.

THE SCOPE OF THIS BOOK

This book has been written with three primary mass media industries in mind: the news media (journalism), advertising, and public relations. Although entertainment media, such as television and the movie industry, are certainly worth investigating, these three are the ones most likely to attract the future practitioners now learning their craft in the journalism and communication programs so prevalent in our colleges and universities today. The lessons learned concerning truth and harm as they apply to these three industries are lessons that can be applied to any other form of communication, information based or otherwise.

In addition, much has already been written concerning the entertainment industries and their effect on our culture. And, certainly, volumes have been penned bemoaning the state of modern journalism. However, advertising and, especially, public relations are often given short shrift or—worse—compared with journalism, assuming that the moral dictates of the one will apply across the board to the others. That is rarely the case, and this book is designed to point out the differences that exist among these three practices in hopes that reasonable and specific guidelines can be developed by which they may be analyzed and, if need be, judged according to their specialized functions within our society. Ultimately, the dicta of truth and minimizing harm should apply to all mass media, but in differing doses and for decidedly different reasons.

THE STRUCTURE OF THE BOOK

The only possibility of arriving at anything approaching a satisfactory response to our moral dilemmas lies not with rote answers to prepackaged questions, but with real sweat that comes only from real thinking. And real thinking can only happen if the thinkers understand as much how to think as what to think about.

The ethical dilemmas faced by the mass media are not unique to them alone; however, the appropriate responses to those dilemmas are often dictated by the position of importance the media hold in our society. The media are different enough from the rest of society as to require a different set of ethical guidelines. And they are different enough from each other so that no single set of standards suffices for all of them. They differ in a great many ways: Chief among these are their differing goals and loyalties. In chapter 1, we look at their similarities and differences and discuss whether there is any common ground on which to evaluate media behavior.

The media are powerful but, like the rest of us, they do not operate in a vacuum. Because they are an integral part of our society, everything they do affects everything else. And, like the rest of us, they are obligated to a great many people by virtue of those effects. Many journalists will say that they are not obligated in any way except by their "natural" charge to serve the public interest. However, no media institution can ignore the potential harm it does by ill-considered or knee-jerk decisions. Obligation is at the heart of much that is presented in this book. Although our society strongly favors individual freedom, we also recognize that without community we are simply isolated and self-interested beings. Somewhere, a balance must be struck between individual autonomy and community interests. The news media have traditionally shown a mistrust of anything that smacks of subjectivity. They claim that their professional autonomy is impugned each time they are asked to care. On the other hand, both advertising and public relations are nothing if not subjective. They, however, are asked to care as much for their audiences as for their clients—a task that may be as difficult to carry out as that of the subjective journalist. To whom the media are obliged and why are discussed in chapter 2, and frequently throughout the book. It is a central theme of this text.

If the media are professions, as some claim, then they must consider the consequences of their actions on all affected parties. This doesn't mean that they must cater to all interests. It means that they should at least recognize all interests. Professionals value autonomy, possibly above all else. Without the ability to make decisions free from outside pressure, the education and expertise of the professional would be wasted. However, part and parcel of being a professional is the charge to serve the public interest and to mitigate harm to those affected by any actions taken on behalf of a client or a "public good." Professional status brings with it a duty to honor professional standards; it does not imply a total disregard of personal ethics or societal norms. Professional ethics are discussed in chapter 3.

A good portion of this book is devoted to exploring how ethical theories can be applied in modern-day moral decision making. Don't be afraid of these theories. After all, they represent merely the thoughts of those who would have us act "morally," or in the "right" way. It is clearly impossible to bring every relevant theory to bear in any single book; however, there are certain theorists who are repeatedly mentioned in leading texts on applied ethics in fields from business to medicine, law to mass media. You will find that they, like us, don't always agree with one another. You will also find that parts of their theories are arguable. That's the nature of theories. As Mark Twain said, "There's . . . [a] trouble about theories: there's always a hole in them somewheres . . . if you look close enough." Ethical theory and its application to the modern media is discussed in chapter 4.

No media professional can justify lying. To tell the truth is the first (and some would say, the only) commandment of professional communicators. Certainly, it is as important to advertising and public relations as it is to journalism; however, the way in which the truth is revealed can be quite different and can offer special challenges to media professionals. Both truth and lying can hurt, and mitigating harm is one of the chief obligations of the media. Harm can be confined to a few or encompass millions. At the heart of any attempt to avoid harm is a responsibility to care about those whom we affect by our actions—care enough to honor their dignity and preserve both their integrity and ours. Ultimately, telling the truth and avoiding harm is what media ethics is all about. Virtually every dilemma faced by the media today boils down to either truth or harm, or both. We must recognize the different "truths" of the media professions in order that we may set realistic standards for this greatest of obligations. We must also care enough about our audience that the thought of harming them, even incidentally, will give us pause. And if we pause long enough, we may come up with a solution to our dilemmas that results in the least amount of harm being done to anyone. After all, the media exist to help, not to harm. The vital considerations of truth and harm are taken up in detail in chapters 5 and 6.

Finally, chapter 7 outlines a method for ethical decision making based on the many questions dealt with in this book and on a thorough understanding of the theories presented here. This worksheet is an admission that there are multiple factors affecting moral decision making and myriad approaches to solving ethical dilemmas. It is also designed to lead you through the process in a way that encourages you, as a moral agent, to consider the full range of variables inevitably involved in moral decision making.

CAN IT WORK?

A great many decisions are made under deadline pressure, nearly all of them the result of experience. Let us add to that experience the ability to weigh the pros and cons of the ethical facets of our decisions. Certainly it is true that practice makes perfect and that the more we practice moral decision-making skills the more finely honed they will become. After all, the public doesn't necessarily fault the media for coming down on one side of an issue or the other as much as it faults them for doing so in a seemingly knee-jerk way, or for falling back on their First Amendment rights as the only justification for their actions. If we can simply prove to them that we thought about these dilemmas seriously before making an educated decision, we may actually gain some respect.

Ultimately, the lessons learned in each such process serve not only to better our ability to make decisions, but also to better our professions as we become more productive, and more ethical, members of the mass media.

CHAPTER

1

What Makes an Ethical Issue?

ETHICS OR MORALS

Would you feel worse if someone called you unethical or if someone called you immoral? Most of us react differently to these two words, but we can't quite pin down the reason why. From a purely definitional standpoint, "ethics" comes from the Greek word *ēthikos* which, in turn, comes from *ēthos*, which means *character, custom*, or *manners*. "Moral" comes from the Latin word *moralis*, which comes from *moris*, which means essentially the same thing as *ēthos* did to the Greeks. However, ethics has come to be recognized as the study of concepts such as *ought, should, duty*, and so on, while "moral" tends to be attached to activities that are either good or bad and to the rules that we develop to cover those activities. Some prefer to think of morals as being culturally transmitted indicators of right and wrong and of ethics as merely a way to determine what we ought to do.

Let's go back to our original question: Would you feel worse if someone called you unethical or if someone called you immoral? If you're like most respondents, you picked "immoral." Why? Because we tend to associate immorality with the Judeo-Christian concept of sin; and, because of the long-standing Puritan heritage within our culture, sin is most often equated with evil. "Unethical," on the other hand, has become a more acceptable term in our modern culture because it tends not to carry the connotation of *evil* doing; rather, it is used most often to connote *wrong* doing (versus doing right). In a sense, to be called ethical or unethical rather than moral or immoral seems to be a reflection of modern connotation rather than representative of any real differences in meaning. In fact, it wouldn't be improbable to suggest that the words "ethical" and "unethical" would more likely be heard (if at all) in newsrooms and media agencies than "moral" and "immoral."

For our purposes, however, the terms will be used pretty much interchangeably, except when noted otherwise. In fact, the technical term for making ethical decisions is *moral decision making*, a term that will be used throughout this book.

ETHICS AND THE ACT OF COMMUNICATION

Communication is basic to being human and is essential for social interaction. But because communication plays a significant role in influencing others and because intent is so important as a motivation, the likelihood that ethical issues will arise as a result of communication is great indeed. The fact that media practitioners consciously choose specific means of communication in order to reach a desired end generally guarantees that issues of right and wrong will arise.[1]

Most of us accept that much media-originated speech is designed to influence, in one way or another, our attitudes and behaviors. We distinctly do not, however, accept that speech will or should be allowed to force us into a particular attitude or behavior through such methods as coercion. According to First Amendment scholar C. Edwin Baker, "speech generally depends for its power on the voluntary acceptance of the listeners. . . ." Thus, speech would normally be considered noncoercive. (This point becomes clearer in chapter 5 when we discuss the extent to which audiences recognize speech as being either one-sided or balanced.) Baker contrasts this normally benign nature of speech with its counterpart, coercive speech:

> In general, a person coercively influences another if (1) she restricts another person to options that are worse than that other person had moral or legitimate right to expect, or (2) she employs means that she had no right to use for changing the threatened person's options.[2]

Coercion, thus, does not refer to how severe or effective the pressure or influence applied is but to the impropriety of the form of pressure—for example, deceptive speech. Seen in this light, coercion would have to force another into a position he or she would not have been in but for the act of the communicator. Further, Baker suggests that speech may be deemed co-

---

[1]Richard L. Johannesen, *Ethics in Human Communication*, 5th ed. (Prospect Heights: Waveland Press, 2002), p. 3.

[2]C. Edwin Baker, *Human Liberty and Freedom of Speech* (New York: Oxford University Press, 1992), pp. 57–60.

ercive if a "speaker manifestly disrespects and attempts to undermine the other person's will and the integrity of the other person's mental processes."[3] We have a great deal more to say on the concept of respect for the "other person" in later chapters, especially chapters 5 and 6.

It is clear, then, that the act of communication is inextricably bound up with the potential for ethically questionable practices. How mass media communicators unravel that knot is the subject of the rest of this book.

THE MEDIA AND MORALITY

Whether the media simply reflect our cultural morality or whether they directly influence that morality is a question of considerable debate and disagreement. Undeniably, the media influence our lives in myriad ways—some good, some not so good. We rely on them for information vital to our daily lives, including everything from hurricane alerts to the variety of products available for headache relief. They also sell us ideas and images we might not otherwise be exposed to were it not for the "mass" nature of the media. They can, and sometimes do, remind us of the joys of being human; but just as often they pander to our basest instincts.

The media reflect our lives in a number of ways as well. We see ourselves in newscasts, we wonder with commentators at the seeming increases in violence and other undesirable cultural trends, and we increasingly enjoy ever speedier and flashier entertainment. In fact, the debate over whether the media contribute to or merely reflect societal mores is really a false one. It is ridiculous to think that they don't do both. They do reflect what we are right now, sometimes distilled so much as to be simply a caricature, but reflective none the less. They also constantly test our reactions to change, and back off only when it becomes unprofitable for them not to do so. They may not innovate as much as many would like, but they do evolve, and so influence us in often subtle ways. Is this necessarily bad? No. All societies are organic in the sense that they are constantly changing. Modern mass media are both reflective of that change and effective agents of it.

Are the Media Prone to Ethical Dilemmas?

Truth be told, we are all probably prone to as many ethical dilemmas in our daily lives as most media people. Why, then, do we seem to attach so much importance to what the media do? The answer is varied and complex. First of all, the ethical dilemmas we face each day may not affect large numbers

[3]Baker, *Human Liberty*, p. 59.

of people. Our decision to tell that white lie when our best friend confronts us with a new (and questionable) hairstyle affects only the two of us, at least initially. But an editor's decision to run a questionable photo on the front page of the paper affects a great many people. An advertising executive's decision to run an ad symbolically demeaning women affects more than just the agency and the advertised product. Likewise, a public relations practitioner's decision to defend a political candidate's character when that character is clearly questionable certainly has ramifications far beyond the candidate himself and his personal life. These examples, and thousands like them, serve to point out the very public nature of media.

The media are not called mass media for nothing. Our individual daily actions aren't, in Humphrey Bogart's famous words, "worth a hill of beans" when compared to actions that affect the lives of millions. It is only logical, therefore, that the decisions the media make should come under closer scrutiny than our own. Additionally, there is some feeling that the media are playing a very different role from the one average citizens play, in that they are acting to inform us on matters about which we would otherwise have little knowledge. In fact, the rationale used by nearly all forms of media (journalism, advertising, and public relations included) is that they are performing a public service by adding to the "marketplace" of information. However, that public service is certainly questionable given the amount of criticism leveled at all forms of media today. In fact, the notion that the media *should* perform a public service tends to set them apart from the rest of society and sets up an "us–them" attitude that is not totally without basis.

The Media Are Not Us

In other words, although the media in some cases represent us (as consumers of media) and in other cases represent others, in only the rarest of instances do they represent us directly. There is a school of thought that paints the news media, for instance, as the representative of the people, acting on their behalf in a watchdog function over government and other public agencies. However, that function is as much self-serving as not. We must never forget that the media also operate within a capitalistic system, not just a democratic one, and that we purchase the news as much as we purchase any other commodity. That relationship is, therefore, not totally one of representation; it is one also of exchange.

The democratic foundations of this country clearly indicate a place for the media. Many of the top thinkers of the 18th and 19th centuries held the role of the press to be a necessary component of a democratic system. Thomas Jefferson called the press "the best instrument for enlightening the mind of man."[4] In his later life, however, even he spoke out against the abuses of the media of his day. The problem in understanding the place of the media in our democracy is that the media today are not constituted the same way that the media of our country's founders envisioned. By the 20th century, they had become imbued with all the trappings of modernity, and critics of the media such as John Dewey and Walter Lippmann were starting to believe the media no longer played an influential role in the democratic process. They had become, in the opinions of many, ineffective and self-serving, seeking only to entertain or impart their own opinions. The media had become estranged from the very society they were supposed to serve. Certainly, they, especially the news media, changed as a result of such scrutiny in the early part of the 20th century. Objectivity became the driving goal of journalism. Despite these changes, however, the media remain different from the people they serve, so different, in fact, that the average person doesn't really know what the media do—and, especially, how they makes their decisions.

To realize that the media are not us is not necessarily to denigrate them or their role in our society. It is simply to realize that the decisions the media make today are not always on our behalf (a subject treated in more detail in chap. 3). For example, when a local television news program airs a segment on a town meeting, it is, ostensibly, in the public interest. However, are the segments filled with entertainment also in the public interest? How much of the news is there simply to attract our attention? How much is there to help us? When an advertising agency decides (with its client's approval) to run a series of ads depicting violence or using sexually charged visuals, is it in our best interest or in the interest of selling the product? Do public relations practitioners act on our behalf when they use spin control to obfuscate the facts? The point is that the media are separate entities existing in a complex and competitive environment, and they can't always afford to act in our best interest. They must, of necessity, sometimes act in their own interests. What we would hope for, however, is that those instances would be limited to necessity and become not the rule but the exception.

Media Culture and the Clash of Priorities

When shiny new journalists, advertising executives, or public relations practitioners take their first jobs, they often do so with great expectations that they will be able to honor their personal ethical codes above all else. What a shock it is for them to discover that the industries in which they have chosen to work already have a pretty fair idea of how things should be

[4]Thomas Jefferson, letter to M. Corey, 1823, Washington ed. vii, 324, Archived at Monticello. Can be accessed through the Jefferson Digital Archive, http://etext.virginia.edu/jefferson/

done and have set their own principles that they expect will be used. This socialization is common to all media industries and even begins when many of these neophytes are still in school.

Ask a budding young journalist whether there are any circumstances under which the media should be censored (by others or even by themselves), and you will invariably receive an instantaneous and emphatic, No! Similarly, ask an advertising major at any leading university whether there is a definition of "taste" that he or she would be willing to follow in creating ads for their clients, regardless of what the client wants. Guess what the answer will be?

A good example of how quickly socialization takes place was detailed by students from the School of Journalism and Communication at the University of Oregon recounting their experiences when thrust, suddenly, into the real world of crisis news gathering. A number of students were pressed into service by leading news organizations during the shootings at Thurston High School in Springfield, Oregon, in 1998. Their experiences make for an interesting case study in media socialization. Some simply accepted the roles they were assigned, adrenaline pumping. Others, not yet having shaken the thinking processes forced on them by the routine of daily education, worried over the ethicality of their actions when asked, for example, to confront grieving parents for interviews mere hours after the deaths of their children.

We should not be surprised, then, that longtime media practitioners adhere, almost religiously, to principles and codes derived from real-world experience rather than any ivory tower contemplation. For example, at a recent meeting of a student chapter of the Society of Professional Journalists (SPJ), a local news director was asked whether an incidence of undercover reporting by a local television news organization was deceptive and thus in violation of the ethical code of the SPJ. The news director responded that such codes were made up by people who didn't understand the realities of real-life journalism. He was wrong, of course. The SPJ code was drafted by working journalists, the same as the major codes of both public relations and advertising were drafted by professionals in those areas. Unfortunately, this attitude pervades newsrooms and advertising and public relations agencies all across the country and is one of the chief obstacles to moral decision making.

In his book *Democracy Without Citizens*, Robert Entman says that the key to understanding modern journalism is to realize that it operates within the context of organizational structures and routines, and that these structures and routines provide for what he calls "news slant." In other words, the very way in which news is gathered and the routines of the process itself have had a detrimental effect on journalism. According to Entman, the media "are stymied on the demand side by the lack of public hunger for relevant information, and on the supply side by overreliance on elite services and the industrial imperatives of efficiency and profits."[5] The hunt for greater profit has led, in turn, to a need for efficiency, resulting, finally, in a routine of dependency on whatever method of news gathering is easiest and fastest.

This media laziness, although not universal, is prevalent enough to be of concern. Deadline pressure has always been a part of news gathering but the move toward greater efficiency is the direct result of economic pressure. The proliferation of magazine news programs on network television speaks directly to this approach. Hidden cameras, exposés, and other "investigative" techniques are very often the easiest methods of gathering some kinds of information (and certainly more attention getting), and the resulting magazine news programs are often cheaper to produce and run than sitcoms and dramas, which are most often purchased from production companies.

When the priority of news gathering becomes to get the story fast, the temptation is great to shortcut not only the process but also any inclination to ponder troubling questions of ethicality. In short, the economic imperative may far outweigh the moral imperative.

The Effects of Organizational Structure on Moral Decision Making

Pressures on decision makers are not limited to economic factors. The roles we take on as media practitioners also imply a responsibility to perform certain functions associated with those roles. "Responsibility" could be defined as a *bundle of obligations associated with a job or function*. In other words, responsibility refers to more than just the primary function of a role; it refers to the multiple facets of that function. Reporters are responsible for covering newsworthy events, for example. As part of that responsibility, they are expected to present a fair and balanced account from an objective viewpoint. However, a more important question can be asked when assessing the ethical implications of roles associated with the media (or any occupation, for that matter): Does responsibility naturally equate with accountability? "Accountability" refers to *blaming or crediting someone for an action*—normally an action associated with a recognized responsibility.[6] The assumption, therefore, would be to hold a person responsible for an action also accountable for the results of that action. This

[5]Robert Entman, *Democracy Without Citizens: Media and the Decay of American Politics* (New York: Oxford University Press, 1989), pp. 17–18.

[6]Bernard Gert, *Morality: A New Justification of the Moral Rules* (New York: Oxford University Press, 1988), pp. 214–215. Gert prefers to use *credit* instead of *praise*, as some others hold, since it is the proper opposite of *blame* as a "responsibility standard"; whereas, *praise* and its opposite, *condemnation*, are considered to be moral standards.

position assumes that the responsible person is relatively autonomous, or free to make decisions associated with his or her job without outside pressure or influence. And, under normal circumstances, we would hope that media practitioners—especially journalists—would have that autonomy. However, the nature of outside influence has changed considerably over the past 25 years or so. Today, the most troubling influences on all forms of media can, and often do, come from the inside.

For example, can a major news organization that is overseen, or run directly, by an entertainment division make entirely autonomous decisions about its reportage? As the three major network news operations (ABC, NBC, and CBS) can attest, the job of news becomes undeniably complex when the news division is subsumed by a large, non-news-oriented organization (Disney, General Electric, and Viacom, respectively). And when entertainment value is believed by nonnews people to supersede news value (and those people are tacitly in charge), the groundwork is laid for a decision-making hierarchy that will gradually dilute the authority of media practitioners to follow their own personal and professional directives.

Furthermore, the temptation to pass the buck on decisions of all types, including moral decisions, increases mightily as the organizational hierarchy becomes more complex. Increasingly, media are becoming big business. Newspapers are owned by conglomerates; public relations and advertising are often partners under the same ownership; and everywhere the entertainment function often overrides the information function. Decision making, likewise, is becoming attenuated, with accountability spread thin throughout large and complex organizations. As pointed out earlier, the structure of the modern news organization, for example, plays a determining role in how news is gathered. In the same way, the structure of large organizations of any type tends to affect the way in which decisions are made.

Complex organizations tend toward decentralized decision making, which, in turn, calls for professionalized decision makers at every level.[7] The ideal would be for both the responsibility and the accountability of decision making to correlate. However, these same organizations lend themselves too readily to a dilution of accountability in decision making. "Moral buck passing" becomes the rule rather than the exception. It is too easy to blame others for decisions over which we have had minimal input or control. The public relations practitioner who is caught in a deception can, too easily, blame her client. An advertising executive can attempt to justify a tasteless ad as a client-based decision. Reporters can slough off blame for invasion of privacy on their editors. The softening of network news can be

---

[7]James Grunig and Todd Hunt, *Managing Public Relations* (New York: Holt, Rinehart, and Winston, 1984), p. 100.

blamed on pressure from above. This failure to assume accountability for our actions because of "orders" from above is frequently referred to as the "Bormann defense," after the Nazi war criminal who uttered the now famous excuse, "I was only following orders." Although this analogy may seem to some to be extreme, the tendency toward moral buck passing will not lessen as long as organizational hierarchy encourages the dilution of responsibility and accountability.

As human beings, we seek accountability. We want to know who is responsible for certain actions and who is accountable for the consequences of those actions. The dilution of accountability now common to most large organizations (including media organizations) frustrates onlookers who can't determine who is to blame when something goes wrong. This confusion is exacerbated when factors other than media influence play a role in certain consequences. Consider the string of school shootings in 1998–1999. It was not uncommon to hear parents and others place much of the blame for what they considered copycat shootings on media coverage—and on media violence in general. The tendency to place blame is entirely normal; however, the degree of accuracy involved in assessing accountability is problematic at best.

Moral Excuses

Are there circumstances in which rational people will hold others not accountable for their actions, even though they are responsible? Most of us recognize a legitimate excuse when we hear one. There are several common excuses that we typically accept as valid when assessing blame. *Constraint*, for instance, refers both to physical imperatives and lack of alternatives. For example, if a person is coerced into doing something that he normally would not do, we tend not to blame him for that action. A bank clerk who is robbed at gunpoint is certainly responsible for the money in his till, but is not accountable for its loss. This is a physical constraint. The same would apply in a situation in which a person is constrained by lack of alternatives. For instance, a company is ordered to comply with new EPA regulations, but the technology needed to comply hasn't been fully developed yet. It cannot be held accountable for noncompliance until the technology is ready to go on line (as long as the company is attempting to comply in a timely fashion.).

We also tend to forgive in instances in which the outcome of an action could not reasonably have been predicted. An excellent example of this occurred in 1996 when *Newsweek* magazine decided to run a story on the U.S. Chief of Naval Operations Admiral Jeremy Michael (Mike) Boorda. It had come to the magazine's attention that the admiral was possibly wearing bronze Vs, signifying *valor*, on two of his 16 merit ribbons—an honor he had not technically earned. Although Boorda had been on combat duty aboard ship during the Vietnam War, he had not actually been in combat—a requirement for the attachment of the V to his ribbons. The admiral's office was contacted by *Newsweek* and an interview date was set. Shortly before the interview was to take place, Boorda committed suicide. Was the magazine in any way accountable for this tragedy? The newsworthiness of this story could certainly be questioned. Boorda had already discontinued wearing the ribbons several years before. What possible motive could *Newsweek* have for wanting to run a story this long after the fact? Even assuming for the moment that the story might have had some news value, we must still ask ourselves whether *Newsweek* could reasonably have expected that the subject of its story would commit suicide over the disclosure that he was assuming an honor he did not, in fact, earn? Probably not. Despite this, however, we must still consider in what way the magazine contributed to the final outcome and question whether or not the harm could have been mitigated or avoided altogether. This is a subject we take up in detail in chapter 6.

Let us return briefly to the notion that accountability for moral decision making has become diluted in modern mass media organizations. If this is, in fact, even partly true, what is to become of our personal ethical standards once we become enveloped in the complexities of mass media structures and routines?

CAN PERSONAL ETHICS BECOME PROFESSIONAL ETHICS?

So far, we've been talking about the elements of modern media that make compromising personal principles highly likely; however, there are other principles not usually questioned by the media that also potentially compromise personal values—the importance of privacy, for instance. For journalists, personal views on the importance of privacy can potentially be overridden by a professional principle of providing the public with information useful to them. The obligations incurred by an individual assuming a professional role may, in fact, differ radically from personal obligations. For example, it may never be appropriate for a private individual to reveal secrets about someone that might result in that person's reputation being ruined, even if the information is true. Take that same private individual and make her a journalist whose job is to investigate the extramarital love affair of the president of the United States, and her actions might not only be deemed appropriate, they might prove to be necessary.

The point is that when we adopt a profession whose entire reason for being is to provide information, we may find that the obligations of that job supersede those of our personal lives. By letting our personal principles take first priority, we could be compromising our professional principles. The question then becomes, which do we want most to be, a private citizen or a media professional? Although the two roles are not mutually exclusive, there is an awareness that one assumes the mantle of professionalism willingly, accepting that a muting of personal values is part of the payment for doing so.

This does not mean that we suddenly become immune to human suffering or deaf to pleas for civility or good taste. It simply means that professional values may, and often do, outweigh personal values. A good example, and one that is dealt with in more detail in chapter 6, has to do with harm. From a perspective of needing to mitigate harm that might be caused by our actions, we must decide how much harm we will allow before the option that would bring about that harm is no longer viable. The first two choices are easy: If more harm than benefit will occur because of our action, we should refrain from taking it. If more benefit than harm is likely to accrue, we should take the action. However, what are we to do when the harm and the benefits are equal? A personal principle might tell us to err on the side of caution and not take the action. But what about our professional obligations? What do they dictate? As a journalist, for instance, the decision about whether or not to run a story may depend on the amount of harm versus benefit that might transpire as a result. If the benefit outweighs the harm—publish. If the harm outweighs the benefit—don't publish. If harm and benefit appear to be equal—publish. Why? Because our default position as a professional journalist is to provide information unless there is a good reason not to. And although this may differ from our personal obligations, it should none-the-less be honored. After all, that is the path we have chosen to take.

To some degree, personal and professional principles will certainly mesh. However, deference is usually, and possibly rightly, given to professional principles. After all, those principles ideally have been established for good reasons—reasons that go beyond satisfying personal values. The ultimate test of any principle, personal or professional, must be the efficacy of the resulting actions based on those principles—not just for the person acting (the moral agent), but for all those involved in or affected by the action.

MEDIA SIMILARITIES: THE COMMON THREADS

The media are alike in a number of ways. The most common connection is that they are all mass media; that is, they deliver their information to mass audiences and/or seek to inform or influence large audiences through mass distribution of messages. Aside from their mass nature, however, the media are similar in other ways as well.

From an ethical perspective, they all are obligated to moral claimants: those who have some stake in our decisions, who are affected by what we do or say. We discuss the nature of this obligation to our moral claimants in detail in the next chapter. For now, we can assume that journalism, advertising, and public relations all have claimants to whom they are obligated, be they employers, clients, or various other constituencies. In fact, as discussed in chapter 3, some degree of obligation to the public interest is, at least tacitly, part of the assumed duties of all of these occupations.

The media under discussion here all profess a duty to truth telling. The ideal of truthful information is at the heart of all communication and is assumed as the normal default in our everyday exchanges with each other. Any mass medium without a basic obeisance to truth would fail to impress any of its constituents. This is not to say that all mass media treat truth the same way, or even define it the same way. It does indicate, however, the place of truth telling in our basic conception of communication. Truth is discussed more fully in chapter 5.

In addition to truth telling, the mass media share a duty to avoid harming their constituents. This is one of the most difficult areas to assess because each of the mass media, again, tends to define harm differently. However, to the extent that harm is an undesirable outcome of most, legitimate mass communication, its avoidance is a shared desire among the media. It serves no purpose, for instance, for advertisers to intentionally harm their markets. When this does occur (as in cigarette advertising), we are quick to grasp the ethical implications. Harm is discussed in more detail in chapter 6.

Finally, the mass media also share a need for credibility, for without credibility their messages are less effective, even unbelievable (regardless of how truthful they may be). Credibility is closely tied to truth telling. Sources known for their veracity are more likely to be held as credible, and looked to for information in the future. Credibility can be damaged in a number of ways. News outlets can lose credibility by lack of accuracy or by seeming to be biased. Advertisers lose credibility by peddling false claims or by insensitivity to market tastes. Public relations practitioners lose credibility by not being open enough in their dealings with news media. And these are only a few examples of how credibility can be compromised. A mass medium without credibility is doomed to have its message ignored by its proposed target audience. Credibility also implies trust, a topic taken up when we discuss the professional nature of the mass media in chapter 4.

Ultimately, however, it's not by their similarities that we tend to distinguish among the media, but by their differences. It would be a false assumption to believe that we can judge the ethicality of any action taken in one form of media by the template used to judge another. To some degree, the similarities will help us reach a common ground from which we may then depart into an exploration of the differences. In order to successfully discuss media ethics, we must fully understand what sets the media apart, but we must not ignore the ways in which they are alike—despite protestations to the contrary.

MEDIA DIFFERENCES: A COAT OF MANY COLORS

Although the media are set apart from society in some ways, they are also set apart from each other in ways that are often even more significant. For instance, while truth telling may be a primary value among all the media, how that value is constituted and how it is honored may be quite different. And, while the public is definitely a major stakeholder in any media activity, the ethical obligation to that public may be conceived of in very different ways by the different media. Perhaps the most instructional way to envision the key differences among the media is to investigate two important aspects: their goals and their loyalties.

Media Goals

What do the media hope to accomplish? The answer to that question points directly to the major differences among the media. The goals established by the various media are sometimes explicit, sometimes implicit. Increasingly, those goals include turning a profit (a goal we sometimes pretend is unique to today's world). Profit is certainly an acceptable goal in a capitalist system, but it should not be the only goal—especially given the expectations we place on our media in this country. Our expectations, to a large degree, also shape the goals of the media. However, all communication has in common a primary set of goals. Which of the set is used at any given time depends on the medium and the purpose to which the communication is being put. The most common of those goals are information dissemination, persuasion, and entertainment. Naturally, each of these approaches to communication can overlap the others, and each can be used in support of the others. For example, an advertisement may be entirely informative; however, its ultimate goal may be to persuade. Entertainment may be used to introduce information or to make the persuasive process more palatable. In most public relations campaigns, for instance, informational communication usually precedes communication aimed at attitude or behavioral change. With this in mind, let's take a look at the most likely goals of each of the media in question.

Goals of the News Media. What would you imagine to be the primary goal of the news media? The received ideal, of course, is that the United States is based on the notion of popular rule. Public opinion (the basis of that rule) is to be expressed periodically through elections, and opinion, in turn, can best be cultivated by a free and vigorous press. Can we infer from this ideal, then, that the goal of the news media (or journalism in general) is to keep the electorate informed? If we still believe in the ideals of journalism, we must accept this as the primary goal. After all, doesn't the First Amendment guarantee the right to a free press? Although not explicitly stated in that amendment, the obligation of the media is generally understood to be as stated above: providing, first, information we need to fulfill our roles as citizens.

As we've come to expect, however, there is more than one goal involved here. The news media also give us what we *want*, which typically leads to a sort of dynamic tension between the two extremes. It is a given that in order to provide us with what we need, the media also often have to provide us with what we want. In the early part of the 20th century, philosopher John Dewey envisioned a press that would combine insider information and popular appeal. He knew that giving us only what we needed would prove a useless endeavor. Striking that balance between the "medicine" and the "spoonful of sugar" needed to get it down may be modern journalism's greatest test. In the words of communications scholar Richard Johannesen: "The search is for an appropriate point between two undesirable extremes—the extreme of saying only what the audience desires and will approve and the extreme of complete lack of concern for and understanding of the audience."[8]

Clearly, then, the goal of the news media is to bring the public information that both informs and interests them. Let's leave it at that for the time being and move on to two other, vastly different, forms of media: advertising and public relations.

Goals of Advertising. The argument has been made, somewhat successfully, that both advertising and public relations, like the news media, provide important information to the public. Advertising, for instance, has long claimed that the information it provides is of vital interest to (and in fact is needed by) the public. This view has been supported by the U.S. Supreme Court, which held that the public's decisions regarding commercial purchases need to be "intelligent and well informed" (Virginia Pharmacy Board v. Virginia Consumer Council, 1976), clearly placing advertising communication in the category of *needed* information. Given this, what then would you suppose the goal of advertising to be?

---

[8]Richard L. Johannesen, *Ethics in Human Communication*, 5th ed. (Prospect Heights: Waveland Press, 2002), p. 4.

Certainly one of the goals is to inform the public about the availability of various products and services and give details about them. But couldn't we also say that the ultimate goal of advertising is to sell something? Although the first goal seems to align nicely with that of the news media, in that the information provided is designed to lead us to a knowledgeable decision, the second goal tends to strike us as indicating a decidedly vested interest. However, couldn't we say the same sort of thing about the news media? Isn't the combination of information and entertainment now so adroitly packaged by nearly every news outlet designed to "sell" us the news? Is this any different than advertising? The answer, of course, is yes. Even conceding that news may be packaged to sell, the "product" we end up with is still information we need (in the ideal sense, at least). The product we end up with in response to advertising is vastly different. The primary goal of advertising, then, is more likely to be to sell a product than to impart information. Like public relations, however, advertising may inform or entertain in order to persuade eventually.

Goals of Public Relations. Like the news media and advertising, one of the primary goals of public relations is to inform. The goal of information dissemination can be the sole purpose of communication, as when performed by a government public information officer or as published in those countless booklets from the FCIC in Pueblo, Colorado. As mentioned earlier, public relations often begins with information, then moves to persuasion; however, depending on the overall goal of the campaign, public relations communication, like advertising, can begin directly with persuasion. And, like advertising, the information produced by public relations can also be viewed as contributing to the marketplace of ideas. In fact, this is a point that needs to be made on behalf of both advertising and public relations. There is a school of thought that holds that public communication of any kind potentially contributes to public debate.

I. F. Stone, in *The Trial of Socrates*, traces the history of Western democracy to the living democracy of the ancient Greeks—specifically the Athenians—who valued open discourse above all else. In fact, the idea that human beings had intelligence sufficient to be reached by reasoned argument was so embedded in Athenian culture that they designed a goddess of persuasion.[9] Stone suggests that such a divinity represented not only democracy, but also the ideal way to achieve it: persuasion through reasoned discourse. To many early Greek philosophers, *rhetoric* implied persuasion. So important was the ability to represent oneself in open debate, that an entire class of teachers of rhetoric evolved (Sophists) whose purpose was to

---

[9]I. F. Stone, *The Trial of Socrates* (Boston: Little Brown & Company, 1988), p. 207.

teach the methods of persuasion to those unfortunate enough to not have been born into the landed aristocracy.

If we trace the rise of modern democracy to those Greek roots, we can draw a parallel as well between persuasion as a cornerstone of the entire political system and the necessity for providing each citizen a voice in that system, regardless of the issue or political alignment. It could be said that the provision of such ability serves the public interest in the ideal way—by providing for a free, balanced, and open debate among democratic equals. In this sense, both advertising and public relations parallel the theory of journalism, which is based on the belief that the public good is being served through the free expression of its practice. The very notion of a free press relies on the understanding of how such a device fits into and contributes to the ideal of free speech, which is most often construed to mean a citizen's right of access to all sides of an issue.

Ultimately, however, public relations must admit to sharing with advertising the time-honored goal of persuasion through communication—a goal not in the least ignoble. But it must also not succumb to the temptation to make more of its motives than they legitimately merit. Public relations is not journalism, and needn't have any pretense to the goals of that practice in order to become legitimate. Both it and advertising are justifiable professions in their own rights.

Media Loyalties

One of the major differences among the media is the issue of loyalty. "Loyalty" can be defined as *faithfulness* or *allegiance*. Loyalty also implies that something is owed to that to which we are loyal. Loyalty can be contractual, as in advertising and public relations (at least in most cases), or it can be implied, as in the news media's obligation to their public. In either event, the sense of owing or being obligated is part and parcel of what being loyal means. Here is where we begin to see real differences among the media, for where our loyalty lies is generally where our best efforts are devoted.

Loyalty in the News Media. Once we concede that the implied goal of the news media is to inform us, it is easier to understand where their loyalties should lie. Clearly, there would be an obligation to their primary constituency (the public) to bring them information that both informs and interests them. (Interests in the sense that it is information the public wants.) Because we discuss claimants (ethical stakeholders) in detail in chapter 2, it is sufficient here to say that the loyalties of the news media are necessarily split. As noted, the primary claimant here is the public; however, loyalty must also extend to stockholders, publishers, owners, and so on. Thus, the reality of economic viability will certainly intrude on loyalty to the public; but for our purposes let us assume that, in an ideal sense, first loyalty goes to the public receiving the information. In fact, the value that most journalists place on autonomy (the ability to remain largely free from outside pressure) practically insures that they will consider the public as their number one claimant.

Loyalty in Advertising and Public Relations. At this point, it should be coming clear that for many purposes advertising and public relations have a good deal in common and are, thus, separated from journalism in some important ways. Loyalty is one of the most important of those ways.

Both advertising and public relations are client-based occupations. That is, they serve clients rather than the general public. The degree to which the purpose of either advertising or public relations is advocacy rather than counseling will determine the priority of loyalties. An advocate usually acts as an agent of the client, performing some service on the client's behalf or representing the client's interests.

Advocates are expected to be subjective—that is the nature of advocacy. Subjectivity brings with it an implicit understanding that one's first allegiance is to the client. To the advocate falls the job of bringing skills of persuasion to bear through methods and on issues often predetermined by the client. Since advocates often have no hand in arriving at either the focus or the nature of their advocacy, the question arises as to whether they can be expected to consider the broader implications of their actions—a question we take up shortly. At this point, suffice it to say that client loyalty generally supersedes loyalty to any third party for both advertising and public relations.

FORMING ETHICAL STANDARDS FOR THE MASS MEDIA

Can we arrive at shared standards for the mass media? Probably not. Shared standards are not possible if we look at the various mass media as having different goals and differing sets of obligations to their constituencies. Whether they are shared or not, ethical standards of any type will require a devotion to ethical action, and ethical action often comes in conflict with our instinct to act in our own self-interest. This tendency toward egoism is manifested at every level of our lives and is reflected not only in our actions but also in our deep-seated sympathy for the tenets of self-interest. We innately understand the desire of our employer to turn a profit, or of our media conglomerate to expand, or of our client to want to sell her product. We understand in the same way that we justify our own decisions to move ahead in life. That is why it is important to understand ethical standards from at least three perspectives: the personal, the professional, and the societal. By understanding the ethical principles associated with each level, we are less likely to act self-interestedly. However, it would be erroneous to assume that these levels are interchangeable or that a decision made using personal ethical standards would automatically apply at the professional or societal levels or vice versa.

Most of us tend to act at each of these levels with no particular priority assigned to any one of them, forgetting that we are obligated differently at each level. These obligations can, and often do, conflict. However, since we tend to assimilate ethical principles at each of these levels, we cannot truly separate them, nor should we. Instead, we must learn to recognize when professional standards override personal standards, or when obligations to society outweigh obligations to our employers or to ourselves. In other words, we must learn how and when the standards of each level apply. We cannot, try as we may, divorce ourselves from any of these standards and obligations and exist only on one level. How our standards develop at each level has much to do with our values and ideals, for from these two sources come our principles—the basis for our ethical actions at every level.

VALUES, IDEALS, AND PRINCIPLES

When we say that truth is of paramount importance to journalism, we are stating a professional value. When we talk about believing in the sanctity of life, we are expressing a personal value. When we tout journalistic objectivity, we are really talking about an ideal in the same way that being virtuous may be a personal ideal. When we say that we will not print the names of rape victims, we are talking about a principle based on the value of privacy. Likewise, a principle of not printing the names of alleged perpetrators could be based on the ideal of "innocent until proven guilty." The differences among these three concepts may seem at first to be small, but there are some distinct definitional contrasts.

Educator and ethicist Clifford Christians defines *values* as those things that "reflect our presuppositions about social life and human nature."[10] Values cover a broad range of possibilities, such as aesthetic values (something is harmonious or pleasing), professional values (innovation and promptness), logical values (consistency and competency), sociocultural values (thrift and hard work), and moral values (honesty and nonviolence).

---

[10]Clifford G. Christians, Kim B. Rotzoll, and Mark Fackler, *Media Ethics*, 5th ed. (New York: Longman, 1997), p. 2.

Values are also further defined by philosophers as being either instrumental or intrinsic. An *instrumental* value is one that leads to something of even more value. For example, money usually is seen as having instrumental value, because possessing it leads to other things of greater value, including (we suppose) happiness. Other values, such as happiness, are said to possess *intrinsic* value; they are sought after because they are ends in and of themselves, and don't necessarily lead to greater values. As journalists, for instance, we could value truth telling because it leads to an honest account of what's happening in the world, which leads to our fulfilling our goals as reporters, which leads to our being satisfied with ourselves, which leads to happiness for us. Conversely, we could simply value truth telling as an end, as did Immanuel Kant (about whom we talk more in chap. 4). However, we need not trace every value through to its intrinsic conclusion; rather, we should simply be aware that some values can be ranked as more important to us because they are ends to be sought in themselves and not means to other ends.

Ideals, on the other hand, are a bit easier to define. Vincent Ryan Ruggiero defines an *ideal* as "a notion of excellence, a goal that is thought to bring about greater harmony to ourselves and to others."[11] For example, our culture respects ideals such as tolerance, compassion, loyalty, forgiveness, peace, justice, fairness, and respect for persons. In addition to these human ideals are institutional or organizational ideals such as profit, efficiency, productivity, quality, and stability.

As Ruggiero noted, ideals often come in conflict with each other. In such cases, decisions become much harder to make. Ruggiero, like many other ethicists, simply suggests that we honor the higher ideal. Of course, the higher ideal may not be that easy to determine. For example, a choice to place the journalistic ideal of providing information an audience wants over the societal ideal of honoring privacy, could result in a decision to run a story that may, in fact, violate someone's privacy.

Principles are those guidelines we derive from values and ideals and are precursors to codified rules. They are usually stated in positive (prescriptive) or negative (proscriptive) terms. For example, "Never corrupt the integrity of media channels" would be a principle derived from the professional value of truth telling in public relations. Or, "Always maximize profit" might be derived from belief in the efficacy of the free-enterprise system.

The ideals, values, and principles of the media will differ according to the differing goals and loyalties of each. Of course, there will be some com-

---

[11]Vincent Ryan Ruggiero, *Beyond feelings: a guide to critical thinking* (Port Washington, NY: Alfred Pub. Co., 1975), p. 147.

mon ground. Truth telling is an ideal agreed upon by all mass media. On the other hand, objectivity would be an acceptable ideal for journalism all the time, but only in rare cases for advertising and public relations. Freedom of speech is not only an ideal, but also a value. We value freedom of speech, but attaining total freedom may be idealistic (or even unrealistic).

When we begin to establish principles, we are committing ourselves to a course of action based on our values and ideals. When we act ethically, we typically act on principle. Principle can serve as a guideline for ethical action. That is why principles often tend to become codified, either as policies, codes, or laws. A newspaper's policy against publishing the names of rape victims is probably based on a belief in privacy for victims of violent crimes. The principle of that belief (value) is to withhold the name—or nondisclosure. In the same way, valuing human life can lead to a principle of nonviolence. In both cases, action (or inaction) is the result of the principle and is derived from it in the same way that the principle is derived from the value or ideal. The next step would be to formalize the principle.

Policies, a step removed from codes, set principles into standards that we can then use to guide our actions. Policy standards are not intractable; rather, they serve as indicators of our values and principles. As such, they are open to scrutiny and question, and even change as our values and principles may also change. Policies, even ethical policies, must be amenable to change in order to remain applicable to an often changing environment. The key is to use a policy standard as a default position, subject to evaluation as warranted but acceptable at face value in most cases. Thus, deciding to reveal the name of a rape victim would have to be justified on grounds that superseded a newspaper's standard of nondisclosure based on its belief in the privacy of crime victims. Those grounds might include the victim's desire to be heard publicly combined with the paper's desire to put a real face to a crime statistic, for instance.

Keep in mind that policies are usually developed not for entire industries but for individual entities within those industries—newspapers, television newsrooms, corporate public relations departments, advertising agencies, and so on. Industries and professions tend to codify policies, the next step up the ladder of formalizing our ethical values (Fig. 1.1).

PROFESSIONAL CODES AND THE LAW

Everyone knows that being legal doesn't necessarily mean being ethical. All media, at one time or another, have used the "It's not illegal so it must be all right" dodge. And, in truth, legality certainly plays an important part in ethicality. The law, however, can only serve to prohibit the most obvious vi-

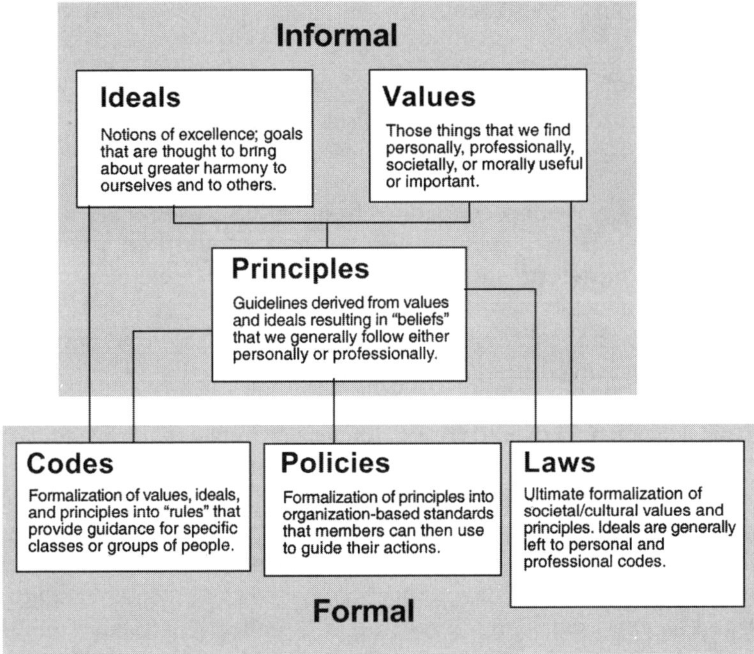

FIG. 1.1. Construction of moral guidelines.

olations of societal standards. Its basic function is to codify the customs, ideals, beliefs, and moral values of a society. It is unreasonable to expect the law either to establish moral standards or to cover the vast array of human conduct. So although it may be legal to use sex to sell a product, for example, it may not be entirely ethical. That's where professional codes come in.

Professional codes tend to establish a general goal or ideal, or define the ideal practitioner, and generally indicate how to attain that goal or become that practitioner. Additionally, codes usually indicate to whom the practitioner is obligated and how. Because codes are typically occupation specific, there tend to be as many different codes as there are professions, each with its own set of highly specialized prescriptions and proscriptions. However, there seems to be no set agreement as to the value of professional codes, a topic we take up in more detail in chapter 3. For now, it is sufficient to say that codes are the logical next step in the progression from identifying values, to developing principles, to setting standards, to creating policies. After codes would come the law, and, as we have seen, the law doesn't usually deal with moral matters.

CAN THE MEDIA BE ETHICAL?

The real question is, Do the media want to be ethical? The problem, as we shall see, is that the dictates of the various media professions often impose a "way of doing things" that clashes dramatically with societal norms. The routine of media work and the accepted standards that rapidly socialize neophytes into the media occupations frequently serve to blunt personal or societal principles. The accepted decision-making norm for most media is situational; every determination is made on a case-by-case basis, rendering consistency practically moot. The result is that the reputation of the media (in all its forms) has increasingly suffered in the eyes of the public. Every time a journalist invades a grieving family's privacy, the reputation of the entire profession suffers. Each deceptive or misleading advertisement is a black mark against all of advertising. And every public relations dodge used to avoid bad press results in achieving just that.

The single greatest roadblock preventing the media from ever conceding to constraint (even self-constraint) is their abiding belief in their "right" to do anything they want free from outside interference. However, rights are best served when tempered by obligation. As we shall see, the media are as obligated as any other entity by virtue of the effects they have on others. The web of obligation woven by every action having moral consequences is far-reaching and unavoidable. Those wishing to live without obligation to others would do well to heed the warning of 17th-century philosopher Thomas Hobbes, who proposed that human beings without a sense of obligation to each other (in the form of a "social contract") would be but "solitary, poor, nasty, [and] brutish" creatures. In the words of philosopher Henry Rosemont Jr., "[The] manner in which we interact with others . . . will clearly have a moral dimension infusing all, not just some, of our conduct." That moral dimension would demand conduct effected with reciprocity, and governed by civility, respect, and affection for others.[12]

The modern mass media exist in an increasingly interrelated world, one in which every action has the potential to affect increasingly broader constituencies. We have only to look at the recent events of September 11th, 2001, and the subsequent war in Afghanistan to understand how profoundly 24-hour news services and satellite delivery systems can affect global interaction. The key to moral decision making is to understand the interrelationships inherent in the actions of the mass media, and to consider the potential outcome of those actions from a perspective infused with care for others and a sense of obligation to serve rather than to prevail.

---

[12]Henry Rosemont, Jr., "Whose Democracy? Which Rights?: A Confucian Critique of Modern Western Liberalism," Unpublished paper (St. Mary's College of Maryland).

EXERCISES

1. Using C. Edwin Baker's definition of coercive speech, recall three instances in which you felt you had been personally coerced by language—printed, broadcast, or in other forms.
2. Cite an example of how the media is reflective of society. This could be a television show, a magazine format, an advertisement, or any other media example. Give as much detail as you can showing how it is either a literal reflection or a symbolic reflection. (Literal examples might be realistic cop shows. Symbolic examples might be television commercials for certain products, such as laundry soap.)
3. Cite an example of how the media directly affect our daily lives. Give details and relate the effect your example has had on society or any part of it.
4. Author Robert Entman cites the Washington press corps as being slavish to routine to the point that they often simply repeat what they are told by elite government sources rather than ferret out the stories for themselves. Cite a specific example of how you think the news media might be ignoring other possibilities of news gathering because of a routine they currently practice automatically.
5. What do you see as the benefit of taking the blame for something (especially if you played some part in the outcome)? What are the drawbacks? How would you assess blame if more than one person had affected the issue, and they were all your superiors?
6. Cite an instance in which your personal ethics might come in conflict with a professional media duty. This could be any form of media, not just journalism.
7. Give an example of a loss of media credibility. How could this loss have been avoided?
8. Do you think it is appropriate for advertising and public relations to owe first loyalty to the client? Why or why not?
9. Give one example each of a value, ideal, and principle that you hold or believe in. Explain why you believe the way you do.

CASE STUDY: *NEWSWEEK* AND THE DEATH OF A STORY

On May 16, 1996, Admiral Jeremy Michael (Mike) Boorda, chief of U.S. naval operations, committed suicide at his home at the Navy Yard in southeast

Washington, D.C. Boorda had been at his high military post since being nominated by President Clinton in 1994.

Apparently, he had chosen to commit suicide rather than face the press over a question of whether he had been wearing a combat citation in error, either intentionally or unintentionally. The decorations in question were two combat Vs (for valor) that the navy says go only to "individuals who are exposed to personal hazard due to direct hostile action." Boorda had, in fact, received two commendations for serving in combat areas during the Vietnam War: first as weapons officer aboard the USS *John R. Craig* in 1965, and later as executive officer aboard the USS *Brooke* for 14 months from 1971 to 1973. However, neither of these citations indicated that Boorda was qualified for the combat V.

In addition, the combat Vs were among the 13 awards and commendations that Boorda listed in the official résumé he gave to the Senate Armed Services Committee in his 1994 confirmation hearings. Boorda signed the résumé, stating that the information was "to the best of my knowledge, current, accurate and complete." He could be seen wearing the V pins in photos as early as 1985. Yet when reporters began digging into his navy records a year before his suicide, he stopped wearing them.[13]

Mike Boorda had been in the navy nearly all his adult life. He had enlisted at 17 (lying about his age) in order to escape a troubled family life. He was married at 18 and spent the next 40 years working his way from an enlisted man to the highest ranking officer in the navy. Along the way, Boorda served two tours of duty in Vietnam, commanded various ships, held several Pentagon posts, and served as chief of NATO's forces in southern Europe in 1991. When he was appointed as chief of naval operations in 1994, he took over a job rocked by scandal. His predecessor, Admiral Frank Kelso II, had to retire early in response to criticism of his handling of the 1991 Tailhook sex-harassment episode.[14]

About a year prior to Boorda's suicide, the National Security News Service, a watchdog group that feeds tips to news organizations, began filing Freedom of Information Act requests for the medal citations of all the members of the Joint Chiefs of Staff. After discovering what seemed to be discrepancies in Boorda's record, a correspondent for the service approached *Newsweek's* contributing editor for military affairs, retired Colonel David Hackworth. Hackworth subsequently scheduled an appointment to meet with Boorda to talk about the allegations; however, when the editor was unable to attend the meeting, *Newsweek* sent two of its Washington bureau correspondents to cover the interview. About two hours prior to the meeting, a navy spokesperson contacted *Newsweek* to discuss the interview. He was

---

[13]*Time*, May 27, 1996 v147 n22 p30(3).

[14]*Time*, May 27, 1996 v147 n22 p30(3).

told about the allegations–information that he passed along to Boorda.[15] Just prior to the meeting, Boorda declined a lunch that had been ordered for him, drove himself to his home, and shot himself in the chest just outside his house. The reporters were still waiting to meet with him at his office.

Following the suicide, many questioned the validity of pursuing such a small story, especially given the outcome. Others pointed out that Boorda's life was not a simple one. His highly public position had increased the pressure he felt to see the navy through its time of trouble. He was accused of being too political, and of acting out of a sense of public responsibility rather than out of loyalty to the navy. He had even been publicly accused of disloyalty by a senior officer in a recent speech. Obviously, his life was extremely complicated and involved many more worries than just the unearned decorations. However, in one of two suicide notes, Boorda alluded to the potential scandal and wondered whether people would believe his error had been an honest mistake.

In several articles covering their investigation of Boorda, *Newsweek* called its actions "defensible." In their words, "The suicide took place not only before any article appeared, but two full days before the reporting was complete. And the reporting that did take place was not duplicitous; Boorda was given plenty of time to respond or provide additional documents."[16] The magazine justified the newsworthiness of the story by citing the concern of many in the military over the significance of medals and the entitlement of those who earn them. At the same time, *Newsweek* editor Jonathan Alter wrote that this case was "a good reminder that even if reporters don't really kill, what we write and say can have grave consequences. This shouldn't make the press less aggressive in pursuing stories, just more thoughtful."[17]

CASE STUDY QUESTIONS

1. Was *Newsweek* on solid ethical grounds in pursuing this story? Consider the difference between investigating a story and actually publishing it.
2. Define in what ways you see this story as newsworthy or not newsworthy.
3. To what degree should journalists be interested in the overall picture they are investigating and not just in the story they are hoping to write? Do you think that backgrounding would have helped *Newsweek* better understand Boorda's frame of mind?

---

[15] *Newsweek*, May 27, 1996 v127 n22 p24(6).
[16] *Newsweek*, May 27, 1996 v127 n22 p24(6).
[17] Jonathan Alter, "Beneath the Waves," *Newsweek*, May 27, 1996, v127, n22, p30.

4. If you had been an editor at *Newsweek* prior to this incident, would you have handled this investigation any differently?
5. Which ethical theories could help you decide what might have been the correct action to take in this case?
6. Could harm have been avoided or mitigated in this case? How?
7. Assume you are the editor of *Newsweek*. Write a letter to your readers explaining why you are going to run this story (assuming the suicide hasn't taken place). Now, assuming the suicide has taken place, write a second letter explaining why you aren't responsible for Boorda's death.
8. Assume you report directly to the editor of *Newsweek*. Explain why you don't think you should run the story of Boorda's citation error (assuming the suicide hasn't taken place).

CASE STUDY: PATRIOTISM IN THE NEWSROOM

On September 17, 2001, Stacey Woelfel, KOMU TV8 news director notified staff via e-mail of the station's policy regarding on-air displays of symbols for any cause, including patriotism.

"Leave the ribbons at home when reporting or anchoring for KOMU News," Woelfel's e-mail said. "What you do on your own time is up to you, though I would urge you to consider the fact that you are always 'on the clock' in terms of being known as a reporter and a representative of the station."

The pressure, both economically and politically, mounted almost immediately. KOMU is owned by the University of Missouri and employs students as interns year round. Some Republican state representatives, in particular Representative Matt Bartle said that they would be "evaluating far more carefully state funding that goes to the school of journalism." KOMU is an "auxiliary enterprise" of the university and is funded solely by outside revenue; however, some faculty members who work at the station are funded by the university.

Columbia, Missouri, public schools board of education member, Don Schoengarth, in a letter to the editor stated:

> What kind of reporters are we training at the journalism school? Is the goal to produce a bunch of androids with no feelings or independent thoughts, who simply smile and read the teleprompter? If our news media remain neutral, we are providing a great moral victory for bin Laden.

The e-mails that Woelfel received from legislators and the public on the newsrooms' policy ranged from scolding to belligerent. Representative Rod Jetton of the 156th district said:

> I will ask you to PLEASE USE COMMON SENSE [author's emphasis]. This is not a political dilemma or an ethical one. What our country is facing right now is a test of our survival. This is war and there are evil opponents out there who hate Americans. There will be a winner and a looser. Good people will die!!!

Tammy Sachse, a member of the public had this to say:

> The media staff is responsible for reporting unbiased news, however that should be only unbiased as it relates to the internal workings of the United States. Outside of that, the news media should be very pro US. This lack of support is part of the decay of our nation's unity that initiated these attacks.

Many of the e-mails were far more menacing; they used foul language and thinly veiled threats directed toward Woelfel. At least two advertisers also removed their spots from KOMU.

Woelfel had adhered to this policy for more than 20 years. He had defended the policy as a matter of journalistic ethics. The faculty at the University of Missouri School of Journalism voted in early October to defend Woelfel's decision and show their support for the controversial policy. The curators of the university made the opposite decision, determining that students and employees were allowed to display patriotic symbols. Woelfel stayed consistent with the original policy and did not make any changes, despite being at odds with the university.

Ultimately, the state legislature decided to withhold some $50,000 from the university because of Woelfel's decision.

CASE STUDY QUESTIONS

1. Do you believe that Woelfel's decision was correct? Why or why not?
2. Are there any circumstances under which it might be acceptable for journalists to show bias? If there are, why would it be acceptable?
3. Put these levels of obligation in the order you believe they should go for working journalists: human being, citizen, professional.

CHAPTER

2

Moral Claimants, Obligation, and Social Responsibility

Whenever we make moral decisions, we affect other people. In fact, anyone who is affected by our decisions or has some effect on us could be considered a *stakeholder*—or, in the language of ethics—a *moral claimant*. This claimant could be our reading or viewing publics, the people who pay our salaries, our families, those we are reporting on, their families, our fellow professionals, or virtually anyone. The fact that the media affect so many seriously complicates moral decisions, because we must consider all those affected or be found lacking by those we do not consider.

As mentioned in chapter 1, our daily decisions as private individuals don't usually affect that many people, but the influence of even those private decisions may have repercussions far beyond our immediate circle. Imagine, then, the impact the media have on vast numbers of people every day. If we are to act as responsible media practitioners, we must consider all of those people every time we make a decision affecting them. In order to accomplish that, we must first decide exactly who those people are and what likely effect we will have on them.

For all media there are four primary claimant groups: our clients/customers, the organization for which we work, the profession of which we are a part, and society as a whole.[1] Naturally, the order in which we address these groups will depend on a number of variables, including the media job we hold (in journalism, advertising, or public relations); the environment in which we are having to make a moral decision (political, economic, and so-

[1]Clifford G. Christians, Mark Fackler, Kim B. Rotzoll, and Kathy Brittain Mckee, *Media Ethics: Cases and Moral Reasoning* (New York: Longman, 1998).

cial factors included); the nature of the decision itself; and the constraints we feel as a result of these other variables. The danger is that because of these constraints, we are more likely to view our choices from a skewed perspective, resulting in a pragmatic allegiance to those who most affect *us* rather than the other way around. It is imperative, therefore, that we develop an organized method of identifying stakeholders and potential moral claimants that will help us understand our relationships with them. If we understand our functional relationships with these various constituencies, we can then begin to sort out our ethical obligations to them.

Considering the consequences of our actions is one of the primary ways in which we define our relationships to others. We tend to avoid actions that result in negative consequences for others, and to promote actions that bear favorable consequences. An advertising agency, for example, promotes its client's interests because the consequence of not doing that would be the loss of the client. In other words, the client has potentially greater effect on the ad agency than vice versa. Likewise, the agency has a potentially greater effect on its target audiences (consumers) than the other way around—at least under normal conditions. And, what about the advertising industry in general? Don't the actions of each agency affect the whole of the industry for better or worse? The same applies to news outlets. The mistake of one network television news anchor reflects not only on her, but on her network and on broadcast journalism as a whole. In effect, we are linked to our stakeholders (constituents, publics, markets, audiences, whatever) by the effects our actions have on them and by the effects they have on us. These *linkages* are nonmoral; that is, they have no moral implications under most circumstances. However, we can derive moral implications from these linkages depending on the situation and on how we are obligated to each of them. The first step in defining these obligations is to define the nonmoral linkages.

THE LINKAGE CONCEPT

All organizations, including media organizations, survive and prosper by dealing successfully with their environments. According to *organizational systems theory*, all organizations exist in an environment that is relevant to their survival. From this environment they derive the resources necessary to do whatever it is that they do. Their relevant environment also provides them with an outlet for whatever it is they produce. For example, a newspaper takes in all the raw materials it needs to produce its "product": financial backing, paper, ink, printing presses, employees, and (of course) information. What it produces is "the news." If it does its job well and gets along with its environment, the paper survives, maybe even prospers.

Identifying the most important other entities in that environment is the key to survival, because seriously misjudging the effects of our actions on any one of these entities (or misjudging their effect on us) could spell disaster for the organizational system. Misreading a market can cause huge losses in revenue for manufacturers, for example. In the same way, misunderstanding an important constituency can seriously injure a public relations practitioner's effectiveness; or failing to deliver the kind of news your community expects can injure your newspaper's reputation and, ultimately, its viability.

Educator James Grunig proposes that organizations are linked to other entities in their environment through consequences—either when the actions of the organization have effects on another entity, or when the actions of another entity have effects on the organization.[2] There are two primary types of linkages: those that provide input into the organization, and those that receive output from the organization. *Input* linkages might be suppliers of raw materials, labor unions, employees, or virtually anyone or any group that provides something the organization needs in order to do its job. *Output* linkages are those that accept the organization's output (product, service, information). For most media, these are the consumers of the media product: newspaper readers, television news watchers, or target publics and markets for public relations and advertising. It is essential to remember that the organization's output has some effect on those to whom it is targeted. The idea of consequence is vital to an understanding of moral obligation, as is discussed later.

Grunig further identifies the four key linkages that are common to most organizations.[3] In order to apply his concept to media organizations, including news-gathering organizations, we will identify these linkages as *providers*, *suppliers*, *receivers*, *associates*, and *issue-defined constituents* (Figs. 2.1 and 2.2).

- *Providers* are those that "provide the authority and control the resources that enable the organization to exist."[4] These could include lending institutions, government agencies, legislative authorities, stockholders, and boards of directors. These entities generally are classified as input linkages because they tend to have more effects on the organization than vice versa.

- Two of the most important linkages are those "with organizations or publics that provide inputs and take outputs."[5] *Suppliers* would include those

---

[2]James E. Grunig, and Todd Hunt, *Managing Public Relations* (New York: Holt, Rinehart and Winston, 1984), p. 140.

[3]Grunig, following on previous research, labels these linkages as enabling, functional input, functional output, normative, and diffuse.

[4]Grunig and Hunt, *Managing Public Relations*, p. 140.

[5]Grunig and Hunt, *Managing Public Relations*, p. 141.

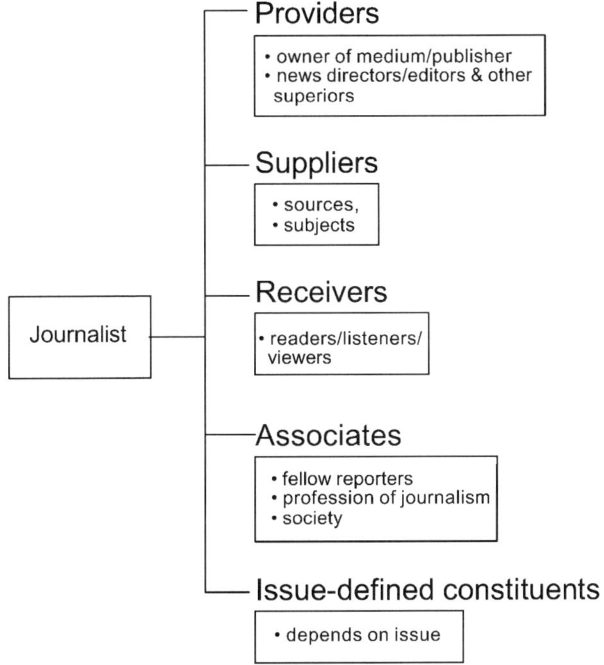

FIG. 2.1. Linkages for journalists.

who furnish raw materials, labor unions, employees, and any other source of needed input for the organization (sources for news stories, for instance). *Receivers* use the organization's output–usually in the form of products or services, but for our purposes, also its public relations messages, its advertisements, or its news and information output. Receivers typically include consumers and target audiences.

• *Associates* are those organizations with similar interests or that face similar problems. It is not unusual to find associates linked through coalitions with the organization. Trade and professional associations are the foremost example of this type of linkage. The inference here is that the linked organizations can affect each other equally or, if presenting a united front, affect other linkages.

• *Issue-defined constituents* are those that arise as issues dictate. These could be groups not normally associated with the organization in a formal way. Whenever the actions of the organization have effects on its environment, these linkages arise. The issue-defined constituents could be special-interest groups, the community in which the organization operates, environmental groups, or basically any representative of public opinion affected by the organization's actions.

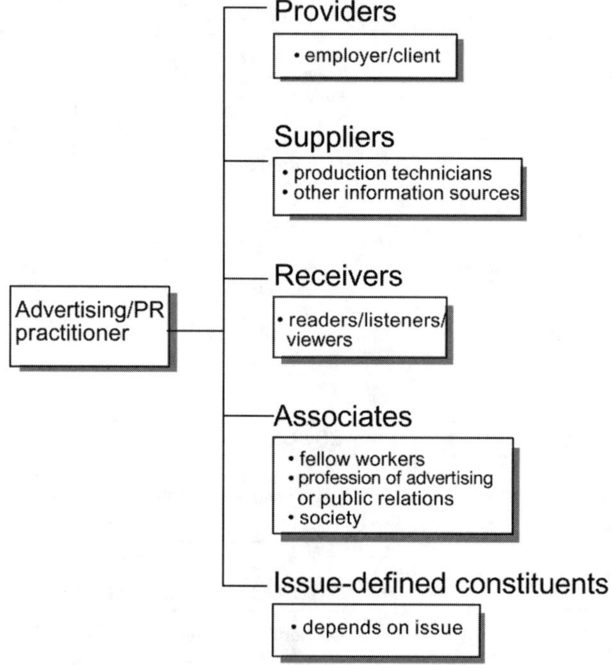

FIG. 2.2. Linkages for advertising and public relations.

It is important to remember that those linkages that have effects on the organization are least likely to be owed a moral obligation, simply because they generally control the relationship. Those on whom the organization has effects, on the other hand, are most likely to incur the organization's ethical obligation.

THE IMPORTANCE OF CONSEQUENCES

Some duty-based ethicists, notably Immanuel Kant (whom we discuss more fully in chap. 4), suggest that consequences be ignored when determining which action is the right one to take. In this view, the right act is the one that is driven by recognition of a duty and a willingness to perform that duty. Obligation, taken in this light, is automatically owed and recognized as universally binding. This assumes that we can recognize our duties through application of some guideline such as Kant's categorical imperative. Although this is a good starting point, we cannot make all our decisions based solely on a single maxim, nor is it possible that our actions can be categorical in the sense of being applicable in every circumstance at all times. To operate based solely on a single guideline may force us to ignore the multiple obligations that we are faced with at every level of our existence: personal, familial, occupational, and societal.

To more completely discharge our obligations to the array of moral claimants we face at every decision point, we must also consider consequences. As noted earlier, the effects of our actions on others are the main reason we recognize obligation in the first place. This fits nicely with the linkage concept of identifying constituents by our effect on them and/or their effect on us. In short, the linkage concept recognizes the importance of consequences when dealing with other people. However, when taken alone, this method falls short of recognizing those to whom we are obligated ethically or of identifying in what way we are obligated to them. So, although we may be able to identify an issue-based linkage in the form of a special-interest group, this only tells us that we must deal with that group through some practical, nonmoral activity. It does not indicate our ethical obligation.

THE NATURE OF OBLIGATION

Obligation usually implies a bond, either legal, social, or moral—an owing of something to someone or something. That obligation exists whether we choose to recognize it or not. Obligation is a natural concomitant of living within a society. Because of our social interactions, we incur obligation, and we tend to recognize that we have done so.

The term "obligation" is roughly synonymous with the term "duty," as used by a number of philosophers. The general assumption about moral duties is that we have them. These duties are not merely those that we create through such actions as making promises or incurring debt. We also have "natural" duties to others "simply because they are people who could be helped or harmed by our actions."[6] We also are obligated merely by being members of human society. Confucian philosophy, for example, holds that obligations are multilayered. One is obligated at the personal, familial, occupational, and societal levels—each representing differing intensities of obligation and differing levels of formality. Educator and ethicist Louis Day reminds us that "our moral calculations affect other humans, regardless of whether these individuals are known personally to us or are members of that amorphous mass known as the public."[7] Philosopher T. M. Scanlon suggests that "what we owe to others" is determined, to a great degree, by

---

[6]James Rachels, *The Elements of Moral Philosophy* (New York: McGraw Hill, 1993), p. 76.

[7]Louis Day, *Ethics in Media Communications: Cases and Controversies*, 2nd ed. (Belmont: Wadsworth Publishing Company, 1997), p. 29.

what they can justifiably expect of us.[8] In other words, we must treat others as they expect to be treated—a version of the Golden Rule.

Obligations arise not only from general social relationships but also from relationships described by our roles and functions in life, including our jobs. Thus, we are obligated explicitly and implicitly in our relationships with others we come in contact with through our daily work. In the view of philosopher Bernard Gert, duties are primarily connected with jobs, offices, positions, and the like.[9] Duties are both voluntarily incurred and forced (as the duty to obey the law). "Do your duty," in the sense of natural obligation, is one of the key rules set down by Gert. However, he emphatically points out that doing your duty is not synonymous with simply doing what you are paid to do. "One's job involves duties only to the extent that the job does not require one to kill his innocent victim, though he may have been paid a sizable sum to do that. One cannot have a duty to unjustifiably violate a moral rule."[10]

Moral philosopher William David Ross defined six areas he believed all human beings would recognize, in one form or another, as being morally binding.[11] He referred to these obligations as prima facie duties, in that they should be considered binding, all other factors being equal—in other words, if no other duty or complication interferes with the consideration of the obligation in question. Ross believed that we would recognize these duties because we are human beings, and as such we are inclined to live in social structures held together in part by obligation. Ross's six categories of obligation are as follows:

- *Duties of fidelity*—If you promise (explicitly or implicitly) to perform some act or to abstain from performing some act, then you are obliged to perform that act or to abstain from performing that act. For instance, most relationships, professional and personal, assume a duty to tell the truth, or at least not to lie. Duties of fidelity would also include remaining faithful to contracts, explicit or implicit, and keeping promises. This category also includes *duties of reparation*; that is, if you perform a wrong action with respect to another person, you are obliged to undo the wrong.
- *Duties of gratitude*—If any person performs some service (favor) for you, then you have some obligation to the person who performed the favor. This would apply both to relationships between friends and to relationships be-

[8]T. M. Scanlon, *What We Owe to Each Other* (Cambridge: The Belknap Press of Harvard University Press, 1998), pp. 360–361.

[9]Bernard Gert, *Morality: A new Justification of the Moral Rules* (Oxford: Oxford University Press, 1966), p. 154.

[10]Gert, *Morality*, p. 156.

[11]William David Ross, *The Right and the Good* (Oxford: Clarendon Press, 1930).

tween employer and employee. For example, if your employer treats you in an exceptionally favorable manner, above that normally expected in an employee–employer relationship, your obligation would deepen to honor your employer's wishes beyond the duty of fidelity.

- *Duties of justice*—If any person merits a distribution of something (typically something that will result in pleasure, happiness, or satisfaction), and you can bring that distribution about (or prevent an unmerited distribution), then you are obliged to distribute what is merited (or prevent/withhold what is not merited). In practice, this can often mean giving greater consideration to the claims of those who deserve it rather than to those who demand it, regardless of their position or power.
- *Duties of beneficence*—If you can make some person better with respect to their state of existence, then you are obliged to do so. An example of this would be corporate philanthropy or the pro bono work of professionals. In a decision-making situation, this duty may oblige you to act when nonaction is preferred or recommended by others.
- *Duties of self-improvement*—If you can make yourself better with respect to your state of existence, then you are obliged to do so. This can cover anything from preserving your own integrity to taking advantage of a favorable situation for self-improvement.
- *Duties of noninjury*—If you are in a position to avoid hurting someone, then you are obliged to do so. This contrasts with the duty of beneficence. Although not injuring others incidentally means doing them good, Ross interprets the avoidance of injuring others as a more pressing duty than beneficence. This may, in fact, be the most important of Ross's duties, since it implies that the possibility of injury to any claimant to whom you are obligated must be assigned some weight. However, this very often results in a form of cost-benefit or risk-benefit analysis, which is counter to the underlying premise of duty-based theory: that rules can, and should, be moral in and of themselves, and not based on considerations of outcome.

What is most useful about Ross's categories of obligation is that we can employ them to help define our claimants and how we are linked to them. The relationship between moral claimants and ourselves as moral decision makers can best be represented through the linkages formed by obligation. For example, a newspaper editor is obligated to a number of claimants. To the consumers of the paper, the obligation is one of fidelity—in the sense of an implied promise to deliver news and information that is useful and interesting. However, editors also are obligated by fidelity to turn a profit for the owners, and to employees (again, through fidelity) to provide a fair wage and good working environment. They may be further obligated by other duties incurred on an issue-by-issue basis. For example, gratitude to a source

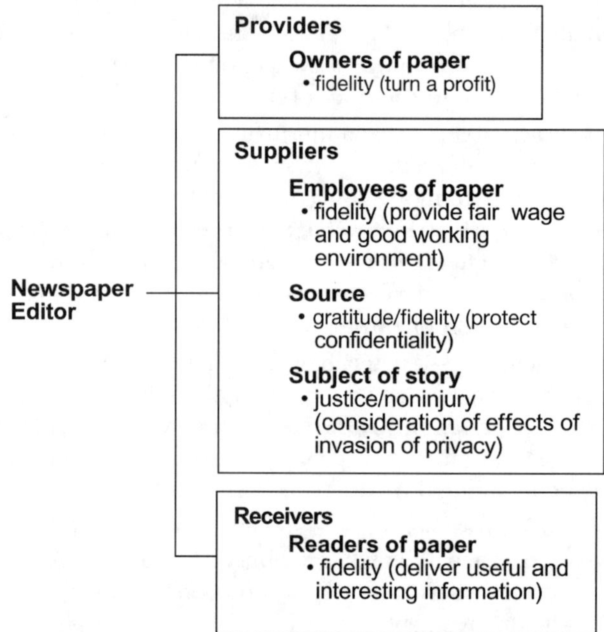

FIG. 2.3. Example of typical obligations of a newspaper editor deciding whether to run a story that might violate someone's privacy.

may prohibit disclosure of the source's name (fidelity may also apply here). Consideration of someone's privacy may follow recognition of a duty of justice (maybe the subject doesn't deserve to have his privacy invaded). Or the opposite—the person does deserve being exposed (the duty of justice as well) (Fig. 2.3).

On the other hand, a public relations consultant is obligated by fidelity to her client. A contract, either explicit or implicit, exists that outlines that obligation. In public relations, this obligation is generally viewed as the primary duty. However, from an ethical perspective, other obligations may have precedence or, at least, be of equal weight. For example, the consultant may also be obligated to her profession to uphold its highest standards (fidelity). And she may be obligated to tell the truth to those to whom her client's message is targeted (fidelity again). However, she may be further obligated by a sense of justice to object to the client's message if it serves to reward those who are undeserving at the expense of those who are more deserving, or by a duty of noninjury if any third party may be harmed by any action she takes (Fig. 2.4). It quickly becomes clear that these obligations may, and often do, conflict.

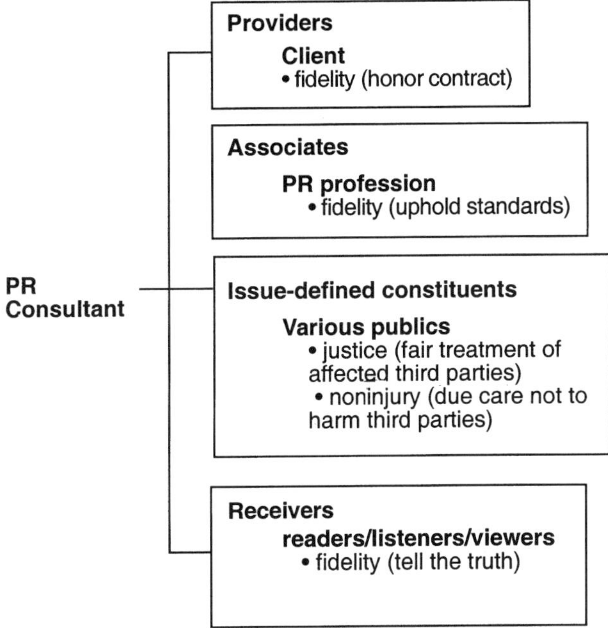

FIG. 2.4. Example of typical obligations of a public relations consultant working for a single client.

One of the methods by which we can begin to identify potential conflicts and thus, begin to sort out the priority of our obligations, is to conceive of these obligations as linkages.

SYNTHESIZING THE APPROACHES

The linkage concept of identifying relevant constituencies provides us with a way to conceptualize primary relationships based on consequence. Remember, however, we are more likely to seek out the linkages that have consequences for us (providers and suppliers especially). This is normal for those attempting to enter or remain in the good graces of these important linkages. We don't want to upset the owners of our television station by our actions, or our clients by ignoring their input—after all, they control the purse strings. However, can we balance our obligations to them with our obligations to those for whom the consequences usually run the other way? Issue-defined constituents and, to some extent, receivers are most often affected by our actions to a greater degree than we are affected by theirs. *These linkages are, therefore, more likely to incur obligation of an ethical nature*—obligation that is least likely to be recognized or honored in the decision-making process, given the special attention that must be paid to those linkages that most affect us.

Obligation, as outlined by William Ross, can be used to further identify those linkages and assign ethical, rather than functional, priority to their status. We can assume that in any decision-making circumstance the relationships among the various entities will be defined by the issue as well as by preestablished and recognized obligations (such as fidelity to the client). However, these preestablished obligational relationships may be altered or even overridden by issue-related obligations, depending on the seriousness of the potential consequences driving the obligation. For example, in a situation in which the outcome of a public relations message may be to "corrupt the channels of communication" through distortion or deception, the obligation of fidelity to the client is overridden by an obligation of fidelity both to the media and to the profession of public relations. The media, in this instance, would be viewed as a receiver, the profession as an associate. Another example might be a circumstance in which a newspaper's obligation to turn a profit is overridden by its obligation to inform its readers. The result might be not giving readers what they want, but giving them, instead, what they need—even at the risk of losing readership. In this case, fidelity to an ideal (or professional standard) may supersede economic considerations. At the very least, the obligation should be identified and recognized.

A diagram of these potential linkages would show that certain obligations are more likely to be linked with certain stakeholders/claimants (Fig. 2.5). For example, because providers such as regulatory agencies have considerable consequential impact on a regulated business (such as broadcasting), that business is more likely to be obligated through fidelity to that linkage. Gratitude may also come into play, but usually in a lesser degree because these linkages rarely occur between friends. (Friendship is not a requirement of gratitude, but gratitude generally implies a closer or more informal relationship than a formal or contractual one.) Remember, also, those linkages that result in the consequences being felt by the organization are least likely to incur ethical obligation—at least from the organization's side.

Fidelity may also be owed to a receiver. For instance, dealers who receive a product from an organization and then sell the product on the organization's behalf are bound to the organization by an explicit contract (television affiliates that must carry certain network programming, for example). However, other receivers, such as consumers, potentially are bound to the organization in additional ways. Certainly, a manufacturer of a product implicitly, if not explicitly, promises that customers will receive

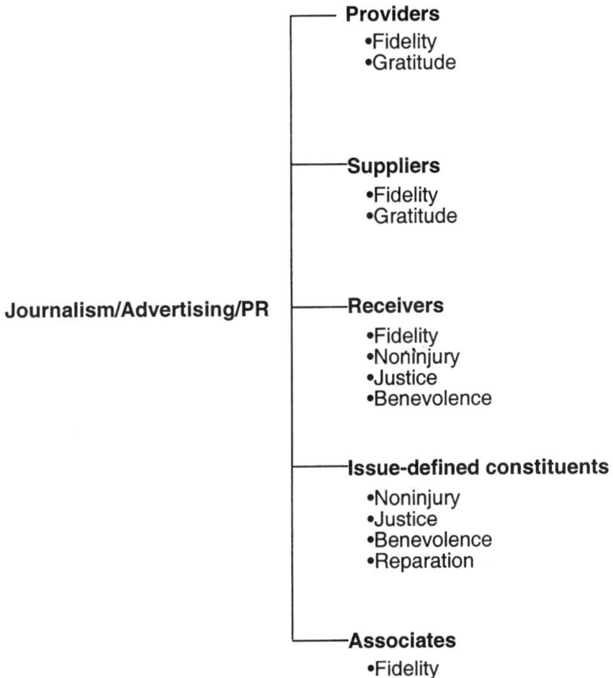

FIG. 2.5. Obligation by linkage type.

their money's worth. To break this promise could involve reparation. The obligation of noninjury requires, for example, that the organization's products are free of safety hazards, or that no hazardous waste is produced as a byproduct of manufacture. Justice can come into play in hiring practices in which minority groups are underrepresented, or when plants are closed without due consideration of the needs, loyalty, and merit of the employees. Obviously, benevolence comes into play as philanthropic giving, but may also become an obligation to provide products and services that contribute to the well-being of society as a whole. This is especially true of journalistic obligations to serve the public interest—also viewed as a duty of fidelity.

The linkages that are most likely to incur ethical obligation are issue-defined constituents. Here, the nature of the issue will play a central role in how these obligations are ordered and whether or not they supersede predetermined obligations to other linkages with stronger effects on the organization. As with receivers, issue-defined constituents often require actions based on noninjury, and justice. Fidelity is noticeably absent, because the linkages between issue-defined constituents and the organization are rarely formal. Added to the list of obligations, however, is reparation. The likelihood that the organization will have done something that requires reparation is much greater with these claimants than with others with whom it is linked. Invading a family's privacy in order to get a story, for example, requires that those most affected by the action be considered.

Naturally, all of the six obligations listed by Ross might be applicable to each of the five linkages; however, it is more likely, given the direction of consequences, that more of them will come into play with receivers and issue-defined constituents. This potential imbalance in obligation should help to offset the traditional tendency among media practitioners to honor the obligations to the linkages affecting them most directly, especially providers and suppliers in the form of employers and clients.

The key is to remember that we are tied to our stakeholders by more than just economic or political linkages. We are tied to them socially, and social links imply obligation. We must always ask not only to whom we are linked, but also in what way we are linked, observing both functional and ethical ties. We may, after determining our obligations, ignore them. But we cannot avoid the likelihood that others recognize these same obligations and are very likely to hold us accountable when we do not honor them. As you might imagine, however, not everyone agrees that the media have any obligation at all toward their claimants.

THE LIBERTARIAN APPROACH

In a sense, the United States was founded on the concept of libertarianism. Roughly speaking, *libertarianism* holds that freedom should be unbounded; there should be no restrictions on an individual's freedom to do what he or she pleases. If we remember how the United States was founded—as a reaction to tyrannous authority—we can better understand the libertarian position. When we hear the word "libertarian," we often conjure up an image of gun-toting cadres of nonconformists holed up in some remote region of the country awaiting the inevitable government attack. What we don't usually think of is the modern media.

Modern journalism maintains a very strong flavor of libertarianism in its refusal to bow to outside pressure, especially governmental pressure. The First Amendment of the Constitution literally guarantees this freedom. Journalists are free to report on anything they deem important to their constituencies. In many states, they are even free from prosecution if they choose to withhold the names of sources. In fact, some would say that journalists are and should be free from any obligation save that of providing the news; for by providing the news, they are serving the public interest—and that is responsibility enough.

This thinking is a reflection of the "invisible hand" theory of Adam Smith, who pointed out that the duty of a capitalistic endeavor was to make a profit and remain viable, for by doing so the rest of society was duly served. The modern conservative economist Milton Freedman echoes this sentiment when he states that the job of business is not only to survive but also to do well. A business that thrives will employ more workers, provide more products and services, and strengthen the overall economy in the process. If business is left alone, free from government intervention, it will either thrive or it will not—but it will do so in a marketplace immune from restrictions.[12]

It is not difficult to understand why the modern press grew from this libertarian model. After all, the job of journalism is journalism. The modern journalist gathers the news and reports it with as much objectivity as can be mustered. In fact, objectivity is the mainstay of a libertarian press. If reporting is truly free from bias, then no one can justifiably intervene in its process. And although objectivity is recognized today as an ideal rather than an absolute goal, the belief that the press should not owe allegiance to anyone or anything but itself is a very powerful one. After all, allegiance implies obligation, and obligation implies reciprocity. A press encumbered by debt is not, by definition, a free press. An interesting question arises, however, as to whether the press discharges its only obligation to the public it serves by simply providing them with a balanced account of the day's news.

THE SOCIAL RESPONSIBILITY APPROACH

The other side of the rights coin is responsibility. The idea of social responsibility developed originally as a means of indicting American business, whose sense of obligation to the public was decidedly lacking in the early part of the twentieth century. With the increasing realization that everything that business does affects huge numbers of people came a concomitant call for greater accountability. In the social responsibility model, businesses are seen as operating at the behest of the public; thus, their rights are really privileges—and privileges come only at the expense of reciprocation in the form of agreed-upon responsibilities.

James Grunig offers three categories of responsibility that he suggests are recognized as binding to some degree on all organizations. At the very least, an organization should perform its basic task (gathering and dissemi-

---

[12]Milton Freedman, "Social Responsibility and Compensatory Justice," in Joan Callahan, *Ethical Issues in Professional Life* (New York: Oxford University Press, 1988), pp. 349–354.

nating the news, for example). Beyond that, it should take care of any potential consequences of its primary task, such as cleaning up pollution it has caused, or being a good employer, or responding to complaints. Finally, organizations may move into the area of general societal concerns such as literacy, disease prevention, hunger, and so on.[13] Grunig proposes that the first two categories of responsibility are naturally binding on all organizations. Anything less would be unacceptable to most of society. The third category, however, is more difficult to measure for effectiveness; and although organizations would certainly be encouraged to take on larger societal issues, most citizens wouldn't fault them if they did not. But how does this apply to the media?

As far back as 1942, the role of the press in our society was recognized as one including both rights and responsibilities. In that year, a commission was established, originally by Henry R. Luce of *Time* and later by the Encyclopedia Britannica, to assess the state of journalism. Robert Hutchins, chancellor of the University of Chicago, was appointed head of the commission composed of 13 members from industry and education. The Hutchins Commission of Freedom of the Press studied the sticky question of a "free and responsible press" and presented its report in 1947. In its report, the commission called for a press that today might be deemed "socially responsible." The five obligations of modern media, according to the Hutchins Commission, were

- to provide a truthful, comprehensive, and intelligent account of the day's events in a context that gives them meaning;
- to serve as a forum for the exchange of comment and criticism;
- to develop a representative picture of the constituent groups in society;
- to be responsible for the presentation and clarification of the goals and values of society;
- to provide full access to the day's intelligence.

In other words, the Hutchins Commission believed that the media should not only do their job and attend to the ramifications of carrying out that job, but they should also involve themselves in the well-being of society as a whole.

It is clear, therefore, that a certain level of responsibility is owed society by the news media; but exactly to what degree are the media expected to give up their traditional autonomy in order to serve the public interest (or

[13]Keith Davis and Robert L. Blomstrom, *Business and Society*, 3rd ed. (New York: McGraw Hill, 1975) cited in Grunig and Hunt, *Managing Public Relations*, pp. 54–56.

cater to its needs)? Today, further indications of media responsibility have surfaced in the concept of *civic* or *public journalism*—a model in which the news media become actively involved in the well-being of the community in which they operate. Social historian Christopher Lasch argued that the press today has abdicated its role as a proper forum for public debate by subscribing to the notions that information alone is the proper product of the media. In Lasch's words, "What democracy requires is public debate, not information." He decried the decline of the partisan press of the 19th century and proposed that the

> rise of a new type of journalism professing rigorous standards of objectivity do[es] not assure a steady supply of usable information.
>
> Unless information is generated by sustained public debate, most of it will be irrelevant at best, misleading and manipulative at worst.[14]

Journalist and educator Jay Rosen also finds objectivity outmoded as a concept and unworkable as an ideal. Rosen believes that "journalism should be involved in re-engaging people in public life." According to him, public journalism "recognizes the overriding importance of improving public life."

> In the next few years, it will be critical for people in journalism to declare an end to their neutrality on certain questions. For example, whether people participate or not, whether we have genuine debate in this country, whether the political system works, whether public life draws the attention of citizens, whether political leaders earn our respect.[15]

These questions, he proposes, can best be answered by a press that is not afraid to take sides. Others argue that a partisan press, a press that loses its objectivity, will be incapable of giving us information that we can trust is balanced enough to allow us to make up our own minds, therefore limiting our autonomy as decision makers.

Thus, the arguments in favor of a press free from outside control are likewise strong. By permitting, or expecting, a less-than-objective account, consumers of news increase their own burden of gathering the facts for themselves. This dilemma is what prompted Walter Lippmann to call for an objective press in the first place. The question then becomes, what level of responsibility can the media accept before they lose the autonomy they

---

[14]Christopher Lasch, Journalism, "Publicity and the Lost Art of Argument." *Gannett Center Journal*, Spring 1990, pp. 10–11.

[15]Jay Rosen, "Beyond Objectivity," *Nieman Reports*, Winter 1993, pp. 48–53.

need to remain fair and balanced? Obligation implies outside pressure, and we have already seen that the disparate media are obligated by the very nature of their jobs. And although the press may be obligated increasingly toward promoting the public welfare, there is a danger that such leanings may result in the news media becoming more like their cousins in advertising and public relations—professions in which bias is expected. Like journalism, advertising and public relations also value autonomy, but bridle to a lesser degree at outside influence—especially if that influence is wielded by those controlling the purse strings. However, as we see in the next chapter, the nature of professionalism works against the most egregious infringements on social responsibility for all of the media, including advertising and public relations, through the ideal of serving the public interest.

In summary, the media are obligated to a vast array of claimants and must discharge those obligations satisfactorily in order to act ethically. And while obligations may differ among the various media, commonalties do exist in such areas as truth telling and prohibitions against harm—topics we visit in detail in chapters 5 and 6. As we see in the next chapter, the type of relationship that exists between a profession and those it serves dictates, to a very great extent, the level of ethicality that can be expected of that profession.

EXERCISES

1. Make a list of the key functional linkages that operate in your organization or school. Explain why each linkage is where it is on your list.
2. Take your list of linkages and assign ethical obligations to each entity. Why did you choose the obligations you did?
3. Make a list of personal linkages. Notice whether the linkage concept you used for your organization has to be adjusted in any way for personal use. If you had to adjust, explain why. Apply Ross's list of six obligations to your personal linkages.
4. Do you believe the press should be free from obligation beyond that of providing news of interest and importance to the public? Why or why not?
5. Do you think the press presents a representative picture of the constituent groups in society? Why or why not?
6. How far should the press go in providing its publics with what they *want* versus what they *need*?

HYPOTHETICAL: EDUCATION FOR SALE

You have been working for over two years now for EduMark, a marketing firm specializing in educational products for grades K through 12. The company regularly works with educators, parents, and corporate sponsors in developing course supplements at a small cost to schools. For example, in your first year at EduMark, you helped develop a political science module for middle schools that explained the electoral process. The package included print material, a one-hour video tape, and referenced an online Web site developed specifically for the educational component. The entire package was sponsored by a large wood-products manufacturer whose name and logo appeared prominently on the cover of the various elements of the module.

When you began work for EduMark, you believed there was nothing wrong with providing corporate sponsors with a way to enhance their reputations through educational philanthropy. Until now, you haven't had occasion to doubt your choice of occupations.

Recently, however, EduMark has taken a contract from a coalition of product manufacturers to develop a satellite-delivered television program consisting of news segments (both hard and soft news), public affairs pieces (mostly political reporting), and some innocuous music and entertainment industry features. On the whole, the two-hour-a-day feed is balanced and harmless and provides a simplified version of what appears on most nightly news programs—which, research shows, are not regularly watched by school-age children. The intent is to sandwich the program into regular classes with which one or more of the segments would be an appropriate fit (political reporting in a class on government, or current events in a history class, for example). Other options are to run the entire program throughout a lunch period on special televisions donated to school cafeterias by the sponsors.

What gives you pause, however, is that sandwiched between the news and entertainment segments are commercials. The sponsors claim the commercials are the only way they can afford to provide the free programming to over a thousand subscriber schools around the country. The coalition of sponsors includes a clothing manufacturer, a soft drink company, a fast-food chain, and a toy company. The commercials appear approximately every 20 minutes and consume less than one fifth of the total programming. The sponsors rotate their commercials so that not all sponsors' messages appear in each daily two-hour feed.

Apparently, most of the schools that have presubscribed to the service find the trade-off between the program content and the commercials a reasonable one. You have begun to wonder, however. Many of the educational components you have worked on to date have had no overt advertising save the sponsor's name attached to the various modules they pay for. This new approach strikes you as different in that the sponsorship is blatant and is sales oriented. You liken the difference to that between the approaches of commercial broadcasting and public television. You also realize that the students viewing this programming are something of a captive audience that can't simply turn off the television. You also wonder if you might be overreacting.

QUESTIONS FOR HYPOTHETICAL

1. Who are your moral claimants in this issue? Consider everyone potentially affected by your (and your company's) actions. Make a list and state in what way you feel you are obligated to each.
2. What do you see as the differences, if any, between the typical corporate sponsorships mentioned and this one?
3. To what extent, if any, does the type of sponsorship that appears on public television differ from that of commercial television?
4. Think about the nature of advertising, especially television advertising. Is there anything inherently unethical about television commercials in general? What are the differences, if any, between commercial television advertising and this project?
5. Do you think anyone could be potentially harmed by this project? If so, who and how?
6. Would you personally take on this project if you had a choice? Why or why not?

CASE STUDY: PROFITS VERSUS PROFESSIONAL OBLIGATION

On March 19, 2001, Jay Harris, publisher of the San Jose *Mercury News* resigned. Harris's stated reason was that he felt that Knight Ridder (parent to the *Mercury News*) had put profit goals above fulfilling the public trust. In his resignation letter, Harris stated that the demand for higher profit margins would "necessitate deep and ill-advised staff and expense reductions at the *Mercury News* [that] . . . would poorly serve our readers, our advertisers and Knight Ridder shareholders."[16]

Earlier, executives of the *Mercury News* and Knight Ridder had met to discuss how to respond to the sharp decline in the newspaper's ad revenues

[16]Jack Hart, Nomination for the Payne Awards for Ethics in Journalism, April 2002.

and how best to achieve the company's goals for the year. According to Harris, what troubled him the most was that there was "virtually no discussion of the damage that would be done to the quality and aspirations of the *Mercury News* as a journalistic endeavor or to its ability to fulfill its responsibilities to the community."[17] The budget cuts proposed by management would have included newsroom layoffs—layoffs that Harris thought would severely damage the paper's ability to fulfill its obligation to the public it served.

Harris had argued that the *Mercury News* could achieve the near-term goals sought by management, but that those savings would be "more than offset by a long term diminution of the vitality and potential profitability of Knight Ridder's Bay Area franchise."[18]

The Knight Ridder CEO, Tony Ridder, had a different perspective and questioned Harris's framing of the issue.[19] According to Ridder, the effects of the bursting of the high-tech bubble in 2001 had strong repercussions throughout the entire economy, including, especially, media supported by advertising. Noting that the *Mercury News* specifically serves the "high-tech heartland," Ridder pointed out that the paper is directly subject to the ups and downs of the economic roller coaster of Silicon Valley. Ridder also suggested that the primary commitment of a publisher, such as Harris, should be to "the ongoing health of the underlying enterprise."

Ridder and Harris also differed on several details. According to Ridder, potential newsroom layoffs were not the reason for Harris's resignation. In fact, such layoffs, said Ridder, were contemplated by Harris himself prior to the executive meeting in March. Ridder also disagreed that the quality of news would suffer, even if the news staff were smaller.

News analyst John McManus backed Harris's position when he pointed out that as long as customers are "able to distinguish high from low quality goods, enjoy choices, and those choices don't harm society . . . it may be reasonable—even a moral duty—for executives to maximize shareholder profits."[20] However, he wondered what happens to society when all but a handful of daily newspapers are owned by monopolies and when the executives in charge "try to generate the largest possible audience at the lowest reporting cost." He suggested that although shareholders will probably come out ahead in the short term, "most of us will lose in the long run."

Ultimately, according to Harris himself, the resignation was caused by a "fundamental disagreement over business strategy and an equally funda-

---

[17]Jay Harris, "Remarks to the American Society of Newspaper Editors," April 6, 2001.

[18]Ibid.

[19]Tony Ridder, "Mercury News Will Remain Strong In Hard Times," Poynter.org, "Today in Journalism," April 11, 2001.

[20]John McMannus, "Does Wall Street Have to Trump Main Street," gradethenews.org, February, 13, 2002.

mental disagreement over whether the company's values and priorities had been changing over the years."

> My argument . . . is that a freedom, a resource so essential to our national democracy that it is protected in our Constitution should not be managed primarily according to the demands of the market or the dictates of a handful of large shareholders.[21]

CASE STUDY QUESTIONS

1. Whom do you see as the moral claimants in this case? List all of them.
2. In what ways is a publisher obligated to them? Use Ross's duties of obligation to help you here.
3. How do you reconcile the tension between turning a legitimate profit and serving the public interest? Can a balance be struck? Who is hurt by leaning too far in either direction and what could you do to minimize that harm?
4. Given that, in this case, the publisher himself is obligated to the parent organization to turn a profit, what do you think Harris's options were? List at least three alternatives.
5. Do you think Harris made the right decision in resigning? Why or why not?

---

[21]Harris, "Remarks to ASNE."

CHAPTER

3

The Media and Professionalism

The question of professionalism in media looms large within the overall landscape of ethical behavior. Professions are supposed to have strong ethical standards that, in some ways, set them apart from other occupations. At the same time, because these standards set them apart, the potential for deviation from societal norms is much greater. For example (assuming for the time being that journalism is a profession), a journalist is typically more obliged to gather a story than to become a part of it. That is how most journalists justify not interfering in a story–not coming to someone's aid, for instance. In fact, the long-held standard of noninterference is a mainstay in modern journalism, for without it a journalist might lose his objectivity. However, professions carry with them much baggage. Licensing, restrictions on membership, codes of conduct, prescriptions for proper actions, all tend to put off working journalists. Thus, most journalists shy away from the notion of their occupation becoming a full profession. On the other hand, public relations has historically embraced the trappings of professionalism, seeking to gain the respectability normally associated with other professions, such as law and medicine. Why the difference? In fact, why would members of any occupation want it to become or not become a profession?

Before we begin to explore whether or not the various media are or should be professions, we must define–as much as possible–what a *profession* is. Perhaps the best way to tackle that question is to describe the characteristics common to most professions. Ethicist Michael Bayles sets down three central features and three secondary features that tend to be present in most professions.[1]

---

[1]Michael D. Bayles, *Professional Ethics*, 2nd ed. (Belmont: Wadsworth Publishing Company, 1989), pp. 7–10.

CENTRAL FEATURES

• Extensive training is usually required to practice within a profession. Most professions have academic degrees associated with them (law, medicine, engineering, nursing, and so on).

• The training involves a significant intellectual component. Although occupations in general usually involve practical training, the professions also require intellectual training, which is usually predominant. This is especially important in the counseling professions, such as law and medicine (and, perhaps, public relations). This provision of advice rather than "things" is a secondary characteristic of most professions.

• The result of the training is an ability that provides an important service to society. Most of the traditional professions provide services vital to the organized function of society (law, medicine, engineering, teaching). These services are necessary not only because they contribute to society in general, but also because not everyone in society is either willing or able to provide these services for themselves.

SECONDARY FEATURES

• Another feature common among professions is credentialing. Most professions have some method of certifying or licensing their members. Lawyers are admitted to the bar; physicians are granted licenses, as are architects, engineers, and dentists. Not all professions are licensed, however. College teachers hold advanced degrees but need not be licensed in any other way. Not all accountants are CPAs. However, what sets professions apart from other occupations are their required credentials—usually a college degree, and in some cases, an advanced college degree. This type of credentialing refers back to the aspect of extensive training.

• A professional organization is also a common feature of most professions. These organizations usually strive to advance the goals of the profession and promote the economic well-being of their members. However, the advancement of professional goals generally takes precedence over economic considerations. This is what sets professional organizations apart from trade unions, for instance.

• Finally, and very importantly, most professions stress autonomy among their members. Being able to perform work free from interference (especially interference from those with less expertise) is vital to being a successful professional. After all, most professionals are hired exactly because their expertise is needed. However, as Bayles points out, exactly how far that autonomy should extend is still an open question, and one that is addressed in detail in the text following.

ARE THE MEDIA PROFESSIONS?

Bayles specifically mentions journalism as being one of those fields having an "equivocal status" as a profession, in that it is "still quite open to people with training in other areas."[2] Many prominent journalists did not study journalism in school. Many were educated in the liberal arts. Increasingly, however, those entering the media fields are graduating from college with degrees in journalism or specific areas of communications media. This influx of workers with intellectual training as well as practical training in the media fields may tend to professionalize the practices even further.

It is also important to distinguish between an occupation being a profession and one undergoing professionalization. Becoming professionalized involves developing standards of performance and some training in them.[3] As occupations move further toward professionalization, they may also develop organizations to represent them, core bodies of knowledge to intellectualize the field, and methods of credentialing to maintain standards of performance. Among the media fields only public relations freely admits to wanting to become a profession; both advertising and journalism contain elements of professions.

All three media occupations have relatively strong support organizations—in some cases, several. For example, public relations has both the Public Relations Society of America (PRSA) and the International Association of Business Communicators (IABC). Among the most influential of advertising professional organizations is the American Advertising Federation. The two largest organizations for print journalists are the Society of Professional Journalists (SPJ) and the American Society of Newspaper Editors (ASNE); and for broadcast journalism, the Radio-Television News Directors Association (RTNDA) is one of the largest. Other organizations exist for specialized areas of journalism. For example, the American Association of Magazine Editors (ASME) yearly announces awards for outstanding and ethical magazine journalism and holds a watchdog function over unethical (especially advertising) practices among magazines.

An established intellectual tradition coupled with a strong professional organization is a clear indicator of increasing professionalization among the media. With media internships on the rise, the practical and technical aspects of professionalism are included in the mix. On the final two criteria,

---

[2]Bayles, *Professional Ethics*, p. 10.
[3]Bayles, *Professional Ethics*, p. 10.

credentialing and public service, there is still a great deal of disagreement. For example, neither licensing nor certification is required of any person working in the media. Exceptions would be membership in trade associations and some affiliation with (often, union membership) or certification for specialized technical work such as cinematography, directing, acting, and various other occupations associated primarily with the entertainment media. But for the "professions" of journalism, advertising, and public relations, there is no licensing.

In journalism, especially, the mere mention of licensing raises hackles. Licensing would indicate control, and journalists will abide no control over their jobs. In fact, the feeling of autonomy is strong enough among journalists to forestall any attempt at licensing or even credentialing (despite the increase in college graduates entering the field fully credentialed, at least intellectually). Journalism maintains a strong libertarian stance even today. Although many journalists will admit to having a professional association (SPJ) and a code of ethics (either SPJ's or their own media outlet's), they generally stop short of claiming that they belong to a profession.

Most advertisers, on the other hand, are more ambivalent about the notion of their business becoming a profession. Remember, advertising is different enough from journalism to require an entirely different communication model (information/persuasion versus pure information). In addition, most advertising performs an "agency" function. That is, advertisers work for clients who make the ultimate decisions concerning their products and how they are marketed. In other ways, however, advertising meets many of the criteria for becoming a profession. It has a fairly large professional organization that represents the field and a code of ethics. College degrees are offered in the study and practice of advertising, which requires that the field have a learnable intellectual component. However, advertisers are not licensed, nor is it clear that they have the same level of autonomy associated with other professions or that they provide an indispensable service to society in the way law and medicine do.

Public relations has been striving for 50 plus years to gain acceptance as a profession. The founding of the Public Relations Society of America (PRSA) in 1948 presaged the steady rise of public relations from an occupation to a near profession. Although members of PRSA are not licensed, they are (voluntarily) accredited through a process similar to licensing. This accreditation, however, does not carry the weight of licensing. For example, a PRSA member who loses his accreditation may still practice public relations—unlike a physician who loses her license or an attorney who is disbarred. So, although public relations has most of the trappings of a profession, it is still struggling to develop and maintain enforceable standards in the same way as law and medicine. Of course, this does not mean that public relations is not a profession. We return to that question at the end of this chapter.

Finally, among the three media industries we are concerned with here, there are several other distinctions associated with professionalism that affect their ethical positions. First, professionals may be either self-employed or employees of a larger organization. Most journalists, for instance, are employees, but many public relations practitioners are self-employed consultants. Advertisers are most often employees in an agency, as are many public relations people. Because self-employed individuals encounter different challenges than do employees, we can expect that ethical considerations will differ as well. For instance, self-employed consultants (as in public relations) must deal with the ethics of client acquisition and conflict of interest. Professional employees, on the other hand, may have to deal more often with reconciling their professional ethics with the bottom-line mentality of their employers.[4]

Another distinction is between those professionals who have individuals as clients and those who have larger entities as clients. A journalist's "clientele" is large and amorphous. A public relations practitioner may serve individuals, groups, or organizations. So may advertisers. Obviously, there is a great deal of variation, and each of the media professions may serve, alternatively, individuals and groups or organizations—and be ethically obligated to each in different ways.

SERVICE TO SOCIETY

One of the key features that differentiates a profession from an occupation is service to society as a whole. Certainly, it can be said that both law and medicine provide this service, but so also do professions such as engineering, dentistry, nursing, accounting, teaching, and many others. The question of service to the public or in the public interest is one that has concerned nearly all professions at one time or another. Answers have ranged from the ideological to the practical, and have taken the form of everything from token articles in codes of ethics to complete programs designed to carry out what many consider to be the premier obligation of a profession. The question is, How real is the discharge of this obligation?

Some have called this service orientation an ideology that maintains that "professionals adhere to the ideal of service to all of humanity. . . . They serve anyone in need regardless of monetary reward or the status of the client."[5] This service orientation has become the keystone among *professional values*, those commonly held beliefs that serve to cement individual practitioners into a single profession. And although serving the public interest is

---

[4]Bayles, *Professional Ethics*, p. 10.

[5]John Kultgen, *Ethics and Professionalism* (Philadelphia: University of Pennsylvania Press, 1988), p. 114.

not necessarily a criterion used to define professionalism, it is one of the most often cited of the values of professionalism.

According to Michael Bayles, professionals in our society are at the top in prestige, wealth, and power; and because they frequently make decisions that affect others, "The granting [by society] of a license and privilege in effect creates a trust for professionals to ensure that these activities are performed in a manner that preserves and promotes values in society."[6] The professions themselves often attempt to justify the respect with which society holds them, and the level of support they in turn command from society, by frequently citing the public service aspects of their roles.

> The animating purpose of a profession is to contribute maximally and efficiently to human welfare. . . . The same purpose (together with great interest in the work itself) is the motive of the true professional, not desire for compensation. . . . [T]he professionals' aim is to serve mankind and they are expected to affirm ("profess") this by accepting their professions' codes of ethics.[7]

There are some basic ways in which most professions attempt to serve the public interest. First, a profession may serve the public interest in a general sense by simply being there. This postulation is somewhat reminiscent of Adam Smith's "invisible hand," in which the effective functioning of a capitalistic economy ultimately serves all of society through discharge of its normal duties to maximize profits. However, although a successfully functioning economy may benefit as the result of a goal-oriented drive to maximize profits, professionals are generally assumed to be guided by an ethical imperative of service to the client–making the "hand" more visible but nonetheless operative. Medicine and the law fall under this heading. Merely by being available to the public, they serve the public welfare. Availability, of course, has led to serious debates over such topics as national health care and equal legal representation. However, for our purposes, a profession such as journalism ideally serves the public interest by providing citizens with the information necessary to participate in a democratic society. In the United States, access to information is deemed as important as access to health care or legal representation. Thus, as with medicine and law, journalism serves the public interest in this general sense–simply by doing its job. As might be expected, however, not everyone agrees with that proposition.

THE PUBLIC JOURNALISM DEBATE

As noted in chapter 2, Christopher Lasch has argued that the press today has abdicated its role of a proper forum for public debate by subscribing to

[6]Bayles, *Professional Ethics*, p. 112.

[7]Kultgen, *Ethics and Professionalism*, p. 62.

the notion that information alone is the proper product of the media. In Lasch's words: "What democracy requires is public debate, not information";[8] and "Unless information is generated by sustained public debate, most of it will be irrelevant at best, misleading and manipulative at worst." Lasch's warnings have not gone unheeded. The rise of what has been dubbed "public journalism" is a direct response to the idea that journalism itself must become an agent of change in a world crying out for direction. The idea of public journalism is communitarian in nature. *Communitarianism* demands involvement in the community in which one resides—a general focus on the community rather than on the individual. It decries the notion that anyone can be detached and objective in the face of community obligation. This would include journalists as well as other occupations operating within a given community. For example, a newspaper practicing public journalism might spend more time studying problems facing the community, open a forum for debate within its pages, and even go so far as to recommend solutions (or, at least, side with some suggestions over others). At the root of this movement is the suspicion that objectivity is simply an unrealizable, perhaps even counterproductive, ideal, and that journalists might as well admit it and move on.

Not surprisingly, many traditional journalists warn that involvement at this level would erode the trust that the people have in the objectivity of journalists. Where else, they ask, can these people turn for unbiased coverage of the day's events? Without that objectivity, journalism becomes merely another opinionated voice. Others counter that it is possible to do both: to have objective reporting on some issues but take sides on others. What is clear is that, as pointed out in chapter 2, simply doing one's job does not necessarily absolve one of all obligations towards others. Journalistic endeavors that ignore the concerns of the community may not survive in today's competitive media environment, a point not lost on most local news operations. Thus, the debate over public journalism—exactly what it constitutes, and whether it can coexist with the more traditional form of objective journalism—will certainly continue for quite some time.

PRO BONO WORK

A second way in which the public interest may be served is through pro bono work. This approach to satisfying the public-interest debt of a profession is clearly outside the realm of journalism, for although journalism may (and often does) point out the ills of society, it rarely becomes involved in

[8]Christopher Lasch, Journalism, "Publicity and the Lost Art of Argument." *Gannett Center Journal*, Spring 1990, pp. 1–11.

solving them (part of the public journalism debate). Thus, pro bono work is most commonly associated with the consulting professions. "Pro bono" literally means *for good*, and is supposed to be work carried out by professionals in the public interest. We often hear of attorneys and physicians taking on pro bono cases, usually the cases of those who cannot pay for their services. (That is why pro bono work is often thought of as being free of charge.) In fact, many in public relations and advertising also take on pro bono clients: often social service agencies or political causes viewed by most as being public-minded. However, Michael Bayles argues that such endeavors as lobbying and public-interest activity do not completely fulfill the responsibility a profession has to act in the public interest, because the individual professionals are not serving the *public* interest, they are merely serving a *particular* interest—something that they are *personally* interested in. Thus, the public interest cannot be served by professionals working on behalf of any such singular interest or client, even if that client is a social service agency.[9]

The reason is that professionals (especially those acting as agents) typically assume the role of advocate. This implies that the professional, under these circumstances, must remain an interested party; and as long as she favors one side of an issue or another, she cannot serve the public interest. For example, a public relations professional assuming pro bono work on behalf of a prochoice interest group is really acting on behalf of the client—no matter how much that client may believe its actions are in the public interest. In the same way, public relations professionals working on behalf of a prolife group espouse their client's position. Both sides certainly are serving an interest, but neither can be said to be serving the public interest.

One way the advertising industry has managed profession-wide pro bono work is through the Advertising Council. Founded during the Second World War, the Advertising Council was composed of volunteer ad agencies from around the country that dedicated their time and resources, free of charge, to promote national causes such as the sale of war bonds and American Red Cross blood drives. Since that time, the Ad Council has continued to work on behalf of nonprofit organizations by providing them with reduced-rate advertising services through its volunteer member agencies. Among its long-standing clients are the United Way and the forest fire prevention campaign featuring Smokey the Bear. Another similar example is the American Civil Liberties Union (ACLU), which has historically taken on cases that involve Constitutional amendments (particularly, the First Amendment). It represents, in a way, the urge of the legal profession toward pro bono work, and takes on cases regardless of public image. For example, the ACLU has represented both jailed journalists and the Ku Klux

[9]Bayles, *Professional Ethics*, p. 117.

Klan. In this sense, the ACLU is not acting out of a personal like or dislike for the cause or the client, but out of a belief that any party deserves the protection afforded by the First Amendment.

What is clear is that the public interest must be served in order for any of the media industries to become true professions. Whether these fields can or even want to become professions is the subject of much debate, some discussed already. However, the inevitable obligations between the media practices and those they affect cannot be ignored, and one of the strengths of professionalism is that these relationships are carefully drawn and the obligations clearly defined. Let us turn, then, to a different approach to defining the relationship between the media practices and their moral claimants—one based on the professional ethics model.

THE PROFESSIONAL–CLIENT RELATIONSHIP

Much is often made of the distinction among advertising, public relations, and journalism. Advertising is most often viewed as an agency-based practice with advocacy on behalf of a client as its primary goal; public relations as a consulting practice, also with advocacy of a client as its goal; and journalism as a slightly paternalistic practice (in that it sets the news agenda) with the public interest at heart. Of course, each of these views is both partly correct and partly incorrect. One of the key elements of a profession is that it serves a client or customer. Physicians and dentists have patients; lawyers have clients, as do advertising and public relations. Teachers have students (increasingly thought of as customers). But the distinction between a client and a customer is a subtle and important one.

A client is someone to whom you are usually contractually obligated. A customer is someone who utilizes your services or uses your product but to whom you are not usually contractually obligated. It could be stated fairly that both advertising and public relations are client-based occupations, and journalism is customer based. However, because of the special place of journalism in our society and the fact that its "product" is the only one protected by the Constitution, the "customers" of journalism must also be considered differently. In fact, journalists are obligated to their public in some of the same ways that teachers are obligated to their students and physicians are obligated to their patients (not just as customers, but as clients). Of course, a journalist's customers expect a good product at a fair price, but they also expect that a certain level of expertise drives the manufacture of that product, including a service orientation not necessarily present in other customer-based occupations. In other words, they expect journalists to be devoted to the dissemination of news in ways they don't expect their grocery clerks to be dedicated to their jobs or taxi drivers to theirs. In the case of journalism, both the provider and the customer have heightened expectations based, in large part, on the understood importance of the press in the United States. Thus, the beneficiaries of the journalistic product are not simply customers; they are, in fact, clients.

It could be argued fairly, then, that the press does have a client, someone to whom it is contractually obligated. As journalist and ethicist James W. Carey has said, "Insofar as journalism has a client, the client is the public."[10] Since the First Amendment of the Constitution is so often cited as a media directive, and the "public's right to know" (a well-worn euphemism for the media's implied imperative to publish), we might call that relationship between the media and the American public a contractual one. With this construct in mind, let us consider the role of journalism, advertising, and public relations and how they might deal with their relationships to their constituent publics from a professional perspective.

One of the key ethical concerns of the professional–client relationship is that of balance. Who makes what decisions and for what reasons? The division of responsibility and accountability for decision making is what drives most professional–client relationships. Most models of this relationship fall into three categories: the client has most decision-making authority; the professional has most decision-making authority; the professional and client are equals.[11] However, most professional models exist along a continuum with various degrees of professional–client involvement (Fig. 3.1). It is rare to find a relationship that is wholly client controlled or one that is entirely controlled by the professional.

Journalism and the Paternalistic Model

As already mentioned, journalism has evolved with more than a touch of *paternalism* in its character. According to Michael Bayles, "A person's conduct is paternalistic to the extent his or her [sic] reasons are to do something to or in behalf of another person for that person's well-being."[12] Journalists have long held that they provide their constituency not only with what it wants, but also with what it needs; and that determination is generally made by the media themselves. Arguments in support of paternalism make much of the clients' inability or unwillingness to decide for themselves. For example, an extremely diligent person might be able to gather and digest enough of what is happening in the world each day to satisfy his

---

[10]As quoted by Joann Byrd, "Let's Stop Abusing the First Amendment" (Seventeenth Annual Ruhl Lecture, University of Oregon School of Journalism and Communication, 1993).

[11]For a thorough discussion of the professional–client relationship, see Bayles, *Professional Ethics*, pp. 70–100.

[12]Bayles, *Professional Ethics*, p. 74.

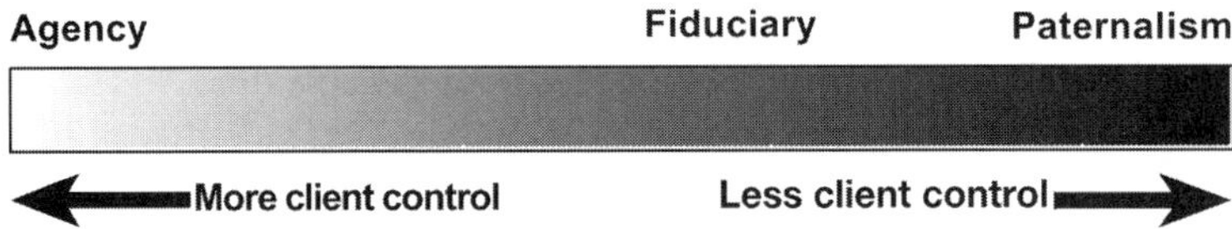

FIG. 3.1. Professional–client relationship models. Professional–client relationship models lie along a continuum from that representing the most client control (agency) to that representing the least client control (paternalism). The fiduciary model represents a more evenly divided relationship, with a slight edge going to the professional. That edge is mitigated, however, by the necessity to foster and maintain the trust of the client.

curiosity. However, not many of us wish to spend our time doing so. We entrust the media to do that for us. We accept the order in which news is selectively presented to us. We assume that the top story is the most newsworthy of the day. We expect that the news will be accurate and balanced. And we do all this because we believe that professional journalists are good at deciding what is news and what is not. At least, that is the tacit understanding. Every time a news director decides what story to run first in the local nightly television newscast, she is acting paternalistically. After all, she has been trained to decide such things, and has the best interest of the clients (her viewers) in mind. The question is, Can the media (especially journalism) provide us with both what we need and what we want?

That balance between serving the public interest by providing people with what they need to become knowledgeable citizens of a working democracy and entertaining them with what they want is a delicate one. Every day, journalists walk this tightrope. Not wanting to appear too paternalistic (and in order to serve very real economic interests), they provide the public with what it wants—whether that is O. J. Simpson trial coverage, endlessly repeated announcements that John F. Kennedy Jr.'s plane has still not been found, or nightly updates on Chandra Levy's whereabouts. In short, journalists tend to be paternalistic a great deal of the time; however, by allowing their audience to dictate much of what they disseminate, they are also tilting toward more client control.

Not everyone sees this as negative. Some journalists view audience involvement in programming decisions as more democratic and far less paternalistic than otherwise. Autonomy has traditionally been a keystone of journalistic practice in this country, but true independence is clearly waning—if it ever really existed. So, although journalism tends to operate according to a paternalistic model, making most of the decisions concerning what to cover, the desires of its constituent public (client) cannot be ignored. The question remains, however, how successful such an arrangement is as a professional model of decision making.

Advocacy and Agency

Both advertising and public relations can said to be advocacy-oriented practices. To *advocate* is to take up the cause of another and to work on that other's behalf to promote that cause. Attorneys become advocates for clients' causes, "zealously" representing their interests.[13] Part of the assumption of advocacy is that the advocate take up his client's cause fully, without regard to his own feelings. An advocate uses his expertise to advance a client's cause. Counseling the client on the most effective course of action may certainly be a part of advocacy, but most advocates proceed pretty much at the client's behest. Thus, advocacy fits well into what is known as the agency model of professional–client relationship.

Under the *agency model*, a professional acts most often under the direction of the client. Advertisers, for instance, may put together elaborate campaigns to serve their client's interests; however, the client picks the agency, determines the product to be marketed, and decides whether or not to use the ideas generated by the agency. Public relations agencies (or "firms," as they are more commonly known) work pretty much in the same fashion. The agency model most clearly exemplifies what has been called the "ideology of advocacy." This ideology assumes two principles of conduct: (a) that a professional is neutral, or detached from the client's purposes; and (b) that the professional is an aggressive partisan of the client working to advance the client's ends.[14] Such a construct allows the professional to absolve herself of moral responsibility for the client's ethical shortcomings. Obviously, this ideology would work well for professions such as the law, in which even unpopular causes would sometimes need to be defended. Without such an ideology, these causes might go unrepresented. But what about other professions, such as advertising and public relations?

There are several reasons why the agency model is not suitable for most professions, including the media. First, as we have discussed in chapters 1 and 2, media professionals are variously obligated. These obligations cannot be discharged properly if all decisions are left to the client. Despite the commonly voiced belief that the primary loyalty of advertisers and public relations practitioners is to the client, we know that serious moral concerns can arise from ignoring third parties. Second, the agency model seriously decreases professional autonomy. Most professionals would strenuously object to abdicating their decision-making authority. Finally, professionals may accept or reject clients who do not meet their moral standards. Ac-

---

[13] *American Bar Association Code of Professional Responsibility*, Canon 7, EC 7-3.

[14] W. H. Simon, "The Ideology of Advocacy: Procedural Justice and Professional Ethics," *Wisconsin Law Review*, 1978, pp. 29–144, as cited in Bayles, *Professional Ethics*, pp. 71–72.

cording to Michael Bayles, "Professionals must . . . be ethically free and responsible persons."[15]

The dilution of decision-making authority is more common in larger organizations in which practitioners most often serve as employees rather than as true professionals. However, even this reduction in autonomy does not reduce a media practitioner's responsibility to act ethically; it only makes the lines of responsibility less clear. Less autonomous practitioners must also determine the ethicality of their actions—even though the major difference between these practitioners and their more independent counterparts, the degree of autonomy, may inhibit the degree to which they might object to actions they determine are less than ethical. Obviously, the independent counselor may advise, and thereby object, from a much stronger position than his counterparts subsumed either within an organization or an agency.

The Fiduciary Model

If paternalism represents the most professional control and agency represents the most client control, what then is an acceptable middle ground? Some have suggested the *fiduciary model*, under which both parties are responsible for decision making and their judgments are given equal consideration. The professional is recognized for his expertise and training (both intellectual and practical); the client is recognized as the driving force behind the professional's activities. Under this construct, a consulting professional (such as an advertising or public relations practitioner) would take the client's problem, canvass all possible solutions, present the most viable options along with costs and benefits of each, and make a recommendation based on professional expertise. Once the client makes the ultimate decision as to which path to pursue, then the professional must work diligently on the client's behalf to carry out the chosen course of action.

While this model has immediate implications for advertising and public relations, its application to journalism requires more explanation. Although journalism is certainly not a consulting profession, it does provide a valuable service to its primary public—its readers, viewers, listeners. The journalist is recognized for her expertise and training and the public is recognized as the reason for journalism to exist in the first place (that is, as the driving force). The ideal of journalism would demand that the press present as complete a picture of the day's important events as possible to its audience. And the implied reason for this presentation of events? To provide the people with the information they need to make educated decisions con-

[15]Bayles, *Professional Ethics*, p. 72.

cerning the environment in which they live and work. They make their decisions based on the provision of this information, much in the same way a client makes a decision based on the information provided by a consulting professional such as an advertiser or public relations professional.

This fiduciary model allows clients as much freedom to determine how their lives are affected as is reasonably warranted on the basis of their ability to make decisions. However, the parties must recognize from the outset that there is a difference between them: The professional is usually at an advantage because she has a better grasp of how to handle certain situations. If this were not the case, the client would do the work for himself. Thus, the weaker party (client) depends on the stronger party (professional), and so must trust the stronger party. According to Bayles, the professional has a special obligation to the client to ensure that the trust and reliance are justified. This obligation of trust is vital to all the media professions.

Trust and the Professional–Client Relationship

At the heart of the fiduciary model is the obligation of trust. Clients must feel that they can trust the professional who is acting, supposedly, in their best interest. As mentioned before, we typically relinquish various decision-making powers to others on a regular basis. We don't want to worry about traffic patterns, the timing of intersection signals, disposing of our own garbage, and the myriad other tasks performed by others on our behalf. We trust that these jobs are being done competently. However, we don't want to give over all our decision-making authority either. It is clear that professionals must engender trust in their constituencies in order to be allowed the autonomy they need to act on their educated judgments; those judgments are what, in turn, perpetuate that trust. As journalist and ethicist Joann Byrd has said concerning journalism, "[The public's] trust is a gift. And we earn it by being forthright about our reasoning."[16]

Clients trust professionals to do what they are supposed to do. What they are supposed to do is defined both by the client and the professional. For example, contracts between public relations professionals or advertisers and their clients stipulate what each will provide. On the other hand, the expectations between the press and the American people have been fairly commonly held over the years. And although those expectations may be, and probably are, changing, their implication is usually clear. Some of these expectations include:

- For consulting professionals, to use professional expertise to analyze the problem. In the case of journalism this means using journalistic

---

[16]Byrd, "Let's Stop Abusing the First Amendment."

training to decide what is news, how to gather it, how to organize it in a meaningful way, and how to present it in a timely manner.

- To formulate alternative plans or courses of action and determine their probable consequences. Journalists are supposed to present a balanced picture, giving as many points of view as are relevant in order that their constituents may make informed decisions.
- To make recommendations, or carry out certain activities on behalf of the client. In the case of journalism, this last expectation depends on how far along the road to public journalism the particular news outlet has moved. To a traditional, libertarian journalist, making a recommendation outside the editorial pages would be a literal sin. To a communitarian journalist, it would be an obligation.

In order to engender the trust needed for a successful fiduciary relationship, professionals generally must fulfill 7 obligations to their clients.[17]

Honesty. The client always expects that the professional will be honest with him. This would extend to others as well, because not being honest with others would necessarily reflect on the client as well. Being honest with clients might include recommending options that are legitimately in the client's best interest, not just the professional's (for example, by providing for more work for the professional instead of leading to an immediate and successful conclusion for the client). Honesty would also include not stealing from a client (by padding bills or providing unneeded services, for instance).

For the professional journalist, honesty is an obvious obligation and requires that all information be truthful, complete, and balanced. However, it could also mean not using deceptive news-gathering techniques, or not obscuring the line between entertainment and news on a television magazine program.

Candor. Candor refers more to truthful disclosure than to honesty. A professional could be dishonest yet open about it. In other words, a person can tell the truth about being dishonest. Some believe that candor is at the heart of the professional–client relationship, at least for consulting professions. In those professions, including advertising and public relations, the client must be able to trust the professional to consult her and to respect her informed judgment in all-important decisions. A client enters the relationship to receive information from the professional. If the professional withholds information he has reason to believe would influence his client's judgment, he alters the agreement (i.e., he manipulates the client's information so that her judgments conform to his own, paternalistic, model). Re-

[17]Bayles, *Professional Ethics*, pp. 79–100.

member, we are not talking about disclosure to possible constituents other than the client here. We deal with that in chapter 5.

For journalists, candor might best be exemplified by a felt obligation to be as complete as possible in covering news stories. A lack of completeness, as is seen in chapter 5, can result in misrepresentation or misinformation, a cardinal sin among professional journalists. In addition, disclosure of conflicts of interest is becoming more commonplace in journalistic circles. For example, *Brill's Content*, a magazine devoted to criticism of the news media, is fairly scrupulous about disclosing its own vested interests when chastising other media. And, with the rise in the digital manipulation of photographs appearing in both news and entertainment media, many are calling for increased emphasis on disclosure—that is, stating clearly which photos have been digitally altered and why.

Competence. The most crucial characteristic of a professional is her ability to do what she says she is capable of doing. It is unethical for professionals to hold themselves out to do or accept work they are not competent to handle; in fact, most professional codes require that professionals undertake only that work they are competent to perform, and that they keep learning in order to keep abreast of the field. This seems simple enough, especially for the consulting professions. An advertiser or public relations person should never claim to be able to provide a service he or she cannot provide; however, it is not that uncommon to hear of agencies of both types overpromising on capabilities or potential results. In the areas of advertising and public relations, agencies may be full-service (providing all the major types of service) or specialized (providing one or only a few types of service). To be the latter and to claim to be the former is to make a false claim concerning competence.

Strangely, competency in journalism is often assumed by the public. Many people outside journalism simply don't understand how it works or what it takes to be a journalist. Because journalism has traditionally been an equivocal profession—those without specific training in the field may still practice it—the level of expertise involved in performing the tasks of the profession is often misunderstood. The result is that many in the media audience fail to comprehend the difference between the competent and the incompetent journalist, thereby supposing that an inferior product reflects the abilities of the entire profession. Although the same is true in public relations and advertising, the effect in journalism is more damning because of the higher expectations for the profession.

Diligence—or Zeal. Although diligence is closely related to competence, it is not the same thing. One can be competent but not diligent. Diligence refers to pursuing a client's interest with vigor and intensity. Too often, professionals let important items slide, due either to laziness or to work pressures. A client realizes that a professional may have other clients, but that does not absolve him of serving her interests with diligence. This is an expected obligation of most consulting professions but its place in journalism is not as strong. Certainly journalists must be diligent in their pursuit of important news; however, their audience is less likely to feel neglected if journalists don't pursue every story, only if they fail to cover the big stories. Diligence in journalism may also refer to the completeness of stories, since an incomplete story may be misleading.

Loyalty. Loyalty is probably one of the most important differences among the media professions (as already mentioned in chapter 1). Loyalty here refers only to that owed to the interests the professional is hired to serve, not to the client in all his or her dealings outside this relationship. And there are limits to this obligation. The biggest problem associated with loyalty is determining the boundaries between a professional's loyalty to a client and other responsibilities. For example, third-party obligations, as we defined them in chapter 2, certainly affect the degree of loyalty owed a client. In addition, clients may expect only a loyalty that does not violate a professional's other responsibilities. For instance, a client can't expect a professional to commit illegal acts on his behalf.

Journalists also have divided loyalties. As discussed earlier, they are obligated to provide information that is both useful and interesting to their audience; they must also turn a profit for their owners, and follow the dictates of their professions and their own consciences. For a journalist, however, fidelity to the ideal of news gathering, what its ultimate purpose is and whom it ultimately serves, is the highest order of loyalty.

Fairness. Fairness in journalism is discussed in some detail in chapter 5; the concept of fairness is part and parcel, however, of all professions. For the consulting professions, fairness can refer to equality of service given to various clients. For example, ignoring one client in order to favor another, higher paying client is patently unfair. Fairness also refers to how clients are chosen by professionals (including serving clients regardless of race, religion, ethnic origin, or gender).

Discretion. Discretion usually refers to confidentiality. Underlying discretion is privacy, the control of information that others have about oneself. Consulting professionals generally maintain client confidentiality, and, in fact, confidentiality clauses are among the most common clauses in professional codes. The importance of discretion to professions such as advertising and public relations is obvious. Many of the clients of these professions are in competitive businesses. Their business strategies, including their advertising and public relations plans, are as important as state secrets are to national governments.

For journalists, confidentiality usually refers to that promised to sources in return for information. Sources would generally be considered as third-party claimants rather than clients in the purest sense. However, the concept of source confidentiality is so strong a journalistic ethic that laws have been enacted to recognize it; and journalists not protected by such laws have sometimes gone to jail to defend source confidentiality.

Can the Fiduciary Model Work?

If we consider the media to be professions, consulting or otherwise, then they need to operate from within a model that brings out the best they have to offer and that encourages ethical consideration of their primary constituency. The fiduciary model does that. For advertising and public relations professionals, this model provides for a way to discharge professional obligations while retaining as much autonomy as possible in decision making. Autonomy allows the consulting professional to adhere more closely to professional standards of conduct. In addition, the element of trust, so vital to this approach, has to be developed and maintained through the pursuit and practice of ethical behavior on the part of the professional toward the client.

For the journalist, this model provides a framework for understanding the obligations inherent in the relationship between the profession and its clients, the consumers of news. These consumers must also trust the journalist, in the same way that advertising and public relations clients trust professional ad and PR people. The provision of good advertising and public relations enables clients to be more effective in their pursuits. In the same way, the provision of important information and news to millions of people every day enables them to better understand their lives and their place in the greater society of which they are a part. Without this information, they are far less likely to contribute effectively to society or to themselves. The client of journalism *trusts* the media professional to do the job right. The fiduciary model *requires* that it be done right. If the media professions consider their roles from the perspective of this model, they are far more likely to realize their ethical obligations, both to clients and to others.

CODES

One of the strongest reasons for belonging to a profession is that certain behaviors, peculiar to that occupation, are spelled out and either encouraged or discouraged by its code. For many members of a profession, a formal code of ethics provides a first line of defense against proposed unethical actions. It is a reference point for the profession as a whole and a sounding board on which to test options for action. Ethicist Richard Johannesen states, "For some people, formal codes are a necessary mark of a true profession. For others, codes are worthless exercises in vagueness, irrelevance, and slick public relations."[18]

Philip Meyer, for example, suggests that the main benefit of codes lies in the work of "articulating a professional group's values" which, in turn, forces the group to think about those values. Not only is the thinking of the members of the profession clarified through this analysis and articulation, but also the group's standards are clarified for outsiders. However, there is some question as to how valuable codes actually are. As Meyer has stated, "Written codes are often criticized for being of little help in making decisions. The values they list are obvious values, the behaviors enjoined are clearly bad behaviors."[19] Speaking specifically of journalism codes, Meyer calls them "lacking in muscle," and "full of glittering generalities."

Can codes be useful? Is there a way to codify professional values and principles that will result in useful guidelines for real-life practitioners? Johannesen thinks so. He argues that, despite the many problems pointed out concerning professional codes, "many of these objections might be lessened or removed."[20] He offers the following list of how professional codes function as useful guidelines for practitioners:

1. Codes can educate new persons in a profession or business by acquainting them with guidelines for ethical responsibility based on the experience of predecessors, and by sensitizing them to ethical problems specific to their field.
2. Codes can narrow the problematic areas with which a person has to struggle.
3. The very process of developing the formal code can be a healthy one that forces participants to reflect on their goals, on allowable means to achieve those goals, and on their obligations to all claimants.
4. An effective and voluntary code may minimize the need for cumbersome and intrusive governmental regulations.
5. Code provisions can be cited as justification for saying no to a communication practice requested by peers or employers.

---

[18]Richard L. Johannesen, *Ethics in Human Communication*, 4th ed. (Prospect Heights: Waveland Press, 1996), p. 197.

[19]Philip Meyer (1987), *Ethical Journalism*. New York: Longman, pp. 17–18.

[20]Richard L. Johannesen, "What should we teach about formal codes of communication ethics," *Journal of Mass Media Ethics*, Vol. 3, No. 1, 59–64. Johannesen, *Ethics in Human Communication*, p. 199.

6. Codes provide an argumentative function. They can serve as a starting point to stimulate professional and public scrutiny of and debate over major ethical quandaries in a field.

   There is a range of argumentative claims that critics or defenders of a communication practice might use to assess ethicality in light of a code. It could be argued that a particular practice

   - clearly is contrary to a precise, relevant, well-justified code;
   - is ethically suspect even though it falls outside the boundaries of any established code;
   - is ethical because the code invoked is irrelevant or inappropriate;
   - is unethical because, although the strict letter of the code was honored, the spirit of the code was violated;
   - is ethical because key terms of the code are too vague and ambiguous for precise or meaningful application;
   - is ethically justified because one applicable code is superseded by another relevant code, or because higher values take precedence over the formal code;
   - is ethical because the facts of the situation, including intent and context, are unclear and should be judged primarily by legal statutes rather than by an ethical code.

7. Codes should be seen as having a function not just of serving as rules of behavior, but primarily as establishing expectations of character. In other words, codes reflect a wide range of character traits necessary for someone to be a professional.[21]

Johannesen also cites 11 guidelines gleaned from a close reading of several scholars who have also studied codes of ethics.

1. The code should clearly differentiate between ideal goals and minimum conditions. *Ideal goals* are to be striven for but not necessarily always attained. *Minimum conditions* must be met in order for a practitioner to be considered ethical.
2. Neither heroic virtue nor extreme sacrifice should be expected by the code. Codes should be written for ordinary persons functioning under ordinary conditions.
3. Language should be clear and specific, free from ambiguity. Key terms should be defined, by analogy if necessary.

[21]Ibid.

4. Provisions of the code should be logically coherent. The order and priority of the provisions should be clear, especially as regards the order in which obligations are to be honored among the various claimants.
5. The code should protect the general public interest and that of all claimants with a stake in the decisions of the professional following the code. The code should make it clear that the profession is never to profit at the expense of the public interest.
6. Provisions should go beyond the obvious ethical violations to focus on the potential problems that are unique to the profession for which the code is devised. For example, a public relations code might accentuate the potential for conflict between the client's interest and the public's.
7. A code should make provision for growth and revision—in fact, encourage it. No code should be seen as engraved in stone.
8. The code should make clear which of its admonitions refer to individual action and which to the profession as a whole.
9. The code should declare the moral bases on which it is founded. Most media codes, for example, cite truth as their guiding principle.
10. As many members as possible should participate in the formulation of the code, from every level within the profession.
11. The code must be enforceable and enforced. A code without teeth is a weak or even useless code.[22]

Finally, Johannesen points to two of the most important functions of codes. The first, and not always the most obvious, is a code's argumentative function. Codes can serve as touchstones for debate, providing the public with a reference point from which to criticize a profession's actions. A code can also serve as a defense against being asked to do something that goes against its provisions, can be used to develop policy, or can serve as an ethical focus for an organization or profession.[23]

The second important function of a code is to depict the ideal character of the professional for whom the code is written. In the words of Karen Lebacqz, author of *Professional Ethics*, a "professional is called not simply to *do* something but to *be* something."[24] This goes beyond the common view of

---

[22]Ibid.

[23]Ibid.

[24]Karen Lebacqz, Professional Ethics: Power and Paradox (Nashville: Abington, 1985), pp. 63–91, as cited in Johannesen, *Ethics in Human Communication*, pp. 202–203.

a code as simply a set of guidelines for professionals to follow. It speaks directly to character, an issue we take up again in chapters 4 and 6.

PROFESSION VERSUS PROFESSIONALISM: IF IT WALKS LIKE A DUCK . . .

Do the media need to be professions? Maybe not, but there are certainly benefits that can be derived from acting like professionals. As already mentioned, professionals garner more respect than those in other occupations. They are often paid more and have a higher level of prestige within our society. Despite the common jokes about doctors and lawyers, they are still held in rather high esteem by the rest of us. To be a professional, in this sense, is to have entrée into a particular realm. In addition to the prestige associated with professionalism is the more important concern of how professionals are supposed to act. Professionals are assumed to be held to a higher set of standards than those in other occupations; and while we certainly find much fault with the professions, it is probably because of this increased expectation that we do so. Being a professional assumes a level of ethicality beyond that of societal norms—certainly different, but also enhanced.

As we have seen, the media "professions" all have professional societies, codes of ethics, intellectual bodies of knowledge, some degree of credentialing, and a prescribed level of practical expertise in their fields. They also bear the obligation of service in the public interest. The discharge of this service may be in some doubt (both in the ideal and the execution), but the expectation is still there. Ironically, in journalism, the field least willing to be viewed as a profession, we find the strongest evidence for the performance of public service.

In short, the media may garner the benefits of professionalism by merely acting as if they were professions. However, this facade has its price. In order to be considered professional, we must act professionally, and that means observing the dictates of professional behavior—including its ethical imperatives. The payoff is that the media gain a modicum of respect that other occupations do not have. And it's not that the public doesn't recognize professional activity when they see it. Paparazzi don't strike many of us as "professional" photographers in the way that photojournalists do. Neither do tabloid reporters compare favorably with those who work for the *New York Times* or the *Washington Post*. The difference is professionalism, and professionalism implies a higher standard of behavior. We cannot have the one without the other.

EXERCISES

1. To what extent do you think news journalism is a profession? Why do you think it should or shouldn't be one?
2. Can advertising and public relations maintain client loyalty and still serve the public interest? Why or why not?
3. Discuss how the news media might use the fiduciary model of professional–client relationship to discharge their obligations to the public they serve.
4. To what degree do you think journalism should or should not be paternalistic?
5. Make up a five-point code of ethics for your own newspaper, ad agency, or PR firm. Limit yourself to the top five ethical problems in your chosen medium.
6. Take one of the professional codes from the Appendix in this book and analyze it according to the points delineated by Richard Johannesen on pages 67–69. For example, is the code's function to educate or to prescribe? Pay particular to Johannesen's 11-point list of guidelines to see if the code you are analyzing meets them.

HYPOTHETICAL: THE TERRORIST MANIFESTO

You are the editor of the *Mountain Times*, a daily newspaper in Aimes, Colorado, a town of 130,000 people. Aimes is also home to Colorado Union College, a school of 10,000 students. The college is known for its topflight liberal arts program and its high scholastic achievements.

Despite its relatively small size, Aimes has been the victim of two mail bombings over the past 18 months. In both cases, college professors were injured—neither seriously. The bomber has not been caught and the local authorities as well as the FBI have no serious leads.

Yesterday, you received in the mail a letter from an anonymous person claiming to be the bomber. Enclosed in the letter was a lengthy "manifesto" outlining the bomber's personal philosophy and his or her reasons for sending explosives to the two professors. Apparently, his/her goal is total anarchy, an overthrow of the government at all levels, and a move to a society of totally independent city-states. The two professors were targeted as symbols of the existing social order. (They are a political scientist and a business professor.) The bombs, he/she claims, were not intended to kill—a claim seemingly supported by the fact that neither of the victims was seriously injured. However, the bomber now insists that his/her political philosophy be printed by the local newspaper in its entirety or he/she will soon be sending out mail bombs designed to do more than just injure. The tone of the threat clearly indicates that he/she is willing to take a life in order to be heard.

You have contacted both the local police and the FBI. The letter is now in the hands of the FBI who tell you that, so far, no finger prints, DNA, or any other identifying features have been lifted from the paper or envelope. The FBI is urging you to run the manifesto in hopes that the bomber will further identify himself or herself in some way as a response to the publication.

QUESTIONS ON HYPOTHETICAL

1. Do you think that running this manifesto compromises your autonomy as a media professional? Why or why not?
2. To what extent do you think the news media should cooperate with law enforcement authorities? If they do, what principles, other than autonomy, might they compromise?
3. Give an example of a situation, other than this one, in which cooperation might be an acceptable option.
4. What would you do in this situation and why?

CASE STUDY: DEFINING A JOURNALIST

Vanessa Leggett was released from the Federal Detention Center in Houston on January 4, 2002, after 168 days of incarceration. Leggett was jailed because she refused to turn over her notes for a true-crime book that she was in the process of writing. Leggett spent more time in jail than any other journalist in U.S. history.

Leggett, who lectures at a local Houston college, is a writer. She was working on a book on the death of a Houston woman, Doris Angleton, who was found shot to death in April 1997. Angleton's millionaire bookie husband, Robert, and his brother, Roger, were charged in the case. The brother committed suicide in jail in February 1998. A state court jury acquitted the husband, and a federal investigation of his dead brother soon followed.

Leggett became interested in the case early on. She was already a criminologist specializing in domestic homicide and had decided to write a book on the Angleton case. The day before Roger Angleton committed suicide, Leggett interviewed him in jail. He left a note admitting his own guilt and exonerating his brother, the murdered woman's husband.

Prior to Robert Angleton's trial, Leggett turned over to local authorities the information she had gathered in her interview with Roger. This information suggested that, despite the suicide note, Robert Angleton had asked his brother to murder Doris. The evidence was not used in the trial and Leggett was not asked to testify. Robert Angleton was acquitted. It turned out that he had been an informant for the Houston police and the FBI.

Subsequently, the FBI asked Leggett to become a paid informant. She refused. They also asked her to delay the publication of her book. She refused. The FBI responded with a subpoena demanding that she turn over every note she had concerning her book in progress, which would have prevented her from continuing her work on the manuscript. She defied the subpoena and was subsequently jailed for contempt of court. Texas has no shield laws protecting journalists or their sources.

The essence of the argument for jailing Leggett was this: The prosecution said that she was not a journalist. She only had one published article, in an obscure FBI journal. She did not make her living as a journalist. She also did not have a contract for the publishing of her proposed book.

Leggett's defenders said that she is considered a journalist because she meets the government's own test. In its panel decision of August 17, 2001, the court said that it would consider whether the person "(1) is engaged in investigative reporting; (2) is gathering news; and (3) possesses the intent at the inception of the news gathering process to disseminate the news to the public." According to these criteria, her defenders say, Leggett is a journalist because she was in the process of gathering news for her book.

Leggett was ultimately released because the grand jury before which she was ordered to testify had completed its term, which meant there was no longer any way for the witness to comply with the subpoena. She could be subpoenaed again if another grand jury is convened to deal with the case or if Robert Angleton is ever indicted.

CASE STUDY QUESTIONS

1. Write down your personal definition of what you think a journalist is.
2. Are there any categories of writers you would exempt from your definition? If so, why?
3. According to your definition, do you think Vanessa Leggett should be considered a journalist? Why or why not?
4. Do you think journalists and their sources should be protected from prosecution? Why or why not?
5. Other professionals, such as physicians, have to carry insurance to protect them from lawsuits, for example. How are journalists similarly protected? Do you think they should be?
6. To what extent, if any, do you think a journalist is obligated, like the rest of us, to aid in criminal investigations?

CHAPTER

4

Ethical Theory

Can understanding ethical theory help us make better moral decisions? Yes, it can. Each of us makes these kinds of decisions anyway, based usually on what we feel is right. That "feeling" isn't really just emotional or intuitive. It's a culturally transmitted as well as a learned response to certain conditions we recognize as having ethical elements in them. Our responses to moral dilemmas are based on what we have learned from our culture, our families, our education, and our society. It might surprise you to know that many of the norms that we glean from these sources are the results of serious moral theorizing.

Ethical theory, which comes from the study of moral philosophy, is simply an organized way of approaching ethical decision making. A theory is a method of explaining something we observe in our lives, the formulation of which will then allow us to predict future such events and deal with them more easily. For example, management theories show us different approaches to managing organizations, employees, and business environments. They help managers understand better the variables involved in running an organization, and show them how best to cope with them. These types of theories are simply models of reality; thus, they are best tested in the real world to see if they work. The same is true of moral theory. Although a great deal of moral theory is so complex and esoteric as to be practically useless to most of us, the specific field of applied ethical theory is designed to be used in the real world. That's the theory we're going to discuss here.

WHY CAN'T WE ALL BE RIGHT? THE DILEMMA OF RELATIVISM

Before we get started on our exploration of ethical theory, we must first answer a very big question: Do we have the right to sit in judgment on other people? This question is very much at the heart of a major moral dilemma today—the dilemma of relativism.

Relativism asserts that moral standards are relative to something else: who you are, the society in which you live, or your cultural predisposition. For example, we can claim that we cannot judge what another society (or a member of that society) is doing because they are governed by the rules of their society, not ours. This is called *cultural relativism.*

Cultural relativism suggest that there are no independent standards by which to judge correct or incorrect actions because all such standards are group- or culture-bound. Since different societies have different moral codes, there can be no objective standard separate from society by which to judge these codes. All moral standards are, thus, subjective. This means that the moral code of our own society has no special status either (except to govern internally). Under this concept, the United States has no moral justification for telling the People's Republic of China that it is violating human rights in its country. According to cultural relativism, human rights is a subjective concept that may or may not cross cultural boundaries intact.

In addition, cultural relativism claims that there are no moral truths in ethics that hold for all people at all times. Morality is merely the construct of a specific society's norms at any given time. It is the moral code of a society that determines what is right within that society. Therefore, we have no authority by which to judge the conduct of people in other societies. What we need, instead, is to become more tolerant of the practices of other cultures. If we were to take cultural relativism seriously, no action deemed acceptable by a given society could be called morally wrong. No society could claim that its conduct was morally superior to another. In fact, the only actions we could decide on would be those of our own society.[1]

SUBJECTIVISM

At the individual level, relativism becomes what is known as ethical subjectivism. *Ethical subjectivism* is the idea that our moral opinions are based on our feelings, and nothing more. There is no right or wrong, only expres-

[1]James Rachels, *The Elements of Moral Philosophy* (New York: McGraw-Hill, Inc., 1993), pp. 15–23.

sions of our feelings. Therefore, we can't judge another individual's actions or beliefs as being wrong or right since our judgments are merely based on opinion and nothing else. Here's the kind of argument ethical subjectivism boils down to:

> "Using sex to sell products is morally acceptable." This simply means I approve of it, nothing more.
>
> "Using sex to sell products is morally unacceptable." This simply means I disapprove of it, nothing more.

Using sex to sell products is neither wrong nor right. The practice is simply a choice based on opinion. The guiding principle of subjectivism is based on the perennial demand "Show me the rule."

Like relativism, subjectivism assumes that there are no objective truths. Thus, there are no such things as moral "facts," only our attitudes about morality. If there is no objective truth in morality, if right and wrong are only matters of opinion, and if opinions vary from culture to culture (and from group to group), how are we to decide whether an action is right or wrong? Does it follow that just because people and cultures disagree there is no objective truth?

THE TEST OF REASON

According to philosopher James Rachels, the problem with the basic argument of both relativism and subjectivism is that it assumes only two possibilities: (a) There *are* moral facts in the same way that there are scientific facts, or (b) our "values" are nothing more than the expression of our subjective feelings—in other words, there are no moral facts. This argument overlooks a crucial third possibility, however: Moral truths are truths of reason. That is, a moral judgment is true if it is backed by better reasons than the alternatives.[2] Think of accepting ethical subjectivism as an excuse. We don't usually allow people to do things simply because they feel they're right. We want reasons.

What we have done instead is to develop theories of rightness and obligation based on the notion of reason. For example, each person ought to do whatever will best promote his or her own interests (ethical egoism). Or we ought to do whatever will promote the greatest happiness for the greatest number (utilitarianism). Or our duty is to follow rules that we could consistently will to be universal laws—that is, rules we would be willing to have

---

[2]Rachels, *Moral Philosophy*, p. 40.

followed by all people in all circumstances (the Kantian categorical imperative).

Although we may still pay a certain amount of lip service to relativism, we tend to want order in our lives. And order typically comes from rules and guidelines, not from allowing everyone to do what they want simply because it feels right. In addition, we realize that there are some things that are not morally acceptable, despite being endorsed by an entire society. Nazi Germany's legally sanctioned and systematic extermination of the Jews during World War II was most certainly immoral. Today, ethnic cleansing evokes the same sense of moral outrage in most of us. What relativism *has* accomplished is to force us to be more tolerant of differences among cultures and between individuals. It should not cause us to overlook unethical or immoral actions.

WHY WE REASON THE WAY WE DO

Every time a journalist refers to the public's right to know as a reason for violating someone's privacy, she is using a *utilitarian* argument. When the same journalist points out that her paper has an absolute rule forbidding the printing of a rape victim's name, she is using a *Kantian* appeal. When a public relations practitioner says that upholding his professional integrity is more important than making money doing something he feels is unethical, he is defending his *virtue*. And when an advertiser says that he is using sex to sell a product because that's what works best, he is using *ethical relativism*. The point is that we all rely on ethical theory every day—we just don't realize it. The benefit in realizing it is that we can then begin to make more consistent decisions by having a better understanding of why we are acting the way we are.

As already pointed out, the way in which we respond to ethical dilemmas isn't entirely something we were born with. Although some of the most recent evidence does suggest that, as human beings, we may be genetically disposed to act in certain ways, these studies don't absolve us of the responsibility to try to be better than our genes dictate.[3] Other research seems to show that whether we're male or female may also predispose us to think and act in certain ways—cultural factors aside.[4] However, assuming for the moment that we just might be slaves to our genes, we are also products of our upbringing, our cultures, and our educational backgrounds. And

---

[3]See especially Matt Ridley, *The Origins of Virtue* (New York: Penguin Books, 1998).

[4]See especially James Q. Wilson, *The Moral Sense* (New York: The Free Press, 1993); and Mary Midgley, *The Ethical Primate: Humans, Freedom and Morality* (London: Routledge, 1994), and *Beast and Man: The Roots of Human Nature* (London: Routledge, 1995).

we each live in a society that has its own set of social and moral norms. Add to that the fact that human beings are born with the ability to reason, and you have the basis for much of ethical theory. Together, these are the elements that have the greatest effect on the way we make moral decisions, and these are what we're going to discuss here.

Because what we are considering in this book are basically the media of the West—specifically, the United States—we will focus here on the ethical theories that have had the most influence on American culture and on American media. Those theories are primarily the ones born during the Enlightenment period in Europe and the United States—a period that ran roughly from the 17th to the 18th century, and had influence on 19th century thought. It is no coincidence that the United States was founded on Enlightenment philosophy; most of the founders of this country were not only quite familiar with that philosophy but were also contributors to it. The Enlightenment was also known as the Age of Reason, because the great thinkers of that time were becoming less attached to religious explanations for life and all its complications and more inclined to scientific accounts. And science, unlike religion, is based on the human faculty of reason, not on faith.

However, we will not slight the critics of Enlightenment theory, many of whom are feminist authors who hold that these theories have resulted in a society, and a media, that is contentious and competitive because of our philosophical heritage. In support of such concepts as communitarianism and some feminist concerns, we will make occasional forays into philosophies such as Confucianism, a societal construct based on interdependence rather than independence. Let us begin, then, with a look at a basic question affecting the activities of human beings: why they band together.

SOCIAL CONTRACT THEORY

One of the longest standing Enlightenment concepts is that of the *social contract.* Dating back to Plato and Aristotle and espoused by a number of European philosophers (most notably Thomas Hobbes, John Locke, and Jean-Jacques Rousseau), social contract theory is an attempt to explain why humans prefer an organized and communal state to one of total individualism and independence. Many of today's disagreements over whether journalism should be objective or subjective in its relationship with its audience stem from the argument over individualism versus communalism. How much allegiance do we owe the state? How community conscious should a newspaper or television station be? Are the media active participants in community affairs or objective outsiders? These are questions that have been discussed in different ways for thousands of years, but they have relevance for us today—especially in how we regard the media and their place in society.

You'll recall from chapter 2 that the media are variously obligated to their constituencies. One of the most important, and most often occurring, obligations is that of fidelity. Fidelity often suggests a contractual obligation, either explicit or implicit. For example, journalists are obligated by fidelity to their audiences; an implied contract exists whereby the journalist is responsible for providing useful and interesting news to his readers, viewers, or listeners. In the same way, advertising and public relations practitioners are obligated to their clients, with third-party obligations discharged through other duties such as noninjury and justice. This latter type of obligation is often referred to as social responsibility (discussed in chapter 1). It could be said that all media are, then, socially obligated.

The idea of social obligation has its roots in the social contract, which basically proposes that a government is responsible to its citizens, who, in turn, lend it legitimacy by their willingness to obey society's rules.

As we have seen, some functions in society are also naturally obligated to society as a whole—especially the professional roles. And although the original idea of social contract had to do with the relationship between a government and the citizens it represents, it is entirely logical to extrapolate this sort of obligation between the media and their constituents. Let us look, then, at some of the philosophers who have considered the social contract and what these theorists have suggested is the proper relationship between citizens and their government.

Plato

As far back as the ancient Greeks, Western philosophy has been concerned with the relationship of individuals to society. Two of the most important of the Greek philosophers, Plato and Aristotle, both gave a great deal of thought to the proper role of society and politics in the lives of human beings. In one of history's greatest works, the *Republic*, Plato (427–347 B.C.) pictured a society in which the educated elite would rule, governing by reason and rejecting the emotional entanglements of life such as the arts. Plato also envisioned a society in which individualism would be sublimated by an overriding obligation to serve society first. The primary reason Plato believed so strongly that only the educated should rule was that he doubted the abilities of *hoi polloi* (Greek words referring to the uncultured mob, or the common people). He thought these people simply didn't have a clue as to the reality of life around them.

In what is known as the parable of the cave, Plato likens the existence of most human beings to that of slaves living in a darkened cave. These slaves are chained facing a large wall. Behind them, and unknown to them, a large fire is burning. Between that fire and the chained slaves are people, perpetually moving about, their shadows thrown upon the wall that the slaves must face. To the slaves, forever bound in place, these shadows and the sounds they hear coming from the moving figures are all there is of reality. It is this reality that the slaves talk and think about, since it is all they know. In order to break the bonds of this reality, a person would have to free himself from his chains, turn around and face the fire and the people moving to and fro in front of it. However, such an experience would probably be so frightening that it would result in the slave wishing to return to his original reality. And if the slave were forced to go to the surface, outside the cave, the experience of the blinding sunlight and vast panorama of this new reality would be nearly overwhelming. Even supposing that the slave became used to the reality of the world, he would never be able to explain it to his fellow slaves if he returned to the darkness of the cave, because their frame of reference wouldn't include these possibilities.

Plato believed most people were enslaved in their own bodies, not able to comprehend the reality beyond their humanity. A more modern interpretation, however, might indicate that we are still prisoners of our own illusions—illusions proffered in large part by the media. In fact, it was this very point that was the focus of much of the criticism of the media early in the 20th century. For example, social philosopher and media critic Walter Lippmann referred to the reality painted by an opinionated media as "the pictures in people's heads," alluding directly to Plato's writings.[5] Today, we have only to look at the phenomenon of the recent rash of reality TV shows to recognize how readily people will incorporate fiction into their daily lives. What transpired on *Survivor* each week invariably became the major topic of conversation around the watercooler until the following week's show. Despite the appellation "reality," the shows are decidedly a sort of forced nonfiction at best.

Thus, the parable of the cave has far-reaching implications for those of us today who base most of what we know about the world beyond our walls on what the media tell us. Plato may have been right to assume that most people will be satisfied with the shadows on the wall, given how difficult it may be to accept the real world. Certainly, this story carries an important moral not only for journalism, but also especially for advertising and public relations, whose primary role frequently is to cast those shadows.

A Platonic view of the place of the media in our society was held (at least for a while) by Lippmann. In some of his earlier works, he proposed that information be controlled by an intelligent elite who would then pass it along to the media to be further interpreted for the people (not unlike Plato's con-

---

[5]Walter Lippmann, *Public Opinion* (New York: Macmillan, 1922), pp. 29–38.

cept of the perfect republic). All information disseminated this way would be completely objective and free of opinion. Although this particular utopia never came to pass, Lippmann is largely responsible for the idealized view of objectivity held by the press today. Thus, a Platonic view of the media would also place objective truth above all else, and allegiance to society above individualism. In other words, social responsibility would probably be placed ahead of press freedom.[6] In addition, we would probably find that the entertainment media would be rejected outright as not contributing positively to society, a view becoming a bit more prevalent these days.

Aristotle

Plato's student Aristotle (384–322 B.C.) continued the Greek interest in the social nature of human beings; however, where Plato focused on the group, Aristotle accentuated the individual. In his *Politics*, he suggested that the true aim of government was to aid its citizens in the realization of the good life. He stressed the seeming need for human beings to live in societies in order to become self-fulfilled—something they could not do in isolation. Aristotle believed that humans are by nature political animals, and it is the job of the state to make the acquisition of the good life a reality. Although he placed heavy stress on the individual, he also noted that both the individual and society must work together toward the same ends. Obviously, his political ideal was a democracy that allows—even requires—personal involvement. And, unlike Plato, Aristotle championed the arts, especially poetic tragedy, because he believed that a message embedded within a creative context would have much more impact and staying power. Although he stopped short of describing a social contract between government and the people, he did shape the belief in a strong and cooperative society. We visit Aristotle again when we look at virtue ethics later in this chapter.

An Aristotelian view of the press would probably emphasize its role in helping individuals fulfill their potential. According to this view, the best way for that to happen would be to keep the citizens informed enough to participate intelligently in the process of democracy. Sound familiar? It's not a coincidence that the modern American press is founded on the principal of informing the people. Aristotle would probably also emphasize the rights of the individual over those of the community, thus press freedoms over press responsibility (at least beyond its basic responsibility to inform). He would also probably favor the creative aspects of advertising, since messages creatively expressed are often those with the most impact (a fact that advertisers know well).

---

[6]John C. Merrill, *Journalism Ethics: Philosophical Foundations for News Media* (New York: St. Martin's Press, 1997), pp. 36–37.

Thomas Hobbes

It wasn't until the Enlightenment that thinkers would revisit the relationship between the state and its citizens with such scrutiny. Thomas Hobbes (1588–1679) lived through some of the most turbulent periods of English history. He was born during the reign of Elizabeth I and lived to see the English Civil War brought to a conclusion. Hobbes was among the first of the Enlightenment philosophers to picture the universe as completely material, and he doubted that either heaven or God could be proved to exist outside the real world. Following the ideas of his day, Hobbes was one of the first to present the human being as a machine with all its parts working together to exist in the material world. In fact, the material world itself was machinelike in its workings, or, as he referred to it, "matter in motion." This mechanistic view of both human beings and the universe they inhabit heavily influenced his concept of how societies and governments were formed.

Hobbes believed that without society human beings would be living in a constant state of violent conflict over scarce resources—"a war of every man against every man." In his best-known book, *Leviathan*, he paints a dire picture of people without government, in which individuals live a life in the shadow of violent death, "solitary, poor, nasty, brutish, and short." His solution to this "state of nature" was the social contract.

Under this social contract, human beings would band together in a state of cooperation in which labor would be divided, and the amount of essential goods would increase and be equitably distributed. In order for this arrangement to work, there had to be a guarantee that people would not harm one another—they had to be free from fear of attack, theft, or treachery. And they had to be able to rely on each other to keep their agreements. But Hobbes was not "the glass is half-full" sort of a person. He believed that although people would band together for self-protection and to better their chances of survival, they would not remain faithful to the contract very long without being forced. Why? Because people, even those living together in a social contract, are still self-interested. Ideally, people will cooperate because they know that their interests are affected not only by what they do but by what other people do as well. In other words, if everyone pursued his or her own self-interests then they would all be worse off than if they worked together. However, Hobbes realized that even by using reason, people would still come to the conclusion that being self-interested would be the best individual course to take.

This is how Hobbes reasoned it out. In living together with other people, you could adopt either of two strategies: You could pursue your own self-interests exclusively, or you could be concerned with other people's welfare as well as your own. Given these two possible strategies, there are four options.

- You could be self-interested although other people are generous, in which case you are getting a free ride.
- Others could be self-interested although you are generous, in which case you're a sucker.
- Everyone could be self-interested, in which case we'd all be back in a state of nature squabbling over scarce resources.
- Everyone could be generous—the ideal state of affairs.[7]

Given these choices, what would a rational person do? Hobbes suggested that anyone with half a brain would choose the first option. The dilemma, however, is that if everyone chooses option one, then we're back to option three—and that is unacceptable. The answer is mutual cooperation overseen by a strong government. People must agree to the establishment of rules to govern their relations with one another and to the formation of an agency (the government) with the power to enforce those rules. Hobbes held that such a government must have more power than any individual or any group in order to effectuate control over violations of the social contract, and people would have only as much liberty as they would allow to others. Hobbes thus made allowances for an individual or a group (a sovereign or a legislature) to govern, as long as governance was for the good of all, not the governing body. Above all else, Thomas Hobbes believed that government—any government—was better than social chaos.

John Locke

John Locke (1632–1704) was a well-educated Englishman who, in addition to being a medical doctor, was profoundly interested in politics. His interest led him to become intimately involved with some of the most influential politicians and rulers of his time. His interest and familiarity with the new thinking in science and philosophy led him to write a number of political and philosophical works throughout his life.

Locke was among those who proposed that human beings band together and form governments in order to manage their affairs better. Without society, Locke believed, people would simply exist in a state of nature, as self-interested individuals—although not as brutish as Hobbes depicted. Only by becoming a society of free individuals deciding their fates together would they reach their full potential as reasoning human beings (a bit Aristotelian). Like most of the other Enlightenment philosophers, Locke believed that human beings were endowed with the ability to reason, and that this is what sets them apart from other creatures. And, as reasoning beings, they

---

[7]Rachels, *Moral Philosophy*, pp. 147–148.

would not bear a government that did not respect their rights. Locke believed that sovereignty ultimately remained with the people, no matter what form the government took. In fact, he proposed that the protection of the rights of the people (life, liberty, and property) was the sole legitimate purpose of government.

John Locke was among the first to suggest that if that trust were ever violated, it would become the moral obligation of the people to overthrow the government and replace it with one that worked properly. Locke was also a man who "walked the talk." During the Glorious Revolution of 1688, he was directly involved in helping place William of Orange on the English throne after James II had, with some reluctance, left it vacant. We can see in Locke the roots of the movement that eventually led to the founding of the United States and the philosophical championing of the individual over the group.

Jean-Jacques Rousseau

Jean-Jacques Rousseau (1712–1778) was born in Geneva, but most people think of him as a French philosopher. His concept of the social contract was quite different from that of both Hobbes and Locke, mostly because his frame of reference was so different. Where Hobbes conceived of people as primarily savages without a government to guide them, Rousseau thought of savagery as ennobling. He believed that Enlightenment society itself had the potential to ruin what was best in humankind by its insistence on reason above all else. He thought that society had a knack for repressing the natural (and good) instincts of people—instincts that he believed should be given free reign. His concept of the "general will" was decidedly democratic. By general will Rousseau meant that individual inclinations should be directed toward what is best for society as a whole, not for individuals. So, while Locke championed the individual, especially the property owner, Rousseau supported social responsibility. He also believed that, because the general population was not always capable of self-rule, charismatic individuals would arise whose forceful personalities would assure them of elected leadership.

Rousseau's ideal state was one in which individual interests were subjugated to the interest of the whole of society—that interest being the betterment of society. He is certainly responsible for furthering the split between the rational being and the emotional being, but his idea of the perfect society was more amenable to totalitarian states than purely democratic ones. Despite this remarkable shortcoming, Rousseau is seen as a champion of social responsibility, and he is often cited when debates turn to the role of the media as either a socially responsible force or one that maintains its rational aloofness.

Rousseau's philosophy would not lend itself to the proposal of a free, unencumbered press, but to the proposal instead of a press that expressed the general will: a socially responsible press. Later, we will see how such a concept ran counter to utilitarian thought (especially that of John Stuart Mill); but for now, suffice it to say that Rousseau's impact on modern media ethics is best understood as falling into the communitarian camp wherein individual freedom plays second fiddle to the needs of society as a whole.

On the other hand, Hobbes would probably propose a press that was responsible directly to government as a tool for control of the people (perhaps as a propaganda arm)—a form of forced social responsibility. And in fact the press of Hobbes's day was strongly controlled by the government. To Hobbes, the role of the press would not be to further either individual goals or societal goals, but goals established by society and legislated by the government.

Of the three philosophers, Locke's insistence on the preservation of individual freedom would play best with today's media. His vision of the social contract would place a heavy emphasis on protecting the people against government affronts to their individual freedoms—in other words, a completely free press. From a journalistic perspective, it is clear that we owe much more to Locke than to Hobbes or Rousseau for the conception of our modern press; however, the true value of what Hobbes, Locke, and Rousseau had to offer lies in their theories of the social contract. The idea that people would come together in consort in order to derive a better life for the conglomerate is part and parcel of America's ideology. Although we owe much more of our societal philosophy to Locke, Hobbes's image of the self-interested individual sublimating his own welfare for the greater good (even if that acquiescence is forced) is a persistent one in our society. Rousseau's insistence on social responsibility over personal interest is a practical counter to total press freedom and finds its home in the modern concept of public journalism. In fact, the concept of the greater good, if not born from, at least was strengthened by, the writings of all the social contractarians.

In short, the concept of the social contract is so ingrained in our social consciousness that we take it for granted that the government and its citizens are mutually obligated. An extension of that relationship is the role of the press in American society, and by further extension, the roles of all media. Remember that Aristotle perceived of communication not only as pure information, but also as entertainment; and to the Greeks, especially, persuasion was a noble endeavor. The Enlightenment philosophers assumed the efficacy of rational argumentation and debate, which the Greeks held as essential to a working democracy. Any social contract has to recognize the place of such tactics of persuasion in furthering the discourse so vital to a society's political well-being. We return to the topic of persuasion in chapters 5 and 6 when we try to come to grips with the various concepts of truth and harm.

THE ARGUMENT OVER MEANS AND ENDS

One of the longest running arguments in ethical theory has been that of whether means or ends should decide what is moral. Some philosophers have contended that a moral act is one that uses ethical means without consideration of the consequences, or ends. Others hold that the consequences of an act are what count; good consequences are the result of right action. In other words, the means are ethical only if the results are good. The two camps have been strongly allied with some of the greatest philosophical minds of the ages, and their arguments have been continued right up until the present day. These two points of view are usually called either *teleological* (having to do with consequences) or *deontological* (having to do with rules or duties). To simplify matters, we'll refer to these as *consequential theories* and *nonconsequential theories*.

NONCONSEQUENTIAL ETHICAL THEORIES

Every time you refer to a law, a rule, a code, or a guideline, you are using nonconsequential ethical theory to bolster your position. Likewise, if you are acting out of a sense of duty or obligation, you are using nonconsequential logic. The idea behind *nonconsequentialism* is that the action itself should be the focus of decision making, not necessarily the outcome of the action. Some actions are simply right or wrong by nature; and, as human beings, we intuitively understand this.

The earliest form of nonconsequential ethics came from religion. The Judeo-Christian Ten Commandments are a good example of a rules-based approach to morality. If you keep the Commandments, you are moral. If you break the Commandments, you are immoral. This is pretty simple reasoning and is, therefore, very appealing to many people. In fact, the strong appeal of nonconsequential ethics is that there is something concrete to base your decisions on. You don't have to dig any deeper than the rule that governs this particular action to find your answer. If your newspaper has a policy against running rape victims' names, then you simply don't run their names—no questions asked. If your professional code of ethics says always tell the truth, then you don't have to mull over whether you should lie or not. These guidelines are sometimes referred to as *conjunctive rules*, and specify a minimal cutoff point for a decision.[8] An example of an ethical conjunctive rule might be the admonition in the Society of Professional Journalists' code (see the Appendix) never to distort the content of news photos or

---

[8]David J. Fritzsche, "A Model of Decision-Making Incorporating Ethical Values." *Journal of Business Ethics, 10*, 1991, pp. 841–852.

videos. Application of such a guideline would clearly invalidate an option of doctoring a photo to remove an unwanted or distracting image.

Most laws, codes, policies, and regulations are the result of nonconsequential ethical thinking: generally, the result of people coming together to make guidelines by which to govern their own actions. The process itself is a major triumph of the Enlightenment and a direct result of the social contract ideas of many of the theorists already discussed. Exactly how these rules of conduct are derived, however, has been often debated. Let us look, then, at some of the more important contributors to this line of thought.

Immanuel Kant

Immanuel Kant (1724–1804) was born and lived his entire life in what was then called the Kingdom of Prussia. By all accounts, he was a quiet intellectual whose studious life ran like clockwork, day after day and year after year. Despite his reserved lifestyle, Kant was a popular figure in his hometown of Königsberg, in eastern Prussia, and he became world famous in his own lifetime.

In a period of just under 10 years at the end of the 18th century, Kant produced some of the most influential philosophical work of his or any other time. In various volumes, covering a huge array of topics, he developed a systematic view of the universe such as had not been seen since the time of the ancient Greeks. Along with his other achievements, Kant also created an ethical system based solely on the human ability to reason and the belief that all moral actions were the result of virtuous intent.

Good Will. Kant held that nothing was good in itself except good will. In other words, no action, in and of itself, was either wrong or right. Only the motive of the actor lent the action its morality. If a person acted out of a vested interest (because of a possible consequence) then the act was nonmoral—it had no moral implications whatsoever. But if a person acted because she thought she was doing the right thing, then she was acting out of good will and the act was a moral act.

In Kant's view, actions have true moral worth only when they spring from recognition of a duty and a choice to discharge it. For example, using Kantian logic, an advertiser who avoided untruthful advertising because he was afraid of getting caught and fined would not necessarily be acting morally. However, if the advertiser recognized a duty to his constituents to tell the truth, and that is the reason he didn't lie, then the act would be a moral act.

Kant defined good will as the uniquely human capacity to act according to one's principles, not out of an expectation of potential consequences. In fact, Kant had learned through the writings of the Italian philosopher and statesman, counselor, Niccolò Machiavelli, that basing decisions solely on likely consequences could excuse any action, even the most abhorrent. In his famous treatise, *The Prince*, Machiavelli had proposed that any action taken by a monarch should be based on an assessment of the best outcome for the monarch himself. Under this guideline (which is also known as "egoism"), actions such as murder could be excused if they are in the best interest of the person making the decision.

Like other Enlightenment theorists, Kant believed that human beings were endowed with the ability to reason, and reasoning would logically lead to an understanding of how to construct moral rules to live by. Rational beings would, then, logically abide by the rules they set for themselves. In this, he was in accord with the social contractarians. Rules arrived at in this manner would also become morally obligatory, and Kant saw obligation (or duty) as the overriding determinant of morality. He believed that we would recognize our duty when we saw it because we could reason, and reason would lead us logically to recognition.

For Kant, there were two obvious types of duties: perfect duties and imperfect duties. *Perfect duties* were those that we must always observe. However, he framed these as proscriptions, or negative obligations—for example, "Never lie" or "Never kill." We must always refrain from these actions, no matter what. *Imperfect duties* were those that we must observe only on some occasions. These were framed as positive obligations, or prescriptions—such as, "Give to charity." He realized that some duties, like "Give to charity," could only be observed by those capable of doing so; others, such as "Don't kill," should and could be observed by everyone. Of course, he knew that rational beings would recognize when a duty was completely binding and when it was not. In this, Kant was an intuitionist, believing that human beings naturally know right from wrong. The question remains, however, exactly how we should come up with the rules by which to live a moral life.

The Categorical Imperative. "We should act in such a way that we could wish the maxim of our action to become a universal law." That's the way Kant believed we would be able to develop rules of order, or duties. "Maxim," in this sense, means the principle on which the action was based—the type of principle that people formulate in determining their conduct. So, if a person won't lie out of principle, he should be willing to apply that principle as a law, universally. Under the categorical imperative, we would only act in ways that we would want everyone else to act, all the time. Thus, if we wished everyone to lie all the time, then it would be permissible for us to lie. We could murder with impunity only if we would allow others to do so. However, Kant proposed that the proper use of the categorical imperative would have us act in a prescribed way, regardless of whether we would wish to be treated that way ourselves. Kant reasoned that rational beings wouldn't tolerate a state of existence in which everyone could lie or kill without compunction. And, of course, that's true. How could we live in a society in which we would expect a lie for every question we asked, or one in which murder were the rule rather than the exception? Kant knew that social order could only come from rules formulated by all and obeyed by all. In fact, a key component of his imperative is that those who legislate the laws are also bound by them.

Kant, writing as he did at the end of the 18th century, was probably heartened by the birth of democracy as a potentially viable form of government. In fact, his idea of a moral community was very much akin to the concepts of democracy given voice by the movers and shakers of the American and French revolutions (although he probably disagreed with the methods of both, since he viewed political change as most properly evolutionary, not revolutionary). If we look at his categorical imperative as a method of achieving a political state that promotes individual autonomy along with the general good, we can better understand the importance of his method. For example, using the categorical imperative, we begin by considering the formulation of laws that will be binding on all citizens all the time, with no exceptions. These laws will not only benefit individuals, but also the state as a whole—or the public good. These laws would also be binding on those whose responsibility it is to legislate and enforce them, because they are categorical. And, these laws would respect the citizens of the state and their individual rights as human beings.[9]

This recognition of the inherent worth of human beings is a key feature of Kant's categorical imperative. As part of his method for recognizing moral duties, Kant insisted that we always act so as to treat others as ends in themselves and never completely as means to an end. In other words, we are not to use or treat other people merely as objects. He rationalized that all human beings are owed a minimum of respect simply because they are human beings and capable of reason—in the same way that other natural rights philosophers believed we are all born with "certain unalienable Rights." For Kant, we all have the right to basic respect as human beings. Only if we demonstrate that we do not deserve to be respected would we relinquish that right. In other words, every person's autonomy would be respected except in cases in which the exercise of that autonomy conflicted with the public good (as represented by the laws of the state). So we can see that Kant's method of arriving at moral rules allows not only individuals

---

[9]For an excellent discussion of the political component of Kant's philosophy as well as a clear explanation of his ethics as a whole, see Roger J. Sullivan, *An Introduction to Kant's Ethics* (Cambridge: Cambridge University Press, 1994).

to construct moral guidelines for themselves, but it also permits whole communities to formulate laws for the governance of an entire political system under which individual rights are also clearly recognized.

NONCONSEQUENTIAL THEORY IN MODERN PRACTICE

Kant's theory is still much debated today, mostly because of his seemingly absolutist stance on perfect duties. For example, there appears to be no clear reason why prohibitions against some acts should hold without exception. Is it never permissible to lie? What if the lie is to save another person from harm? Likewise, could we ever be justified in killing another person? How about in defense of one's family? These are important questions over which Kant clearly struggled. On the question of conflicting duties, for instance, Kant, much like other intuitionists, insisted that we would recognize which was the "true" moral duty and act according to our reason. This smacks a bit of the rationale given in this century by William David Ross, a Kantian scholar already introduced in chapter 2. Ross, whose six obligations were discussed as a means of identifying moral claimants, also held that rational human beings would be able to decide for themselves which of these duties were paramount in any given situation. The reasoning here is that the very struggle involved in determining the priority of duties is instructional in itself and will ultimately lead to more thoughtful decisions.

The fact that all of the media professions have codes of ethics, and that nearly all media outlets (journalistic, advertising, and public relations) have their own, individual, codes as well, speaks to the Kantian desire to make and follow moral rules. These rules are almost always made with no exceptions in mind. When the previous Public Relations Society of America code stated in Article 5 that "a member shall not knowingly disseminate false or misleading information," it means "no member—ever." Not surprisingly, most rules are like that.

Kantian guidelines continue to proliferate in every newsroom and media agency. They vary from the overly complex to the exquisitely simple. Former *Washington Post* ombudsperson Joann Byrd has developed what she calls her "Four-Minute Ethics Guide." Her decidedly Kantian rules are:

- Do not kill.
- Do not cause avoidable harm.
- Act justly (meaning, give people what they are due, treat them fairly).
- Help those in immediate need.
- Keep promises.

- Respect persons (as in: Appreciate their dignity and privacy and autonomy).
- Do not lie.

To these, Byrd adds the "only two principles of journalism [that] can be weighed on the same scale with the rules that guide the human race. They are: Inform the public and Serve the public interest."[10]

Another aspect of Kantian ethics apparent today is that of personal integrity. Kant's emphasis on individual autonomy and respect for persons as ends in themselves leads us to respect individual integrity as well. It also insists on our practicing individual integrity in recognition of our duties as moral agents. Legal scholar Stephen Carter, in his book *Integrity*, says that the practice of integrity today has three requirements.[11] First, a person must discern the difference between right and wrong. Of course, Kant believed that, as reasoning human beings, we were capable of doing just that. According to Carter, this first criterion "captures the idea of integrity as requiring a degree of moral reflectiveness." Second, a person must act on what she has discerned, even at personal cost. This brings in the ideal of an integral person as steadfast, which includes the sense of keeping commitments. You'll recall that the key to Kant's morality was good will–acting out of a sense of duty. Finally, Carter states that a person must be willing to say openly that she is acting out of an understanding of right and wrong, "which reminds us that a person of integrity is unashamed of doing the right thing."

Thus, in the view of both Kant and his successors, the moral person is the one who is willing to formulate rules that will then become binding both on her and on everyone else in her society. Then, that person must act out of recognition of those rules and out of respect for the integrity of others as well as her own. We can clearly see the influence Kant has had on modern ethical thought as well as its potential implications for the media. However, the question that must concern us now is whether simply following the rules, no matter how logically arrived at, is the only way we can conceive of moral action. Is it not possible that the probable outcome of our actions should also be considered?

CONSEQUENTIAL ETHICAL THEORIES

Although rules of morality may seem to be the most common approach used, both historically and currently, such is not the case. If you think

---

[10] Joann Byrd, "Let's Stop Abusing the First Amendment" (Seventeenth Annual Ruhl Lecture, University of Oregon School of Journalism and Communication, 1993).

[11] Stephen Carter, *Integrity* (New York: Basic Books (Harper Collins), 1996).

about it, even rules must be arrived at by considering the consequences of actions. For example, by proposing that public relations practitioners should not lie to the media we are also asking, in effect, Why not? And when we ask why not, we're considering consequences. As already mentioned, consequentialism has acquired something of a bad reputation, at least in the Machiavellian form (egoism). However, no one today would seriously propose that we make moral decisions without considering the potential consequences of our actions. In order to better understand the nature of consequential ethical thought, we need to explore its most common forms.

First of all, all consequential theories contend that the moral rightness of an action can be determined by looking at its consequences. If the consequences are good, the act is right. If the consequences are bad, the act is wrong. What is right is determined by considering the ratio of good to evil that the action produces. The right act is the one that produces, or is intended to produce, the greatest ratio of good to evil of any alternative being considered. The two consequential theories we're going to discuss here are egoism and utilitarianism.

Egoism

Egoism contends that an act is moral when it promotes an individual's best long-term interests. If an action produces, or is intended to produce, a greater ratio of good to evil for the individual *in the long run* than any other alternative, then it is the right action to perform. Remember Machiavelli? He basically proposed that a monarch should do anything in his power to improve his position and to gain more power. Any act was justified if it aided the acquisition and maintenance of power, for a good ruler sometimes had to be ruthless if his people were to derive any benefit from his being in charge.

Also recall that Thomas Hobbes saw human beings as essentially egoistic (self-interested), and this is why a strong government was a necessary component of his social contract. Unless being forced to do otherwise, he believed, most people would simply look out for themselves. Although the other social contractarians, such as Locke and Rousseau, took a slightly less callous view of the self-interested nature of people, they still recognized that the temptation existed. In fact, all moral decisions contain an element of egoism. When a reporter writes a story about a social problem, he certainly hopes that some good will come of it. He probably also hopes that some good will come to him as well—recognition, a promotion, a Pulitzer Prize. And there is nothing inherently wrong with self-interest, as long as it doesn't become the overriding reason for making a decision.

Not only people are egoistic. Organizations can act egoistically, as can entire nations (typically called "chauvinism" or "jingoism"). It wasn't that long ago that the infamous line, "What's good for General Motors is good for the nation," was uttered. When a local television news outlet withholds a story critical of a local car dealer because car dealerships are its main source of advertising income, it is acting egoistically. When an advertising agency runs a campaign for a big-name liquor brand directed at a minority with a known predisposition for alcoholism, it is acting egoistically. When a public relations firm decides to drop a controversial client because it is worried about its reputation, it is acting egoistically. This is not to say that these are unethical decisions; however, if self-interest is the sole, motivating factor, they may well be.

There are some misconceptions concerning egoism that give it a worse reputation than it deserves. For example, egoists don't necessarily do just anything they want. An egoist might undergo unpleasant or even painful experiences as long as the long-term outcome is positive. It is also not true that egoists are bereft of such traits as honesty, generosity, and self-sacrifice. Egoists can possess all of these traits, as long as they advance long-term self-interest. For example, an egoistic CEO might be willing to admit to wrongdoing in the short term if the net gain were a better reputation in the long run. In fact, it is not uncommon to hear public relations counselors phrase advice in egoistic rather than moralistic terms to their clients. You'd be much more likely to hear, "I think that course of action will damage our potential sales in the minority markets," than, "I don't think that's the ethical thing to do."

Of course, the most obvious weaknesses of egoism have been pointed out by numerous theorists, including some we've already discussed. First of all, egoism ignores blatant wrongs—actions that, in and of themselves, are morally unacceptable. That is why Machiavelli has such a bad reputation for recommending egoism as a legitimate form of moral decision making. Murdering your rivals just doesn't seem very democratic. We also recognize that egoism cannot be used successfully by everyone at the same time. If all people were egoists exclusively, we would probably end up back in Hobbes's "state of nature." We have seen for ourselves how, in unsettled times, whole societies become egoistic to the extent that they are willing to wipe out other cultures different from themselves. In short, there is simply no way to resolve conflicts of egoistic interests. All egoists are compelled to look out for themselves unless forced to do otherwise. Obviously, the interests of others must be considered as well as the likely consequences of our actions on these other parties. That's where utilitarianism comes in.

Utilitarianism

Although not entirely his idea, the credit for utilitarian philosophy is usually given to Jeremy Bentham (1748–1832). Bentham was something of a radical reformer in his lifetime, pursuing such causes as prison reform, public education, censorship, and government corruption. At the base of all of his activities lay a single, guiding philosophy: The rightness or wrongness of any action can be judged entirely in terms of its consequences. Motives are, thus, irrelevant—completely the opposite of Kantian theory. Good consequences give pleasure; bad consequences result in pain. (This became known as the "pleasure–pain principle.") Bentham's idea was that the right course of action was the one that promoted the greatest pleasure or minimized the most pain. He called this philosophy *utilitarianism*, because it promoted an action based on its utility, or usefulness. In fact, the now familiar phrase, "the greatest good for the greatest number," is part and parcel of utilitarian philosophy.

On the down side, Bentham is also largely responsible for developing utilitarianism into a coldly objective and formulaic method for making decisions. He was convinced, for instance, that pleasure and pain could be arithmetically calculated, and that the more objective the decision maker, the more fair the outcome. Under his conception of utilitarianism, there was no room for emotion or for the individual. Only the greater good was important.

Bentham continued to crusade for utilitarianism his entire life, bringing about numerous reforms in Great Britain. His philosophy was furthered by his disciple, James Mill (1773–1836), who is largely credited with bringing Bentham's works to the forefront of British politics in the early part of the 19th century. Government and social agencies in Britain, even today, are heavily influenced by the utilitarian notion of the greater good and the welfare of all of society as having precedence over that of the individual.

John Stuart Mill. James Mill is probably best known, however, as the father of John Stuart Mill (1806–1873). John Stuart Mill was raised as part of an educational experiment to see how much intelligence could be imparted to a child completely shut off from outside influences. As a result of a strict, and lonely, upbringing, young Mill was reading Greek at the age of 3 and studying the classics, arithmetic, and history before he was 7. He was also inundated with the philosophy of utilitarianism, which he eventually came to view as too objective and cold to be used successfully on human beings. (His odd upbringing probably had something to do with this.) Not surprisingly, by the age of 19, Mill was suffering from massive depression. Fortunately, he discovered poetry and later largely credited the works of William Wordsworth with having cured him of his illness. After some time in France, where he came in contact with many of the great French minds of the age, Mill began his lifelong investigation into and reformation of the philosophy of utilitarianism.

The result of Mill's work has been a utilitarian philosophy much more amenable to the individual and less rigid in its attention to the majority's happiness; and in one of his greatest works, *On Liberty* (1859), he asserted once and for all the rights of the individual. In addition to his more famous work, Mill is also credited with bringing the rights of women to the forefront in a series of works coauthored with his wife, Harriet Taylor, culminating with *The Subjection of Women* (1869). In it, Mill and Taylor (and after Taylor's death, her daughter, Helen) argued forcefully for sexual equality, a subject that had largely been ignored since ancient times (except, of course, by women, most especially women philosophers such as Mary Wollstonecraft, who wrote vehemently about women's rights in the 18th century).[12] We return to John Stuart Mill again when we take up the subjects of free speech and harm.

Modern Utilitarianism

Utilitarianism today has lost much of the mathematical machinery that Bentham developed in order to weigh good and evil against each other. In fact, today we tend to be suspicious of decision-making methods that use calculation as a basis. Think of the negative connotation of the word "calculating." How about the business practice of cost-benefit analysis—reducing everything to numbers (typically monetary)? Modern utilitarianism simply asserts that we should always act so as to produce the greatest ratio of good to evil for everyone concerned with our decision. Ideally, that would include all of the moral claimants affected by our decision. In this way, utilitarianism pays strict attention to third-party interests, thus disallowing client loyalty (for example) to override the best interests of others. In fact, one of the primary benefits of using utilitarianism is that it recognizes the four primary claimant groups: clients/customers, organization, profession, and society.

We can easily see the attractiveness of utilitarianism as a decision-making tool for the media. Every time a journalist argues that publishing a story benefits his readers more than it harms the subject of the story, he is using utilitarian logic. The common claim that the practice of advertising adds to the marketplace of ideas, is also a utilitarian argument. In fact, making a moral decision without considering the likely effect of the action on the various claimants would strike most of us as decidedly errant. One of the problems with utilitarianism, however, is that it causes us to have to make decisions on a case-by-case basis. Every decision requires that we stop and consider how our actions will affect everyone on our list. Then we must balance the potential good against the possible harm caused by our action. If the good outweighs the harm—for the most people—then we go with the decision. Wouldn't following rules be a lot easier?

---

[12]Harriet Taylor's first husband requested that her name not appear on works jointly or almost wholly written by her and Mill with whom she had been carrying on a very close relationship. Following her husband's death and her subsequent marriage to Mill, she was, according to Mill, still reluctant to have her name appear on their works. After her death from tuberculosis in 1858, *The Subjection of Women* was finished by Mill and Helen Taylor, Harriet's daughter. Mill credited both of them with the bulk of this work, even though only his name appeared on it.

In fact, utilitarians have had similar problems with their own philosophy. That's why there are two basic forms of utilitarianism. *Act* utilitarianism, which is what we've been talking about so far, states that the right *act* is the one that produces the greatest ratio of good to evil for all concerned, and is used on a case-by-case basis. On the other hand, *rule* utilitarianism states that ethical actions and judgments can be based on *rules* that promote the greatest ratio of good to evil for all concerned.

For example, a reporter working under the act utilitarian guideline could write a completely fictitious story about a ghetto child hooked on drugs, and how his life is a microcosm of the tragedy of our inner cities. The publication of this story could win the paper accolades and the reporter a major prize and a glowing reputation. It could also prompt intense public concern and stimulate legislative activity to help correct the inequalities suffered by people living in the inner cities of this country. Under act utilitarianism, the publication of this fictitious story could be justified because it serves the greater good via recognition of the problem and probable social reform. However, is lying ever acceptable in journalism? Most everyone would agree that it is not. How, then, can a utilitarian justify *not* writing the story?

Rule utilitarians believe that not every decision calls for a balancing of good over evil. They hold that some types of decisions can be made in advance, because the logical right choice can generally be said to be in the best interest of all concerned. For example, if we assume that lying, in any form, irrevocably damages the reputation of journalism, and that that damage is definitely counter to the greater good, then we can make a rule that says, "Never lie in journalism." The idea is that the greater good is nearly always promoted by following this rule. Any exceptions can be resolved using act utilitarian methods.

The benefits of using utilitarianism as a decision-making tool are that it forces us to consider everyone concerned with our actions, and that it directs us to pick the alternative that generates the greatest good for the greatest number of people—a very democratic concept. In fact, that is exactly what makes a democracy work—majority rule. The majority choice is the one that is put into effect because the majority, by default, is the greatest number of people. The problem, of course, is that the majority may not deserve the greatest good, a point made very clear at the beginning of the 19th century by a French visitor to the United States named Alexis de Tocqueville. De Tocqueville had come to America to study its new form of government for himself, and ended up writing one of the most probing investigations of democracy ever produced, before or since. One of his most cogent insights was that the focus of majority rule under a democratic form of government might well lead to what he termed, "the tyranny of the majority"—a point not wasted on anyone who has ever lost an election. And, in fact, under utilitarianism, the minority basically loses out. Only by balancing utilitarianism with the theory of justice can we account for the often neglected minority interest. The theory of *distributive justice* basically asserts that those who deserve something should get it, and those who are not deserving should not. Thus, a deserving minority might benefit from an action over an undeserving majority—a concept that runs decidedly counter to the purest form of utilitarian theory. In this country, however, we have variously recognized this shortcoming of utilitarianism by enacting laws to help mitigate the effect of the tyranny of the majority. Affirmative action laws are a good example of the theory of distributive justice used as a counter to the "greater good" approach.

This potential conflict was not lost on John Stuart Mill who, in his treatise on utilitarianism, dealt with the connection between justice and utility. Mill admits that certain examples of justice and injustice merit a higher consideration than the mere meting out of pleasure. For example, he agrees that we

- Should not deprive anyone of his or her personal liberty, property, or any other thing that belongs to him or her by law. In other words, do not violate a person's legal rights.
- Should not take or withhold from anyone that to which they have a moral right. This is especially important if a bad law has resulted in someone either being deprived of their rights or having been given rights they do not deserve. The fact that these rights are conferred by law makes them legal rights; however, the fact that the law may have deprived someone of rights that they deserve makes those rights (prohibited by the law) moral rights. Think, here, of the segregation laws prior to the 1960s.
- Should give to those who are deserving, and withhold from those who are not deserving (the notion of distributive justice).
- Should keep promises that we have entered into voluntarily.
- Should not show partiality in circumstances in which impartiality is considered appropriate.

Mill warns us that a blind devotion to the greater good should be tempered first by these considerations.

The final indictment against utilitarianism is that it, like egoism, ignores blatant wrongs. Theoretically, utilitarianism could, and has been, used to justify everything from segregation to genocide. The point is that neither nonconsequential nor consequential theories are totally satisfactory as decision-making tools. Most modern philosophers have merged the two into acceptable hybrid systems that seem to accentuate the positives while attempting to eliminate the negatives. Now, however, let's turn to a totally different approach to ethical decision making—one that deals neither with the act nor the consequences, but with the character of the moral agent.

VIRTUE ETHICS

Virtue ethics, or *character ethics*, has been around easily as long as both consequential and nonconsequential theories; however, the Enlightenment pretty much guaranteed that an emphasis on duty, obligation, and the greater good would dominate Western ethical thought. It is only recently that the study of virtue ethics has elicited new interest. It is surprising, therefore, to find that the study of virtue as an ethical construct is at least as old as the ancient Greeks.

History of Virtue Ethics

The Greek philosophers (especially Plato and Aristotle) chose not to ask, What is the right thing to do? Instead, they asked, What traits of character make one a good person? They called these traits "virtues" and defined them as actions that, if practiced habitually, would ultimately result in a good character. In other words, virtues are needed for human beings to conduct their lives well. Virtues can be acquired, learned, and cultivated by the diligent person. Plato concentrated on what he called the "Four Cardinal Virtues": temperance, justice, courage, and wisdom. In Judeo-Christian cultures, desirable virtues might include these four plus gentleness, fairness, generosity, and truthfulness.[13] Of course, many lists are possible. James Rachels, in his book *The Elements of Moral Philosophy* lists the following as a few of the possibilities:[14]

- benevolence
- civility
- compassion
- conscientiousness
- courage
- courteousness
- dependability
- fairness
- friendliness
- generosity
- honesty
- industriousness
- justice
- loyalty
- moderation
- reasonableness
- self-confidence
- self-control
- self-discipline
- self-reliance
- tactfulness
- thoughtfulness
- tolerance

[13]Richard L. Johannesen, *Ethics in Human Communication*, 4th ed. (Prospect Heights: Waveland Press, 1996), p. 12.

[14]James Rachels, *Moral Philosophy*, p. 163.

Aristotle, Plato's student, took a different approach to defining exactly what constituted a virtue. Aristotle held that a "Moral virtue is a mean between two extremes, the one involving excess and the other deficiency." Aristotle dubbed this concept the "Golden Mean," and called for moderation in all things as the road to a virtuous character. For example, the middle ground between cowardice and foolhardiness would be courage. The mean between shamelessness and bashfulness is modesty; and between stinginess and wastefulness lies generosity.

According to media scholar Stanley Cunningham, however, Aristotle didn't intend that we should begin with the extremes and then identify the mean. This would tend to lead us into mediocrity rather than excellence. Instead, he believed that a person of moral maturity (one who had learned the habits of good character and subsequently gained the acuity of moral reasoning) would naturally seek the action that would further excellent moral character—an action that would logically lie somewhere between two extremes—one excessive, the other deficient. As Cunningham suggests,

> . . . that same quality of goodness in the things we do is ultimately grounded in our perception or judgment about what is the right thing to do. . . . It is the informed choice of a morally developed person whose cognitive apparatus and emotional status are in good working order.[15]

Aristotle also held that the process of reasoning that would lead to the moral mean was dependent on the individual and on the circumstance. The moral mean would, thus, be different for each person; no one, absolute mean would suffice. "[E]verybody who understands his business avoids alike excess and deficiency; he seeks and chooses the mean, not the absolute mean, but the mean considered relatively to ourselves." And he was much in favor of teaching the young to develop the habit of moral reasoning so that when they were adults, they would naturally gravitate toward the moral mean in any given situation. "Arguments and teaching surely do not influence everyone, but the soul of the student needs to have been prepared by habits for enjoying and hating finely, like ground that is to nourish seed."[16] Ultimately, the moral mean can only be discovered by the application of both learned theory and personal perception (the practical application of our natural senses to a situation).

Thus, Aristotle's model of the golden mean is not a simple, arithmetical calculation of an average action. Rather, it is the result of acquired character, a moral maturity, and an ability to perceive a situation accurately as it pertains to the individual involved. He would say that any person of moral

---

[15]Stanley Cunningham, "Getting it Right: Aristotle's 'Golden Mean' as Theory Deterioration," *Journal of Mass Media Ethics*, Volume, 14, Number 1, 1999, p. 11.

[16]Aristotle, *Nichomachean Ethics*, Book X, section 9.

maturity, with an understanding of what is right and what is wrong, would view the situation through the lens of his personal experience and naturally choose the moral mean. As every situation differs, every moral mean will likewise differ.

For example, an editor deciding on a privacy issue might decide to "soften" a story so as not to inflict undue harm on the story's subject; however, this decision would not be based on first deciding on the extremes (for instance, publishing and injuring the subject of the story, or not publishing and depriving the public of information it needs). In other words, the decision is not a compromise between the two extremes. Rather, it is based on the knowledge and experience of the editor, his vision of the place of journalism in society, the obligations inherent in that charge, and the myriad other factors that comprise the whole of the issue. The decision is, thus, a choice to do the right thing under the circumstances, but is based on a well-developed character, honed in the practice of journalism and tempered by both personal and societal morality.

Both Plato and Aristotle believed that a good character would result in good actions; and virtues, in turn, were cultivated by the practice of good actions—so the logic is somewhat circuitous. Regardless, the message is clear: A person's character dictates whether that person will conduct himself morally or immorally. A person possessing the virtue of honesty is not very likely to lie, since telling the truth is habitual with that person. A virtuous person is, therefore, a person of continuity—a person for whom moral action is based on a good character, not on consequences or rules. This sort of person will be consistent in her judgments because her character dictates it. You'll recall that Stephen Carter called for more integrity in moral decision making, and was cited earlier as an exemplar of Kantian thinking. Carter could also be said to be a virtue ethicist in that he views integrity as an essential and desirable character trait—a virtue.

Virtue Ethics in Modern Practice

The real value of virtue ethics is that it places the onus of right action directly on the person making the decision. A person of strong character developed through habitual right action will make the right decisions, most of the time. A person of weak character will not. It's as simple as that. How does this work out for those in the media? First, we must ask ourselves what we would consider virtues in the various media professions. For example, a list of virtues for journalists would probably include truthfulness, tenaciousness, fairness, and self-reliance. Certainly, there are others, but you get the idea. For public relations: truthfulness, loyalty, trustworthiness, honesty, diligence, and discretion. How about advertising? Certainly advertisers would cite truthfulness in common with the other media professions, but also loyalty, diligence, honesty, and tactfulness.

You may have noticed that these virtues all have one thing in common—they contribute to the effectiveness of the practice for which they are considered virtues. But what about other virtues not normally associated with these media roles? Why not consider compassion a journalistic virtue? Or civility, or friendliness? What's wrong with adding fairness, justice, and moderation to the lists for advertising and public relations? The answer, of course, is that these virtues might sometimes interfere with the functions of the media in ways the others would not. However, it is easy to see why so many outside the media often view them as unfeeling and egoistic when the very virtues we would most associate with being a good *person* are those that might hobble media people in the performance of their jobs as *professionals*. Nonetheless, it is hard to imagine a media practitioner of good character opting to override that character simply in order to get a story or keep a client. As Aristotle suggested, a person of good character will gravitate toward the moral mean. If he does not, can we truly say he is virtuous?

Finally, character can tell us something valuable about a person. For instance, one of the most frequently voiced opinions during the Monica Lewinsky–Bill Clinton scandal that lasted nearly a year was that it was a "character issue." Others countered that a person's private life (even a president's) shouldn't be anybody's business but his own. In fact, this is the most often cited journalistic guideline when deciding on invasion of privacy issues. Typically, if a public official's private life doesn't interfere with the public performance of his or her duties, then invading that person's privacy is not called for. However, we might ask ourselves, What does this lapse in a person's private morals say about his or her public morals? According to virtue ethics, an inherently honest person would not lie under most circumstances. Logically, then, a person who does lie (especially habitually) could be viewed as a person of less than sterling character—at least as far as the virtue of honesty is concerned. It may be that, as the Greeks believed, a person cannot be publicly virtuous and privately not virtuous. As we have noted, the idea of a "split personality" being desirable in a leader is a particularly Machiavellian concept.

Are there weaknesses in virtue ethics? Of course. First of all, since the emphasis is on character and not on action, there is no easy way to determine a right action from a wrong one. Virtue ethicists simply insist that a virtuous character will result in virtuous actions. Also, there is no way to resolve conflicts of virtues. For example, should honesty supersede kindness (should I or should I not tell my roommate that her newly dyed green hair is nauseating)?

Nonetheless, we cannot ignore the idea behind virtue ethics if we are to make good decisions. We must consider the character of those with whom we must deal as well as our own character every time we make a moral decision. Some say that inconsistency is the hobgoblin of moral decision making. Having a virtuous character helps exorcise that particular spirit.

FREE SPEECH THEORIES

The United States has the strongest free speech protection in the world. The First Amendment of the U.S. Constitution states that "Congress shall make no law respecting an establishment of religion, or prohibiting the free exercise thereof; or *abridging the freedom of speech, or of the press* [emphasis added], or the right of the people peaceably to assemble, and to petition the Government for a redress of grievances." This amendment, along with the rest of the Bill of Rights, was passed in 1791, and we have been debating its efficacy ever since. Although it is most likely true that the free speech component of the First Amendment was originally directed at political expression and designed to prevent government censorship of criticism, it has been much more widely interpreted over the intervening years. Today, free speech protection has been extended not only to advertising and public relations, but also to nightclub performances, "pornographic" publications, music lyrics, artworks and other forms of symbolic expression, bumper stickers, and T-shirt slogans. In the words of Stephen Carter, the First Amendment has grown into "an apologetic leviathan, able to shield from community scrutiny everything from violent pornography to tabloid rumor-mongering to hurling racial epithets to burning the American flag."[17] However, the Amendment's provisions have not been granted to child pornography, sedition (suggesting the overthrow of the government), some instances of privacy violation, speech that incites to riot, and numerous other small and large exceptions. For example, cigarette advertising was banned from broadcasting nearly 30 years ago and is now forbidden on billboards. However, this is not the place to go into the long legal history of Supreme Court cases affirming and, in some instances, restricting free speech. Suffice it to say that the Court has consistently acted out the theories of free speech that we will investigate here, and, in some cases, has been at the forefront of interpreting those theories.

Freedom of expression in the West has had a long and tumultuous history. The Enlightenment ushered in a new age based on reason and, naturally, on the ability to express the results of rational thought. Much of that voice was muted, however, during the lifetimes of the philosophers who fought so hard for free expression.

---

[17]Carter, *Integrity*, p. 92.

Benedict Spinoza

For example, the Dutch philosopher Benedict Spinoza (1632–1677) was a supporter not only of free expression, but also of freedom of religion—not exactly smiled on by most of the religious and political heads of state in those days. Even his scholarly contemporaries considered Spinoza to be dangerously "ungodly." Generally speaking, Spinoza designed his social theories around one of the same concepts that Plato had used. He insisted that as long as human beings remained unaware of their real surroundings, and concerned themselves only with their personal problems, they would never realize their full potential as free and autonomous agents. This view led him to devise a political philosophy based largely on perspective (the ability to see reality as it is) and toleration. His *Theological-Political Treatise* strongly defended free speech as a major contributor to the public good and to social order—believing as he did that everyone has a right both to think what they want and to speak what they think. In fact, Spinoza stated, "The real disturbers of the peace are those who, in a free state, seek to curtail the liberty of judgment which they are unable to tyrannize over."[18] Unfortunately, Spinoza died without ever fully experiencing the realization of his ideal, tolerant state.

John Milton and the Marketplace of Ideas

Writing at roughly the same time as Spinoza, the great English poet John Milton (1608–1674), may be singly responsible for one of the most time-honored ideals of Western journalism. In 1644, he published a scathing denouncement of censorship that he titled *Areopagitica: A Speech for the Liberty of Unlicensed Printing* (after an ancient Greek term for a speech given before their highest judicial court, which met on the Areopagus, the hill of Ares, in Athens). In this brief but immortal address to the English Parliament, Milton defended his right to publish without government censorship two pamphlets on divorce. These earlier publications had angered not only Parliament, but, more importantly, the Anglican Church (which, as you'll recall, apparently only granted divorces to royalty). In fact, Milton's pamphlets on divorce eventually led to a law disallowing any type of publication without church licensing. The real effect of *Areopagitica*, however, was in its defense of free speech and its contribution to the thinking that ultimately led to the near total protection of expression that exists in the United States today.

[18]Edwin Curley, ed. and trans., *The collected works of Spinoza* (Princeton, N.J.: Princeton University Press, 1985), from chapter 20 of *Tractatus Theologico-politicus* (Theological-political Treatise) originally published in 1670.

In a now famous construction, Milton envisioned a world in which truth would always win out over falsity. In what has come to be known as "the self-righting principle," Milton held that

> . . . though all the winds of doctrine were let loose to play upon the earth, so truth be in the field, we do injuriously by licensing and prohibiting to misdoubt her strength. Let her and falsehood grapple: who ever knew truth put to the worse, in a free and open encounter?

Thus was born the *marketplace of ideas* concept, in terms of which all ideas could, and were expected to, compete with each other in open debate. If truth were as strong as Milton believed it was, it would not need to have its opponents silenced by the government or anyone else. It would win on its own merits. John Stuart Mill, whom we have already visited, gave further impetus to this theory in his treatise *On Liberty*, in which he argues, like Milton, that the truth can best be arrived at through "robust" and open debate. In justifying the marketplace ideal, Mill proposed that

1. if any statement contains truth and we silence it, we lose any chance at having viewed that kernel of truth and possibly exchanging it for error;
2. the result of a clash between two contesting opinions will most likely bring out the truth inherent in both;
3. even if the opposing opinion is wholly false, by not debating with it, the truth eventually becomes uncontested and unquestioned dogma.[19]

The Marketplace of Ideas in Modern Times

Today, the marketplace of ideas theory is still strongly adhered to by most people working in the media. However, the strength of the argument rests on several assumptions that are being questioned by both consumers and critics of the media. The first is that rationality is probably not as widespread a virtue as the Enlightenment philosophers supposed. (Of course, Plato suspected this all along.) Secondly, no matter how much we would like to believe that truth will always defeat falsity, the fact of the matter is that we simply can't always tell the difference between the two—especially since the "truth" often seems so subjective. Thus, the marketplace of ideas theory has evolved into one in which the value of any expressed idea lies more in its public acceptance than in its veracity. Ac-

---

[19]J. S. Mill, *On liberty and other essays*, John Gray, ed. (New York: Oxford University Press, 1991).

cording to First Amendment scholar Frederick Schauer, good arguments do not always defeat bad ones.

> While it would be excessively skeptical to think that Gresham's Law operates in the marketplace of ideas, and that bad arguments invariably drive out good ones, it may be excessively sanguine to suppose that we live in the deliberative environment supposed by the rationalists of the Enlightenment, an environment in which sound arguments prevail just because of their inherent soundness. Rather, we appear to exist in a world in which various superficially appealing but deeply flawed arguments all too often carry the day in public debate.[20]

In fact, some critics have pointed out that under the marketplace theory, as it has developed over the years, a single value now justifies and defines the scope of protection for speech: the *successful exchange of information.* This concept assumes that speech is a commodity and that its success in the marketplace depends solely on its ability to compete for acceptance by the public—whether it is true or not. In other words, efficiency wins out over veracity. Media critic Neil Postman cites efficiency as one of the harbingers of the technical age and discusses its distancing effect on human beings in his book *Technopoly.* According to Postman, the technological engines of progress work most efficiently when people are conceived of as consumers.[21] He posits that the "I have no responsibility for the consequences of my decisions" argument is a direct result of feeling the pressure of being efficient over that of being moral.[22] The implications of this hypothesis are clear for most media practitioners, especially those whose job it is to produce messages that will compete successfully with other messages—and that's just about everybody in the media. For too many in public relations and advertising, for instance, efficiency is the true measure of success, and success is the only thing that counts. That particular measure is not relegated solely to public relations and advertising, however. Any local TV news show (or network news show, for that matter) knows that it has to compete successfully with every other news show on the air. And in order to compete, it generally has to become more efficient. Further, as men-

---

[20]Frederick Schauer in his introduction to: Sissela Bok, *Violence, Children, and the Press: Eight Rationales Inhibiting Public Policy Debates*, Discussion Paper D-16 (The Joan Shorenstein Barone Center for Press, Politics and Public Policy, Harvard University, John F. Kennedy School of Government, 1994).

[21]Neil Postman, *Technopoly: The Surrender of Culture to Technology* (New York: Alfred K. Knopf, 1992), p. 42.

[22]Neil Postman, *Technopoly*, p. 87.

tioned in chapter 1, the pressure to compete is fast becoming the driving force behind the way news is gathered and presented.

What does this have to do with free speech and the marketplace of ideas theory? If efficiency and the success brought about by being efficient result in one message winning out over another, instead of the truthful message automatically winning out over the false one, then efficiency and success will probably be the hallmarks of protected speech. Under this model, all speech would be protected, because only through competition will speech be either accepted or rejected. The result is that the market becomes the sole arbiter of free speech; and, as every marketing student knows, if it sells, it's successful.[23] No tactic is disallowed, no technique is off limits.

In fact, the gradual evolution of speech as a commodity has been lent legitimacy by several Supreme Court decisions, most notably *Virginia Pharmacy Board v. Virginia Consumer Council*, in which Justice Harry Blackmun concurred with the majority when he noted that consumers' decisions needed to be "intelligent and well informed," and that the "free flow of commercial information is indispensable" to that process within a free enterprise economy. In so stating, he likened commercial speech (specifically advertising) to other information competing for attention within the marketplace of ideas, and suggested that some consumers might even prefer commercial information over political information—a point made as well by Walter Lippmann (although more critically). Lippmann had noted in *Public Opinion* that the public appetite for the trivial spelled the death knell for any idealized democratic involvement in the political process. In his view, citizens were more concerned with their individual needs than with the state of the nation.

THE LIBERTY THEORY

An alternative defense of free speech is offered by the *liberty theory*. Developed by First Amendment scholar C. Edwin Baker as a more logical substitute for the marketplace of ideas approach, the liberty theory holds that First Amendment freedom is essential for furthering four values:

- individual self-fulfillment
- advancement of knowledge and discovery of truth

[23]For an exhaustive discussion of the failings of the marketplace theory and a recommended alternative, see C. Edwin Baker, *Human Liberty and Freedom of Speech* (New York: Oxford University Press, 1989), pp. 47–69.

- participation in decision making by all members of the society (which is particularly significant for political decisions but embraces the right to participate in the building of the whole culture)
- achievement of a more adaptable and hence stable community

In other words, the liberty theory places a positive emphasis on protected speech and on the sanctity of individual autonomy. In a sense, this approach is Kantian in nature, with its focus on the autonomy of both speaker and listener. On another level, it is Aristotelian in that it sees speech worthy of protection as something that furthers self-fulfillment and provides for a stable culture and community.

Using this construction, Baker points out that although commercial speech (such as advertising) is protected under the marketplace theory, the liberty theory would not offer it like protection. The reason is that the success of commercial speech is determined by economic market forces. It is not a necessary component of self-fulfillment because its content is likewise determined by success in the market and not by any abiding sense of value felt by the copywriter. Its purpose, contrary to what Justice Blackmun supposed, is to sell a product or idea and not the discovery of truth or even the participation by all members of society in any decision-making role except as that of consumers. In this, the liberty theory is consistent with its own claim that the marketplace approach is based entirely on an economic model rather than a human value model. A *human value model* would presume that not everything is reducible to the status of a product—some values are intrinsic and need not compete for attention or recognition of worth.

The liberty theory differs in other areas as well, but it would be a mistake to think that this approach is more limiting on speech than the marketplace approach. For example, the marketplace theory would allow (except for rare exceptions) speech that harms, but it fails to come to grips with a definition of harm that would eliminate debate over certain types of communication such as pornography. The liberty theory construes harm specifically as coercion, thus clearly stating the reasons for allowing most speech and setting explicit guidelines for limiting speech. Under this theory, speech-caused harms are generally allowed, because speech does not, in most cases, physically harm people. Rather, people are *potentially* harmed only to the extent that they adopt any perceptions or attitudes because of the speech. In other words, the harm-causing speech does not itself interfere with the listener's legitimate decision-making authority (the autonomy of the *listener*). You don't have to listen to it, and if you do, you don't have to change your mind about anything. The listener has no right, then, to control that speech because that would be disrespectful of the *speaker's* autonomy. So, outlawing speech in order to protect people from harms that result simply because listeners might adopt certain perceptions or attitudes disrespects the responsibility and freedom of the listener as well as the speaker.

Under the liberty theory, only if speech is manifestly coercive should it be restricted. In general, speech depends for its power on the voluntary acceptance of the listeners, so speech behavior is normally considered noncoercive. *Coercive speech* would be that which "restricts another person to options that are worse than that other person had moral or legitimate right to expect, or [which] employs means that [the speaker] had no right to use for changing the threatened person's options." Thus, coercion refers to the impropriety of the form of pressure, not to the severity or effectiveness of the pressure itself. Again, like Kant, Baker suggests that motive leads to technique. Improper motive leads to improper technique. It should make no difference if anyone is harmed by the attempt at coercion—coercive speech would be wrong by nature.

> Speech used to influence another person may be coercive if the speaker manifestly disrespects and attempts to undermine the other person's will and the integrity of the other person's mental processes. Both the concept of coercion and the rationale for protecting speech draw from the same ethical requirement that the integrity and autonomy of the individual be respected.[24]

In sum, the liberty theory depicts protected speech as that which: (1) represents the freely chosen expression of the speaker, (2) depends for its power on the free acceptance of the listener, (3) and is not used in the context of a violent or coercive activity. Speech is protected because, without disrespecting the autonomy of other persons, it promotes both the speaker's self-fulfillment and the speaker's ability to participate in change.[25]

FREE SPEECH AND THE INDIVIDUAL VERSUS SOCIETY

One of the triumphs of the free speech principle is that it gives protection to the individual as well as the group. A key interpretation of the free speech doctrine, as embodied in the First Amendment, is that *no* voice can be silenced—not even the faintest. This emphasis on individual rights has come down to us almost untouched since the time of John Locke. You'll recall that Locke championed the rights of individuals over the power of the government, and, by so doing, presented the founders of the United States

[24]Edwin Baker, *Human Liberty and Freedom of Speech*, pp. 56–66.

[25]Edwin Baker, *Human Liberty and Freedom of Speech*, p. 69.

with a fully developed concept of government as the agent of the people. *Libertarian theory*, with its extreme focus on the individual, asserts that individual rights may not be violated, and that there is no natural concomitant responsibility associated with any right.

The liberal viewpoint (especially as expressed through libertarianism) holds that the most important political values are freedom and equality—particularly as they relate to individual virtues. The role of government, under this construct, is to ensure freedom and equality, and to promote toleration and freedom of conscience for all its citizens; otherwise, government is to stay out of the affairs of individuals. Society is, thus, governed by an enlightened state working through the tenets of reason, whose actions are not clouded by the ambiguities of culture or the needs of the whole. As Locke proposed, government's sole purpose is to ensure individual rights. Under this theory, journalists have the right to publish what they want, and are not answerable to anyone except themselves for what they publish (as long as it's not libelous). Censorship by the government is strictly forbidden by the First Amendment, a journalist's right to information has been validated by such laws as the Freedom of Information Act, and the only responsibility recognized by most journalists is "the public's right to know."

Directly contrary to this approach, the *communitarian* perspective asserts that other values are more important, especially those that regard community as the proper focus of the human being. Communitarians believe that the state's primary role is to ensure the welfare of the community, because it is the basis of all human interaction. They believe that we cannot be simply individuals pursuing our self-interests without regard for the society of which we are an integral part. According to this theory, journalists are responsible to the community of which they are a part. As discussed in chapter 3, the new trend toward public journalism is a reflection of this increasing concern for the place of the press in fostering community well-being. Under communitarianism, the traditions of culture and society are vital to the realization of the good life, and we cannot separate ourselves from that whole of which we are a part. In fact, our very roles within that society tie us to the community in ways we could not be as mere individuals. We are what we are, in part because of our roles in society.

In agreement with the Chinese philosopher Confucius (Kung-Fu Tze), communitarians suggest that our various roles define us. As Confucian scholar Henry Rosemont Jr. analogized, the Western individualist is like a peach. While the outside is what most people see and value, what is inside is the real essence of what it means to be a human being. Inside each of us is a center that is wholly ours. We share only that which is exterior to that center. Contrary to that way of thinking, the Confucian sees herself as an onion: Each layer defines her being. One layer may be her role as parent, one as wife, one as colleague, one as employee, one as community member, one as citizen. Thus, the communitarian is defined by her relationship with others, the libertarian by his individuality.

Finally, communitarians disagree that rule by reason alone is sufficient to ensure community health. That can be accomplished only through discourse based on the social goals of the community, as exemplified through its cultural traditions and roles.[26] Again, like Confucians, communitarians hold that communal tradition and one's place within that tradition are vital to the operation of a successful society. In addition, to trust only in reason is to divorce oneself from the reality that human beings are simultaneously thinking and feeling creatures. In fact, Confucius didn't even recognize a separate state of reasoning absent emotion. As pointed out by religious philosopher Huston Smith, "The Chinese idiogram for mind designates heart as well, which shows that the Chinese took it for granted that reason functions in a context of attitudes and emotions. Unless our hearts prompt us to cooperate, reason will devise clever stratagems to further self interest."[27]

As might be expected, the debate over free speech rights has not escaped the long-running conflict between these two schools of thought. As suggested by educator and philosopher John Merrill, most of the major moral philosophers (both past and present) fall into one of these two camps. For example, John Milton, John Locke, John Stuart Mill, and Henry David Thoreau all tend toward libertarianism. Others, such as Plato, Rousseau, and Confucius, favor more communitarian constructs.[28]

One of the most adamant defenders of individual rights over group rights was John Stuart Mill. In *On Liberty*, he firmly asserted that no individual voice should be silenced, especially by the din of the majority.

> If all mankind minus one were of one opinion and only one person were of the contrary opinion, mankind would be no more justified in silencing that one person than he, if he had the power, would be justified in silencing mankind.[29]

Like Alexis de Tocqueville before him, Mill was concerned with the "tyranny of the majority," and the dangers of operating from a greater-good perspective without consideration of minority opinion. That minority had already been recognized by a number of philosophers from Plato to Henry David Thoreau, who pointed out in his conclusion to *Walden*, in 1854, that "If a man does not keep pace with his companions, perhaps it is because he

[26]Jean Hampton, *Political Philosophy* (New York: Westview Press, 1997), pp. 169–185.

[27]Huston Smith, *World's Religions: A Guide to Our Wisdom Traditions* (San Francisco: Harper San Francisco, 1994), p. 107.

[28]John C. Merrill, *Journalism Ethics: Philosophical Foundations for News Media* (New York: St. Martin's Press, 1997), p. 34.

[29]J. S. Mill, *On liberty and other essays.*

hears a different drummer. Let him step to the music which he hears, however measured or far away."

This historical emphasis on the individual has, in part, grown from an Enlightenment period distrust of government—especially totalitarian regimes—and a firmly held belief in a social contract construct that gives the individual power over the group. Dissenters, such as Rousseau, have been more often cited for their focus on the dehumanizing effects of mass society than on their belief in a strict allegiance to the well-being of society instead of the individual. In more recent years, philosophers such as Alisdair MacIntyre and Michael Sandel have written forcefully about the dangers of too much emphasis on the individual. MacIntyre, for instance, decries the "cult of individuality" as presenting human beings as free-will addicts with no relationship to society as a whole. This, he says, is a mistake. We are all born into a society and learn to live within its shelter, developing as part of the whole. In this way, we are not (as the libertarians suppose) disconnected entities living wholly for ourselves.[30]

Likewise, Sandel argues that human beings simply cannot be considered as separate from their social communities.

> We cannot regard ourselves as independent . . . without great cost to those loyalties and convictions whose moral force consists partly in the fact that living by them is inseparable from understanding ourselves as the particular persons we are—as members of this family or community or nation or people, as bearers of this history, as sons and daughters of that revolution, as citizens of this republic.[31]

Sandel says that the "enduring attachments" that arise out of these relationships, "partly define the person that I am." This devotion to relationships as the defining force of our existence is common to most communitarian philosophies. As we saw in chapter 2, relationships naturally result in obligations. Obligations, by nature, restrict our actions. Therefore, the various obligations that the media have toward their constituencies constitute another way of looking at conceivable restrictions on free speech—even if those restrictions are self-imposed. If the media are obligated to present news that has some meaning with respect to people's daily lives, and they are obligated to mitigate harm wherever possible, then some restriction on speech is to be expected.

The conflict between the communitarian and libertarian philosophies, like most conflicts, is based on a false either-or dichotomy. It is unnecessary, and probably unwise, to allow all expression free reign. Harm to fellow human beings is one reason for restricting some forms of expression. Child pornogra-

---

[30]Alasdair MacIntyre, *After Virtue* (Notre Dame: University of Notre Dame Press, 1981), p. 187.

[31]Michael J. Sandel, *Liberalism and the Limits of Justice* (Cambridge: Cambridge University Press, 1982), p. 179.

phy laws attest to our desire to protect our children, antisedition laws reflect our desire to protect our country. Slanderous speech is punishable by law, as is speech that incites to riot. We also tend to recognize the inappropriateness of some forms of speech at certain times and places. Some of these restrictions are recognized by the Supreme Court. Courthouses (especially during trials), schools, prisons and jails, and military bases are some examples. Not surprisingly, these exceptions have been made so that order might be maintained in and around these institutions. Additionally, rulings such as those regulating cigarette advertising on television, and now on billboards, have been made for the sake of society as a whole—an entirely communitarian perspective. Social custom dictates other restrictions—but, of course, social customs change. Fifty years ago, it would have been unusual to hear someone swear in public. Today, a walk across any college campus will alert you to how much social mores have changed.

On the other hand, John Stuart Mill was probably right when he insisted that no individual voice should be silenced by a "tyrannous" majority. And, as Milton pointed out, that one voice might just contain the real truth, while the rest of us are wrong. The trick is to balance a commitment to free expression with a fair amount of respect for others. This respect can be based on a Kantian notion of natural merit or on a more complex rendering of obligations based on the nature of human relationships. The former is often considered a minimum expectation; the latter is sometimes referred to as the lynchpin of social order. Whichever way you view it, it is clear that speech rights are not absolute but are regulated to a very great extent by our social and cultural values—and, if these methods fail, sometimes by the law.

HOW TO CHOOSE APPLICABLE THEORIES

Although the foregoing list of theories and philosophers is far from exhaustive, we can now begin to see where our predisposition to decide in certain ways may have come from. The problem is that without some coherent method of picking among the various philosophies, we often end up contradicting ourselves or arriving at no satisfactory solution to our dilemmas. Or worse, we manage to rationalize, and thus justify, nearly any action we see fit to take. It is this last that is the most troublesome aspect of having so many differing approaches to moral decision making at our fingertips. Some words of caution need to be voiced here.

The *theory of cognitive dissonance* (yet another theory) tells us that human beings tend to pay attention only to that with which they already agree, and that they simply block out unwanted information (especially if it runs counter to their predisposition to act in a certain way). It is no wonder then that most of us tend to latch onto the theories that will bolster our already held beliefs. The same is true of moral decision making. Most of us have some idea of what we're going to do before we ever make a formal decision—and, unfortunately, before we've looked at the possible alternatives. The various publics who are targets of the media have probably suspected this for quite some time. It is little wonder that surveys consistently show media professions at the low end of the credibility scale when most people probably believe that media decisions are either standard-operating-procedure decisions (at best) or knee-jerk ones (at worst).

Part of the solution is to realize that not every theory is applicable to every situation. For example, a rule in force at a local television news outlet disallowing the use of photos of people who have been arrested but not yet indicted could be an example of either Kantian logic or rule utilitarianism. Either way, we need not apply act utilitarianism to the question of whether to run a photo or not. The decision has already been made. At some point, we had to have asked ourselves what rationale would allow us to run these types of photos. We could have used the categorical imperative to arrive at a rule such as, "Never run photos of those arrested but not yet indicted." Our reasoning might have told us that we would not want our own pictures run in such a fashion, especially if we were falsely accused. And, if we further reasoned that no rational person would want the same, then we could make a rule to guide us in similar situations in the future. Rule utilitarian logic might have told us that no greater good is furthered by publishing pictures of this type and that the potential harm to the subject may outweigh any benefit to the community at this point.

It is important to remember that we could also arrive at the opposite conclusion by employing at least one of these theories. Rule utilitarianism might tell us that the community's best interest would be served by running photos of this sort, because people's interest in knowing exactly who is suspected of crimes is important information and has some bearing on how they feel about their community and its level of safety. A Kantian approach, however, might still result in the same decision not to run photos, because this theory is based not on consequences but on a duty to adhere to an already reasoned-out guideline.

As pointed out, the danger here is that we already may be predisposed to run photos of people who have been arrested but not indicted simply because, as a television news operation, we have to rely on images to "sell" our product. In order to make a rule that doesn't reflect this somewhat egoistic reason, we rationalize that the greater good is being served. "Rationalize," in this sense, means *to devise self-satisfying but incorrect reasons for a particular behavior*. It is, therefore, crucial that we understand our reasons for preferring one action over another and to admit them to ourselves. Unless we understand our real reasons, we will be content to rationalize our actions by using other means—even if those means are ethical theories. In this case, by recognizing our need to provide images for our stories, we can factor this element into our decision-making process and weigh our egoistic benefits with the benefits to the community versus the potential harm to the subject of the story. Recognizing that egoism is a variable may help us to make a decision based more on the needs of others than on our own perceived needs. Remember, our actions must be justified, never merely rationalized. When we use ethical theory simply as a way to rationalize our decisions, we are doing ourselves and everyone concerned an injustice.

EXERCISES

1. Explain why you think cultural relativism is a good point of view to hold. What are its drawbacks, if any? Give at least one example of how cultural relativism affects the mass media.
2. What role do you think the modern media play in the American social contract?
3. Do you agree or disagree with Plato that most people don't understand reality? What implications does your belief have on how the media should behave?
4. Make an argument as to why you, personally, should be mostly self-interested. Now, make an argument as to why you should not be mostly self-interested. Which do you think is more accurate?
5. List five rules that you think you follow most of the time in your everyday dealings with other people. Do you think everyone should follow your rules? Why or why not?
6. Are there any rules that you think everyone, everywhere, should follow at all times? What are they?
7. In what way, if any, do you think advertising and public relations contribute to the greater good of society? If you don't think they do contribute, explain how they could.
8. List five personal virtues you hold now or would like to hold.
9. Compare and contrast the marketplace theory of free speech with the liberty theory. Which do you think is the more viable?
10. To what extent do you agree or disagree that the media should be more involved with their communities?
11. Among other things, the First Amendment of the U.S. Constitution states that, "Congress shall make no law . . . abridging the freedom of speech, or of the press. . . ." Many have suggested that this amendment allows the press (and other forms of mass media) undue freedom, freedom that, as Mill would say, often makes the media a "nuisance to other people." Although a literal reading of this amendment indicates neither, both legal and moral philosophers have disagreed widely on its implied meaning.

EXERCISES *(Cont.)*

Write a brief paper examining the degree to which you view the First Amendment as implying media rights and/or media obligation.

Remember, free speech/free press applies not only to the press, but also to public relations, advertising, and broadcasting (and practically every other form of public communication in this country).

HYPOTHETICAL: FREE SPEECH OR FREEDOM FROM FEAR

Jane Franklin worked for a sports merchandising company with stores in three major West Coast cities. Sportsfield Promotions sells sports apparel and equipment trademarked by the names of major college and professional sports teams. Jane worked with Sportsfield Promotions for over 6 years and had recently been promoted to director of marketing for the Seattle outlet.

Jane is also a writer. When she left college 7 years ago with a masters in English, her intent was to become a novelist. She has written a couple of dozen short stories over the past several years, a number of which have been placed in both print and electronic online magazines. However, without her work with Sportsfield Promotions, Jane wouldn't have been able to support herself and her writing "hobby."

Jane was well liked by her fellow employees and by the company president, Vince Rogers. Her progress through the company had been steady, and her recent promotion was seen by all as well deserved.

Recently, Jane had had a new short story placed with an online magazine of good repute. A number of well-known authors have had small pieces featured on the site, and Jane felt fortunate to have her work placed in their company. Her story dealt with a disgruntled middle manager who took out his pent-up aggressions by coming to work one day and shooting several of his coworkers. Although the story was entirely fictitious, many of the characters bore a striking resemblance to Jane's coworkers at Sportsfield Promotions.

Jane had drawn on her personal work experiences to lend a sense of reality to the story. She also knew that this topic was a hot one and would enhance her chances of placing the story; however, she never imagined that anyone would be upset by it. As it turned out, one of her coworkers had come across the story online and had reported its content to the company president. Apparently, the coworker was upset because he recognized himself as the basis for one of the characters shot by the fictitious manager in the story. And, although he liked Jane personally, he believed this story could be a signal of something seriously wrong with her emotionally. The company president agreed.

He called Jane into his office and explained the situation to her. He sympathized with the concerns of the employees over the story (a number of others had now read the piece), and he wanted Jane to take a psychological exam to help prove to her coworkers that she wasn't capable of committing the act she wrote so intimately about in her recent story. Jane explained that the story was pure fiction and that, as a writer, it was easy for her to create fictitious circumstances in which she herself could not have participated in reality. She had already withdrawn the story from the Web and was willing to apologize to any employee whom she had made to feel uncomfortable. President Rogers insisted on the psychological exam. Jane refused and was subsequently fired.

The company president cited employee fears as the reason for the termination, saying that, regardless of his personal admiration for Jane as a trusted employee, she had inadvertently created a hostile working environment. Jane saw the psychological exam as an ultimatum, and the termination as a violation of her freedom of speech.

QUESTIONS ON HYPOTHETICAL

1. Put yourself in the shoes of the employees. Do you think their concerns were legitimate? Why or why not?
2. Put yourself in the shoes of the company president, Vince Rogers. What were his options? How would you have handled the situation?
3. Do you think this is a free speech issue? Why or why not?
4. Using C. Edwin Baker's liberty theory, analyze this situation by considering whether the "speech" in question causes legitimate harm to anyone.
5. Using the marketplace of ideas theory, discuss whether this situation warrants free speech protection.

CHAPTER

5

To Tell the Truth

Of all the possible virtues a media practitioner would like to be known for, truth stands out as preeminent. On the list of virtues the public would like to see the media practice most, avoidance of harm may be nearer the top.

Hardly anyone doubts that the media go to great lengths to tell the truth. With the exception of the tabloid press, which typically runs stories on alien births and Elvis spottings, most media base their reputations on their veracity. In fact, the few laws that limit freedom of speech have mostly to do with protection from harm caused by some form of lying. Laws against libel, slander, defamation, and so on, all deal with false or misleading speech. These laws apply equally to both public relations and advertising. In addition, both public relations and advertising are subject to very strict U.S. Federal Trade Commission guidelines governing deception in print and broadcast ads. In short, truth is the default position for all serious media, both legally and ethically. However, as we will see, truth is defined somewhat differently for journalism than it is for public relations and advertising, and on that definitional difference turns a great deal of controversy.

We have all heard the phrase, "The truth hurts." This simple adage illuminates one of the most controversial areas of media ethics: the avoidance of harm. The media, in fulfilling their role as disseminators of information, often face the invariable conflict between providing news or respecting rights. As mentioned in chapter 1, values and ideals come in conflict all the time. A citizen's right to privacy can be, and often is, ignored by the news media. Every tragedy has its victims and tragedy is news. Unfortunately, so are the victims. The recent rash of high school shootings has illustrated the extremes that some reporters will go to get a story. In the aftermath of the shootings at Thurston High School in Springfield, Oregon, in 1998, reporters obtained the home addresses of the victims and pursued their stories right into the families' homes in some cases. One reporter for a national news outlet even posed as a doctor in order to get nearer the hospitalized shooting victims.

When *USA Today* ran a story making public the fact that tennis great Arthur Ashe had AIDS, much harm was done to both Ashe and his family, who wanted the information kept private. *USA Today*, and a number of journalistic defenders, pointed out that Ashe was a public figure and a role model for a great many people, and that this was, thus, a newsworthy story. Others, journalists and nonjournalists alike, countered that the story was merely voyeurism, and that there are times when respect for others should outweigh public curiosity.

To what extent does the obligation of the news media to gather and disseminate the news outweigh their personal obligation to respect the rights of others? Can personal standards override professional standards? Can the media's allegiance to the truth be bent or even broken in the name of public interest? Do public relations and advertising have to adhere to the same strict standard of truth telling that the news media do? These questions, and others, are probably the most important ones facing the media today. And these are the questions we take up here and in chapter 6.

TRUTH AS A LEGAL CONCEPT

Remember that the law is the ultimate formalization of societal and cultural values and ideals. The fact that we have enacted laws that deal with truth shows that, as a society, we value communication that is truthful and tend to restrict communication that potentially harms others. Although the law doesn't pretend, nor does it need, to cover every potential communication-caused harm, it does deal with the most egregious. It is also worth mentioning that most of these laws apply equally to individuals and to the media. For example, *slander* is generally applied to the communication of individuals; *libel* is reserved for published communication. As an individual, I may slander someone else if I harm him in some way because of something I've said to a third party. Libel would occur if the harm were caused by my publishing the same communication.

The First Amendment is not inviolable. Laws exist that clearly disallow certain types of speech, and all those who deal in public communication are bound by these laws. For the most part, these laws protect others. We are all familiar with the First Amendment rights allowed the press in this country. But, as with most rights, there are concomitant obligations—chief among them being the obligation not to harm others through communication. The most important "don'ts" in the media concern slander or libel (defamation), and invasion of privacy.

Defamation

Although it is variously defined (each case seems to bring a new definition), *defamation* can be said to be any communication that holds a person up to contempt, hatred, ridicule, or scorn. One problem in defending against accusations of defamation is that there are different rules for different people. It is generally easier for private individuals to prove defamation than it is for those in the public eye. Celebrities and politicians, for example, open themselves to a certain amount of publicity, and, therefore, criticism. A private individual suing for libel must only prove negligence, but a public figure must prove malice. In order for defamation to be actionable, five elements must be present.

- There must be communication of a statement that harms a person's reputation in some way—even if it only lowers that person's esteem in another's eyes.
- The communication must have been published or communicated to a third party. The difference here is that between slander and libel. Slander is oral defamation and might arise, for example, in a public speech. Libel is written defamation, although it also includes broadcast communication.
- The person defamed must have been identified in the communication either by name or by direct inference. This is the toughest to prove if the person's name hasn't been used directly.
- The person defamed must be able to prove that the communication caused damage to his or her reputation.
- Negligence must also be shown. In other words, the source of the communication must be proved to have been negligent during research or writing. Negligence can be the fault of poor information gathering. Public figures must prove malice—that is, that the communication was made with knowing falsehood or reckless disregard for the truth.

There are defenses against defamation. The most obvious one is that the communication is the truth, regardless of whether the information harmed someone's reputation or not.

The second defense is privilege. Privilege applies to statements made during public, official, or judicial proceedings. For example, if something normally libelous is reported accurately on the basis of a public meeting, the reporter cannot be held responsible. Privilege is a tricky concept, however, and care must be taken that privileged information be released only to those who have a right to it. Public meetings are public information. Only concerned individuals have a right to privileged information released at private meetings.

The third most common defense is fair comment. This concept applies primarily to the right to criticize, as in theater or book critiques, and must be restricted to the public-interest aspects of that which is under discussion. However, it also can be construed to apply to such communications as comparative advertising.

Invasion of Privacy

Most of us are familiar with the term *invasion of privacy*, which falls roughly into three categories.

- *Appropriation* is the commercial use of a person's name or picture without permission. For instance, you can't say that one of your employees supports the company's position on nuclear energy if that employee hasn't given you permission to do so—even if she does support that position and has said so to you.
- *Private facts* about individuals are also protected. Information about a person's lifestyle, family situation, personal health, etc., is considered to be strictly private and may not be disclosed without permission.
- *Intrusion* involves literally spying on another. Obtaining information by bugging, filming, or recording in any way another's private affairs is cause for a lawsuit.

We should remember that laws are extensions of our moral beliefs, codified so that we, as a society, must follow them. In this way, laws are similar to what Kant would call perfect duties. We must refrain from such acts as murder, stealing, and—most importantly for our purposes here—lying. It is often pointed out that being legal doesn't necessarily mean being ethical; however, if we understand that many of our common laws were designed to help us live together successfully as a society, we should also see that those laws reflect the commonalties in our moral standards. All that is legal may not be ethical, but legality is a good starting point for many ethical situations.

Defamation and privacy issues are at the heart of legal protection from untruthful and harmful speech, and these types of speech are certainly morally troublesome as well. What follows, then, is a discussion of the additional ethical considerations necessary for all media in order that they fulfill both their professional and their social obligations.

TRUTH AND THE ACT OF COMMUNICATION

You would think that in any act of communication, truth would need to be an essential ingredient. After all, what kind of society would we have if lying rather than telling the truth were the default position? When you ask a stranger on the street if he has the time, you don't expect him to lie to you. When you ask the price of a pair of socks, you expect the store clerk to give you a truthful response. In fact, in nearly all of our everyday dealings with fellow human beings, we assume the truth of their statements unless we have good reasons to believe otherwise. As human beings, we naturally seek a state of cooperation, and cooperation can only be gained in the long run by telling the truth. However (and here's the rub), what constitutes telling the truth varies definitionally as well as functionally. Suppose you ask if a particular item is expensive. The store clerk answers that it's not. You ask the price. It's a real killer—at least according to *your* paycheck. Was the clerk lying? It depends. Maybe the clerk is used to selling high-priced items and this is one of the least expensive of the items she sells. But you're not used to buying high-priced items, so your definition of expensive may be different from the store clerk's. Can we say the same thing about the definition of truth?

There is certainly no lack of definitions of truth (and lying, for that matter); however, we must always recognize the limits of those definitions and realize our own limitations in pinning them down. One of the most useful definitions of truth comes from philosopher Sissela Bok, who suggests that lying is a form of coercion. That is, to lie to someone is to lead them to act in a manner in which they would not have acted had you told them the truth. For example, a politician lies to his constituency concerning his stand on a particular issue. His constituency votes for him based, in part, on that stand. They have been encouraged to act in a way they might not have had they known the truth. Recall from chapter 4 C. Edwin Baker's description of coercive speech. He holds that coercive speech is that which undermines another person's autonomy in decision making.

Telling the truth also implies that the teller believes what he is saying as well. This is especially important if the professional communicator is repeating what someone else has said and has no reason to doubt the veracity of that information. In recent years, both public relations and advertising professionals have been called to account for falsehoods they furthered on behalf of their clients. In fact, many agencies now require a contract that includes a no-fault clause absolving them from blame if they unknowingly pass on false information on behalf of a client. All media professionals, including journalists, must believe in the basic truth of their statements and the accuracy of their information, realizing, at the same time, that there is always the chance they may be proved wrong. British philosopher Mary

Midgley explains how important it is to be committed to what we believe to be true, because commitment doesn't carry any claim of infallibility.

> Commitment of this kind is necessary for effective discourse, because if everybody holds back from endorsing everything they say, no speech is reliable and we lose the advantage of speaking at all. (Someone who kept adding, "Of course this may not be true," to every sentence would simply be a public nuisance.) Words like "certain" and "know" and indeed "truth" are part of this language of commitment. Perhaps the strongest form of commitment is to say something like, "I am as sure of this as I am of anything." . . .[1]

Without getting into deep philosophical debates over the nature of language, perception versus reality, and truths of reason versus truths of fact, let's take a look at the possible different ways the media might define truth and put it into practice.

JOURNALISTIC TRUTH

Mark Twain once said that his job as a journalist was to "corral" the truth. When a journalist talks about the truth today, she is generally speaking of the elements that contribute to journalistic truth (ways in which it can be corralled). Among these elements are accuracy, context, and balance.

Accuracy has to do with getting the facts straight. Despite deadline pressures, nearly every journalist will tell you that accuracy is of utmost importance to the truth of a story. Although the term *fact* itself may often be disputed (especially by philosophers), a journalist will strive to verify the "facts" of a story through sources, background, records, experts, and other methods before deciding on their veracity. Some will argue, of course, that truth (including facts) is relative. For instance, once people believed that the world was flat. For all intents and purposes, it was a fact for quite a long time. Of course, it was later disproved and now we all accept the "fact" that the earth is round (or nearly round). But a journalist, on learning from the coroner that a victim was killed at approximately 2:00 A.M., will almost certainly take that information as fact and pass it on as such. And although other facts are more difficult to ascertain, part of a journalist's job is to do just that, using his power of perception and his training to decipher, as much as possible, fact from fiction. A second factor contributing to accuracy is the care with which direct quotes are treated in journalism. No self-respecting journalist would alter a quote. In fact, although some journalists feel that cleaning up grammar is acceptable, others hold that a quote is

[1]Mary Midgley, *Can't we make moral judgements?* (Bristol: Bristol Press, 1991), p. 135.

only accurate if repeated exactly the way it was uttered. Of course, even an accurate quote can be deceptive if taken out of context.

Context is vital to the understanding of a story. We all know how damaging taking quotes out of context can be, for instance. When General William Westmoreland (the former U.S. supreme commander in Vietnam) sued CBS News for libel, he based his case almost exclusively on his quotes having been taken out of context by *60 Minutes*. Another way to look at context, however, is to say that to place any element of a story out of context is to leave out information vital to the understanding of that story—and to do that would be tantamount to lying by omission. Journalists strive, or should strive, for understanding. After all, mere facts alone don't constitute understanding. This sticking point is also central to the debate over the supposed objective nature of journalism—a subject we deal with more fully later.

Balance is integral to the truth of a story because it bears on the concept of fairness, and fairness is viewed by many as essential to ethical action of all sorts. To a journalist, balance simply means presenting as many sides of a story as it takes to achieve a complete picture. So, in a very real sense, balance is related directly both to accuracy and to context. Part and parcel of being objective is to seem not to take sides. It may be for this reason as much as any sense of fairness that most journalists strive for balance. To present an unbalanced account would be to leave yourself open to accusations of partisanship. Either way, it is certain that balance contributes to the truth of a story by strengthening its context.

JOURNALISTIC DECEPTION

Is it ever proper for a journalist to lie in order to get a story? This is the primary question every journalist must ask when deciding whether to engage in investigative reporting, especially undercover reporting. The question is not a new one. At the turn of the 20th century, reporter Nellie Bly (a pseudonym) posed as an insane woman so she could expose New York City's notorious Women's Lunatic Asylum. Carrying on in that tradition in the 1960s, Gloria Steinem became a Playboy Bunny in order to give readers an inside look at what the women employees of the Playboy Clubs had to go through to earn a living. In the 1970s, reporter Carol Lynn Mithers posed as a man to get a job on a sports magazine and then published the results of her investigation in a *Village Voice* article called "My Life as a Man." The *Chicago Sun-Times* sent female journalists into clinics in downtown Chicago that performed costly abortions on women who were not pregnant. Even the venerable Walter Cronkite once voted under false names twice in the same election to expose election fraud. And, in 1977, in probably the most famous undercover scam in decades, the *Chicago Sun-Times* set up a fake bar called the Mirage, run completely by undercover journalists, in order to record dozens of city officials engaged in bribe taking.

In the now famous Food Lion case, ABC's *Prime Time* went undercover to expose what it suggested was the giant grocery store chain's practice of selling tainted meat and fish and ignoring expiration dates on other food products. When Food Lion sued ABC in a North Carolina court, it based its legal position on the fact that ABC undercover reporters had lied on their employment applications in order to gain access to Food Lion stores for the purposes of surreptitious filming. The jury awarded Food Lion $5.5 million in damages (later reduced to just over $300,000). Both journalists and nonjournalists came down on opposite sides of the issue. Writing in *USA Today*, Joe Saltzman painted a picture of investigative reporting as a time-honored tradition, fighting both big government and big business on behalf of the American people.[2] Although most journalistic accounts of the case were in this vein, David Wagner, writing for *Insight on the News* (a *Washington Times* publication), saw it differently. Citing possible collusion between ABC and the United Food and Commercial Workers International Union (UFCWIU), Wagner contended that the report was simply a concerted effort to "get Food Lion" because it had repeatedly resisted pressure to unionize.[3] In the most recent turn of events, an appeals court threw out the original verdict and exonerated ABC. Despite this new ruling, the Food Lion case exemplifies the problems caused by undercover reporting using deceptive practices. The question of using deception to gather information is a sticky one that has troubled journalists for a very long time.

The Society of Professional Journalists (SPJ) code of ethics advises journalists to "Avoid undercover or other surreptitious methods of gathering information except when traditional open methods will not yield information vital to the public. Use of such methods should be explained as part of the story."

The argument in favor of using questionable means to gather news deemed of value to the public welfare is based solidly on utilitarian grounds. According to the utilitarian view, deception must be used at times to further the public interest. Supporting this position, Sissela Bok, in her seminal work *Secrets: On the Ethics of Concealment and Revelation*, holds that journalistic deception, like lying in general, is not an either-or proposition. Rather, it is best viewed as operating along a continuum from unnecessary to necessary.[4] Journalistic deception that clearly benefits the public welfare

---

[2]Joe Saltzman, "A chill settles over investigative journalism: (Food Lion markets' victory over ABC News)" *USA Today* (magazine), July 1997 v125 n2626 p29(1).

[3]David Wagner, "Making news, breaking ethics," *Insight on the News*, March 17, 1997 v13 n10 p10(3).

[4]Sissela Bok, *Secrets: On the Ethics of Concealment and Revelation* (New York: Pantheon Books, 1982), pp. 249–264.

could be seen as permissible; deception that results in a story that merely titillates or satisfies the public's curiosity over some matter is clearly suspect. However, since the guiding ideal in journalism is to tell the truth, any deviation from that ideal must be able to stand up to the closest scrutiny. In other words, the burden of proof for using deceptive techniques in news gathering is squarely on the journalist.

According to educator and ethicist Louis Day, investigative techniques such as undercover reporting and the use of hidden cameras should be employed only after a full and deliberate discussion in which the decision makers: (1) are convinced that the information sought is of compelling public importance, (2) have considered all alternatives to the use of deception, (3) are convinced that the benefit to be derived from the deceptive practice outweighs the possible harm to the various parties involved, and (4) are willing to disclose to their audience the nature of the deception and their reasons for using such tactics.[5] This test, while not solving all the problems associated with undercover reporting, certainly requires a hard look at the justification for using such techniques.

TRUTH IN ADVERTISING AND PUBLIC RELATIONS

Many people would say that the area of truth telling is where journalism and advertising and public relations definitely part company; however, from a professional perspective, truth is just as important to advertising and public relations as it is to journalism. The truth of an advertising claim is quickly verified once the product is tested by the consumer. In the same way, the truth of a public relations claim is likewise verified by proof in the form of action. (For example, a political candidate's claims are quickly confirmed once he takes office.) Both advertising and public relations generally rely on a legal definition of truth to determine whether or not they have erred. But although a legal definition of truth is useful, it does not begin to cover the gray areas produced by vagueness, ambiguity, and puffery.

Puffery is defined by Ivan Preston as "advertising or other sales representations which praise the item to be sold with subjective opinions, superlatives, or exaggerations, vaguely and generally, stating no specific facts."[6] A soft drink commercial showing young people frolicking on the beach doesn't really tell us anything about the soft drink itself. It merely creates an ambiance in which the soft drink plays an apparently critical role. Some, including

---

[5]Louis Day, *Ethics in Media Communications: Cases and Controversies* (Belmont: Wadsworth Publishing Company, 1997), p. 97.

[6]Ivan Preston, *The Great American Blow-Up: Puffery in Advertising and Selling* (Madison: University of Wisconsin Press, 1975), pp. 6–8.

Preston, consider puffery to be unethical by nature; however, anyone who has ever had to come up with an idea for a product that is exactly like every other product of its kind knows that image can be everything.

Carl P. Wrighter in his book *I Can Sell You Anything* defines words that have a vague meaning and seem to say something other than what they really mean as *weasel words*. Such advertising claims as "part of a balanced breakfast," "helps prevent gum disease," and "leaves your dishes virtually spotless," have little meaning when weasel words such as "part of," "helps," and "virtually" are fully defined. Both "part of" and "helps" actually indicate that something else plays a part in the success of the product, while "virtually" literally means "almost."[7] Use of these words is not, on the face of it, unethical, but we should be aware that there is a certain equivocation involved in using them at all and that ambiguity in both advertising and public relations is usually intentional. Is that tantamount to lying? Possibly not. Unless the claim is absolutely false or the information inaccurate, the truth is not being altered–the message is merely being selectively presented. Selectivity of information and the way in which it is presented is what sets advertising and public relations the farthest apart from journalism. One of the ways to discover the basic differences among the various media is to compare the criteria for truthful communication used in journalism with those in advertising and public relations.

If we were to compare the journalistic definition of truth with that of advertising and public relations we would discover that on the criterion of accuracy they would approximately match. Accuracy is just as important to advertising and public relations as it is to journalism. The accuracy of information disseminated by advertising is central to the success of its endeavor. Inaccurate information could be considered a false product claim, which is illegal. At the very least, it could lead to consumer dissatisfaction. For public relations, inaccurate information could result in lack of credibility, the ultimate goal of media relations, for instance. For both advertising and public relations, intentional inaccuracy would be considered unethical (and possibly illegal), just as it would in journalism. When it comes to quotes, however, there is a major difference.

Although quotes used in journalism must be absolutely accurate, quotes in public relations can be, and often are, literally made up. What does a speechwriter do? She makes up quotes. How, then, do those quotes become an accurate reflection of the person for whom the speech is written? That person gives the speech; at that point, the quotes become his, not his speechwriter's. What about the corporate or political speech that is handed out prior to the actual speech being given, as with the State of the Union ad-

[7]Carl P. Wrighter, "Weasel Words: God's Little Helpers," in *I Can Sell You Anything* (New York: Ballantine Books, 1972).

dress given by the president each year? The same thing applies. The quotes, once passed on to the intended audience, are then validated as having been spoken by the person for whom they were written. The same thing applies to quotes appearing in press releases. These are often made up in order to enhance the credibility of the release or simply to get the name of some executive into the release. Once the person to whom the quote is attributed approves of the quote, it is legitimate. The key in both instances is the approval of the quoted person. This form of writing, often referred to as *ghostwriting*, presents a number of ethical pitfalls. Richard Johannesen proposes a series of guidelines that would remove some of the potential for ethical error from this process.[8]

- *What is the communicator's intent and what is the audience's degree of awareness?* In other words, does the communicator pretend to be the author of the words he speaks or over which his signature appears? And how aware is the audience that ghostwriting is commonplace under certain circumstances? If we assume, as most do, that presidential speeches are ghostwritten, then the only unethical act would be for the president to claim to write his own speeches.
- *Does the communicator use ghostwriters to make himself or herself appear to possess personal qualities that he or she does not really have?* In other words, does the writer impart such qualities as eloquence, wit, coherence, and incisive ideas to a communicator who might not possess these qualities otherwise? The degree to which the writing distorts a communicator's character has a great deal to do with ethicality.
- *What are the surrounding circumstances of the communicator's job that make ghostwriting a necessity?* The pressures of a job often dictate that a ghostwriter be used. Busy executives like busy politicians may not have the time to write all the messages they must deliver on a daily basis. However, we don't expect the average office manager or university professor to hire a ghostwriter. Part of the answer to this question lies in the pressures of the job itself, and the other part has to do with the need and frequency of communication.
- *To what extent do the communicators actively participate in the writing of their own messages?* Obviously, the more input a communicator has in his or her own writing, the more ethical will be the resultant image. We really don't expect the president to write his own speeches, but we do expect that the sentiments expressed in them will be his own.
- *Does the communicator accept responsibility for the message he or she presents?* When former president Ronald Reagan's press secretary, Larry

[8]Johannesen, *Ethics in Human Communication*, pp. 138–139.

Speakes, disclosed in his book that many of the quotes attributed to the president were, in fact, either made up or "borrowed" from someone else, he caused quite an ethical uproar. Part of the problem with the Larry Speakes revelation was that the president denied the accusations. In other words, he claimed he never approved Speakes's work. Most communicators simply assume that whatever they say or whatever they sign their names to is theirs, whether written by someone else or not. This is obviously the most ethical position to take.

Context is a more ambiguous concept for advertising and public relations. Although a news story needs to appear within the broader context of its setting in order to enhance understanding, the contextual setting of information for both advertising and public relations can be much narrower. For example, a television ad need only be placed within the context of its own reality, and that reality is often created just for that product (in literature, this is called *verisimilitude*). The make-believe world of the ideal nuclear family is the context from which we are most often sold laundry detergent, bath soap, kids' juice drinks, floor waxes, and dozens of other household products. Does this created context enhance understanding of the typical uses of the product? Of course it does. Is the context true? Possibly not; however, if it actually shows the most typical use of the product, even in a make-believe setting, it does not alter the veracity of the product claim.

For public relations, context may be even more important. The context within which a claim is made or an argument offered decidedly influences the reactions of the receiving audience. Claims not placed within context generally cry out for support. Intelligent listeners typically reject such vacuous statements. For example, a political candidate claiming that violent crime is a problem so great in scope that only severe measures will work to prevent its uncontrolled spread would do well to place that claim within the context of national crime statistics or risk loss of credibility. By the same token, context is sometimes narrowed in order to give an argument more strength. For instance, an impassioned plea for gun control by a state legislator following a school shooting may be placed within the local context for greater effect. It may even be placed within the larger national context, given the "epidemic" of school shootings in this country, and still succeed. However, if placed within the totality of violent crime, which is on the decrease, or if compared with the relative safety of nearly all of our schools (hundreds of thousands in number), the argument may lose some of its edge. So, selective context for public relations, as for advertising, is purposeful and generally done to enhance the marketability of a product, service, or idea.

On the criteria of balance, advertising and public relations diverge widely from journalism. The objective nature of journalism demands balance. The highly subjective nature of advertising and public relations results in no such requirement. In fact, the act of persuasion requires that a side be taken. And although a persuasive claim may very well present both sides of an argument, it will certainly support only one. We must also remember that persuasion is not unethical by nature. As mentioned earlier in this chapter, persuasion within a democratic environment is entirely necessary for that endeavor to succeed. As long as the message isn't intentionally deceptive, or important facts are misrepresented or left out, or blatant lies are told, advertising and public relations communication can be said to be truthful.

Finally, it should be noted that it would be a mistake for us to hold all media to the same standards as newswriting. We must remember that journalistic writing in its present form is an invention of the past 80 years or so and uses standards of objectivity not suited to persuasive writing. In fact, the ideal of objectivity is being argued by many as an unsatisfactory one even for journalism. Regardless, we must be cautious not to assume unethicality simply because of a difference in style or intent.

ETHICS AND PERSUASION

As has been noted, the primary difference between journalism and advertising and public relations is that we expect the latter two to be biased in their points of view. In most cases, we even expect them to be persuasive in their approaches to communication. Both advertising and public relations use language to persuade, and, as mentioned earlier, persuasion is not unethical by nature. Instead, it is a time-honored democratic tradition based on guidelines formulated by the Greeks over 2,000 years ago.

Those who believe persuasion is unethical by nature generally also believe in a very strict version of the marketplace of ideas theory: that if you provide enough unbiased information for people, they will be able to make up their own minds about any issue. Although our political system is based on this theory, to some extent, it is also based on the notion of reasoned argument—including persuasion. People who believe fervently enough in a particular point of view aren't going to rely on any marketplace to decide their case. They're going to get out there and argue, persuasively, for their side.

Since the time of Aristotle, we've had access to a number of persuasive techniques. We also are aware of how easily many of these techniques can be turned to unethical purposes. In fact, the most frequent complaint about any form of communication is that it is trying to persuade unethically, usually through deception. Both public relations and advertising suffer from this charge.

Some believe that persuasion, like lying, is coercive and thus harmful by nature. Feminist theorist Sally Miller Gearhart holds that persuasion is, in fact, "an act of violence." Like a number of other feminist scholars, Gearhart views some communication techniques as reflecting a masculine-oriented approach. Persuasion, in particular, represents a "conquest/conversion mentality."[9] This approach, according to Gearhart, uses persuasive techniques to convince the persuaded that they are better off accepting a particular point of view. The persuaded, in this model, may or may not be willing to change their points of view. She holds that those who are willing will be self-persuaded when presented with the necessary information, and that others should be left to their own beliefs. Gearhart proposes that we develop a "collective" mode, focusing on listening and receiving rather than the "competitive" mode common to the masculine perspective.

Clearly, this runs counter to the assumption of the ancient Greek rhetoricians, who held that persuasion was a necessary concomitant of democracy. And it seems a bit harsh to other feminist theorists. Sonja Foss and Cindy Griffin accept persuasion as one among many techniques that can be used ethically, given the right context. They point out, however, that persuasion based on a model of "domination" is decidedly not the ethical approach. Rather, they suggest that persuasion be grounded in a belief that the most desirable outcome of the persuasive act is one of equality and autonomy among the parties. Their ideal persuasive model is one in which all sides are invited to view the alternatives and decide for themselves. In this model, the likelihood of change is as great for one party as for the other.[10] This same model shows up in other communication theories, such as those of public relations scholar James Grunig. Grunig proposes that the ideal model for public relations is one that provides for mutual understanding as its goal. This "two-way symmetric" communication model presupposes that all sides of an issue are amenable to change, and that change will come with an increased understanding of all points of view.[11]

We must realize, however, that the traditional approach to persuasion (whether or not it is a masculine orientation) is the approach that is in effect today, much as it has been for several thousand years. Advocates of all sorts (legal, commercial, and editorial) still subscribe to the tenets of persuasion set forth by the likes of Aristotle and Cicero. Because this traditional approach is in effect, we must be prepared to deal with the potential for unethical use of both the language and the techniques of persuasion.

---

[9]Sally Miller Gearhart, "The Womanization of Rhetoric," *Women's Studies International Quarterly*, 2 (1979): 195–201.

[10]Sonja K. Foss and Cindy L. Griffin, "Beyond Persuasion: A Proposal for an Invitational Rhetoric," Communication Monographs, 2 (March 1995): 2–18.

[11]James E. Grunig and Todd Hunt, *Managing Public Relations* (New York: Holt, Rinehart and Winston, 1984), p. 21.

The Art of Persuasion

Aristotle left a great body of work, much of which was saved and passed on to us from one generation to the next. One of his most important works, as regards the topic of persuasion, is *On Rhetoric*. In it, he lays out the reasoning process and the techniques of public speaking—primarily, persuasive speaking. Aristotle believed that rhetoric was part method and part art, derived both from politics and ethics; and he classified its use both as a pragmatic, persuasive tool and as an important theory and ethical concept. Like Milton (nearly 2,000 years later), Aristotle believed that rhetoric was a legitimate tool that allows a speaker to debate an important issue and defend a point of view while refuting an opponent with an alternate viewpoint. In fact, Aristotle thought it would be odd not to be able to defend our ideas verbally in much the same way that we defend our persons physically from assault.[12] He did not believe that rhetoric should be used to persuade an audience of something that was untrue or wicked.

Aristotle defined rhetoric as an ability to recognize and use the available means of persuasion. He divided these means of persuasion into two groups: those based on evidence of witnesses, and written contracts (not invented by the speaker), thus *nonartistic* means; and *artistic* means. These were further subdivided into three groups: *ethos*, technique based on the character of the speaker; *pathos*, an appeal to the emotions of an audience; and *logos*, derived from logical argument (further divided into inductive and deductive reasoning). What follows is based, in large part, on Aristotle's *Rhetoric*, with some modern interpretations.

The Strategies of Persuasion

Certain strategies are more appropriate to persuasion than to information dissemination and are typically used in both public relations and advertising to sell products and ideas. For example, emotional appeals are most often associated with persuasion, not information. That's why, for instance, straight news stories are generally free of such appeal. They are supposed to be as objective (informative) as possible. Probably the persuasive strategies most thought of as ethical are the argument strategies, usually because they appeal to logic and generally provide balance.

Democratic debate is at the heart of our system of government. It is no surprise then that argument strategies are among the oldest types of persuasion at a communicator's disposal. Argument strategies, which are persuasive strategies designed to oppose another point of view and to persuade, come in two types: reasoned argument (logos) and emotional appeal

[12]George A. Kennedy, *Aristotle* On Rhetoric*: A Theory of Civil Discourse* (New York: Oxford University Press, 1991), pp. 31–50.

(pathos). Both attempt to persuade by arguing one point of view against another.

Reasoned Argument–*Reasoned argument* (also known as logical argument) uses the techniques of rhetoric as handed down from the ancient Greeks. For persuasive messages it is important to understand the psychological state of an audience and build a message around this. Good persuasive communicators know how their audiences will react to certain techniques and certain types of language. That's why they use them.

For example, good persuaders know that if their audience opposes their position, they must present arguments on both sides of the issue. That's because the audience already knows the communicator has a vested interest in giving her side of the story. By presenting both sides, she portrays an image of fairness and willingness to compare arguments. The process appears to be more democratic that way. The technique of carrying out this strategy involves addressing counterarguments only after the persuader's side of the issue has been presented. Here's how it works:

- The opposing view is stated fairly. This makes the audience believe that the communicator is fair-minded enough to recognize that there is another side and that the audience is intelligent enough to understand it.
- The communicator's position on the opposing view is stated. Now that he's shown he understands the other side, he states why he doesn't think it's right–or better yet, not totally right. This indicates that he finds at least some merit in what others have to say–even the opposition.
- The communicator's position is supported. The details of the argument are given. Logic, not emotion, is used. This shows that the communicator is above such tricks; however, emotion shouldn't be avoided altogether. A balance is usually struck, at the same time leaning toward logic and emotional control.
- The two positions are then compared and the communicator's is shown to be the more viable. By this time, the audience should already see the clear differences between the two sides. The communicator then strengthens the audience's understanding by reiterating the differences and finishing with a strong statement in support of the arguments.

There are similar techniques for audiences who agree with a point of view, for those who are well educated, and for those who are likely to hear the opposing argument from the other side later. Reasoned argument is considered to be the most ethical form of persuasion. It also requires the most audience involvement. That's why most advertising appeals to the emotions. The restrictions of time and space requirements demand an appeal that can be presented in a limited format.

Emotional appeal–Because emotion is common to all human beings, it should come as no surprise that the use of it as a persuasive strategy is widespread. Most advertising uses emotional appeal to sell products. Parity products, especially, benefit from this technique. A parity product is one that is virtually indistinguishable from other similar products. Bath soap, soft drinks, and perfumes are examples of parity products. Think about the type of ads you have seen that deal with these products: They are almost always based on an image created by emotional appeal. And not to let public relations off the hook, think of all those politicians who seem to be pretty much alike. How are they differentiated in our minds? Or, what is the difference in most people's minds between Exxon, Phillips Petroleum, Mobil, and Texaco? For over 20 years, Mobil Oil has been closely associated with public television (most notably, Masterpiece Theater). Most opera buffs know that Texaco has sponsored weekly radio opera broadcasts for nearly twice as long.

Emotional appeal can be fostered in several ways, the most important of which are the use of *symbols*, the use of *emotive language*, and through *entertainment strategies*. We discuss the use of symbols and emotive language later. Here we concentrate on entertainment as a way of creating emotional appeal.

Like the techniques of argument, the techniques of entertainment have been handed down to us from the ancient Greeks. The masks of comedy and tragedy are part of our cultural symbolism in the West. Entertainment, by nature, appeals to the senses. As a culture we constantly refer to a person's "sense of humor" or someone's "sense of the dramatic."

Soft drinks and beer are two of the products most often sold with humor. Like many other products, these are parity items, and parity products are best differentiated by image–which is often the result of entertainment strategies.

Although it's easy to spot the uses of drama and humor in advertising, public relations campaigns frequently use the same approaches in order to persuade. Humor, for example, is especially useful if what you have to "sell" is either opposed by your audience or appears to be distant from their experience. Humor puts people at ease in otherwise serious situations. Politicians and other speechmakers often open with a joke or a humorous anecdote before getting to the heart of the message. Abraham Lincoln was renowned for his folksy humor, John Kennedy for his sophisticated brand.

Emotional appeal, like compliance strategies, may seem to be unethical; however, using emotion to draw attention is not inherently so. It may be manipulative (in the sense that its sole intent is to hook the audience), but it is only unethical if it hides the true objective of the message: to persuade.

Guidelines For Ethical Persuasion

The ethical determinants of most advertising and public relations messages are, thus, those of responsible rhetorical techniques. A number of scholars in the field of rhetoric and persuasion have provided excellent guidelines for determining the morality of both the act of persuasion and the content of persuasive messages. Following is one such checklist for the measurement of the persuasive act itself:[13]

1. Is the communication act or technique right in general and/or right in this specific situation?
2. To what extent is the argument valid?
3. Are the best interests of the audience considered?
4. Does society hold the communication act or technique to be right in general and/or in this situation?
5. Does the communication act or technique appeal to values the society holds to be morally good or bad?
6. Are the "real motives" behind the act or technique admirable or at least legitimate?
7. What would be the social consequences of the act or technique if it were to become widely practiced by others?

Obviously, these questions involve a number of ethical theories including utilitarianism and Kant's categorical imperative. Consequently, they serve to provide the persuader with a checklist for motives when developing—as every public relations and advertising professional must—a proper marketing mix for the dissemination of a persuasive message. This checklist, or another like it, can be applied both to the act itself and to the communication technique. One of the admonitions contained in the Public Relations Society of America Code of Professional Standards, for instance, forbids the corruption of media channels. This checklist also speaks to that problem.

The message itself also has the potential for corruption. Obviously, moral intent and ethical technique do not necessarily guarantee subsequently ethical communication. For this purpose, these eight guidelines for evaluating the degree of ethicality in argumentation and persuasion may be useful.[14]

---

[13]J. M. Sproule, *Argument: Language and Its Influence* (New York: McGraw-Hill, 1980), Ch. 8.

[14]J. V. Jensen, *Argumentation: Reasoning in Communication* (New York: Van Nostrand, 1981), Ch. 2.

- A message should be *accurate*. It should stay within both the facts and the relevant context, and neither exaggerate nor make false claims.
- It should be *complete*. Although advocacy implies bias, it is necessary that all arguments be at least recognized. This also refers to the proper attribution of sources.
- Material should always be *relevant*. Superfluous information only serves to cloud the message.
- *Openness* implies that alternatives be recognized even if the intent of the message is to promote only one of them.
- The message should be made *understandable* through the minimization of ambiguity, and avoidance of oversimplification and distortion of accuracy.
- Sound *reasoning* should be in evidence, containing only appropriate appeals to values, emotions, needs, and motives.
- *Social utility* should be promoted.
- Communicators should demonstrate *benevolence* through sincerity, tact, and respect for dignity.

CAN WE TELL TRUTH FROM FICTION?

As far as advertising and public relations are concerned, the question of whether we can tell truth from fiction is crucial. We expect journalistic descriptions and reports to be "real"—that is, to be factual and accurate representations of reality. Thus, we are shocked to learn that a news story has been fabricated, as in the infamous Janet Cooke–*Washington Post* scandal of over 20 years ago. We are outraged when we learn, for instance, that NBC News would rig a truck to blow up to prove a crash-test point. But what about docudramas, "reality" cop shows, entertainment "news"? These somewhat gray areas, as well as a great deal of advertising and public relations, require a closer inspection of what constitutes truth. Such a discussion also requires that we take sides in the age-old debate over whether people are intelligent enough to make such distinctions or are, as Plato suggested, simply an uneducated mob.

Ethics scholars Tom Wheeler and Tim Gleason have developed a test for ethicality in photo manipulation that is based on the idea of an audience's expectation of reality. They claim that one way to test this ethicality is to ask the viewer/reader if the photograph is plausible. "Or, is the fictional content immediately obvious?"[15] This recognition factor allows for a fairly

[15]Tom Wheeler and Tim Gleason, "Digital Photography and the Ethics of Photofiction: Four Tests for Assessing the Reader's Qualified Expectation of Reality," Paper presented to AEJMC Mag Division, August 1994.

liberal interpretation of what is misleading. It relies on two tests: (1) whether or not the image is implausible and, thus, readily obvious; or (2) if not, if it is appropriately labeled. This *qualified expectation of reality* test (QER), then, is the determinant of ethicality—at least for manipulated photographs. Following on this guideline, we might expect that a photo on the cover *of Mad Magazine* would more likely be manipulated than one on the cover of *Time* magazine. That is why, for instance, the now famous O. J. Simpson photo that appeared greatly altered on the cover of *Time* several years ago drew so much negative attention. The cover was labeled a "photo-illustration" on the masthead, and showed a heavily touched up police mug shot of Simpson with a decidedly darkened countenance. Racial overtones aside, most people felt that the cover of a news magazine was not the place to fool around with reality. The determinant is whether an average reader or viewer would expect the image to be real or not. If he does expect reality, then any manipulation must be admitted to in order not to, either intentionally or unintentionally, fool him.

The QER test also can be useful for determining the "truth" of advertising and public relations claims—as regards image and context—as well as information programming that blurs the lines between fact and fiction. How plausible is the image of a skier screaming down the side of a skyscraper, or of huge draft horses playing football, or of frogs talking with lizards about beer? Do we really believe that the product they are selling is reflected in the image they are using, or are we merely amused? Do we really prefer Pepsi over Coke because of all those clever commercials? Clearly, the examples cited here fall into the implausible category; however, there are many that are not so easily recognized as fiction. Magazine ads that depict young women as unnaturally tall and thin may appear to be real when, in fact, they are subtly manipulated to enhance already gaunt features. What about the celebrity spokesperson who endorses a product he doesn't use? Do we believe him or not? What about the seemingly real testimonial from a person who turns out to be an actor? Do we believe that the "vintage" film footage of Dean Witter urging his employees to care about their customers is what it purports to be? Or do the advertisers think we'll instantly recognize it as an artistic prop meant simply to catch our attention? Is that Jeep really on top of that mountain peak? Is that hamburger really that big? What are our expectations?

So, although selective presentation, as mentioned earlier, may not be inherently unethical, much depends on the receiver's qualified expectation of reality. The clichéd advertising response of caveat emptor (buyer beware) covers only so much transgression. If we follow the model suggested by Wheeler and Gleason, our obligation is to remove all doubt concerning the reality of the context of our message. And although the law has already insisted on some indicators (labeling dramatizations, for instance), our goal should be to eliminate any potential for misunderstanding. If our goal is to intentionally blur the lines between fact and fiction, we are acting unethically.

CONSUMERS: VICTIMS OR INFORMED CHOOSERS?

You'll remember from chapter 4 that not everyone has viewed the "people" as intelligent enough to look out for themselves. This is an important point to come to grips with, as much of the justification for the type of communication that both advertising and public relations engage in is predicated on the notion that listeners are intelligent enough to discern true from false. According to this concept, the views of the likes of Milton and Locke are correct in that truth will prevail in an open marketplace, in part because autonomous and rational individuals will be able to discern the difference between truth and falsity. This belief in the rational abilities of the people who receive media messages is directly responsible for such precepts as caveat emptor. "Buyer beware" assumes that an intelligent consumer will be able to discern nuances in messages—nuances that the designer of the message may have intentionally obscured. And this turns up the other side of the coin: Why do those advertising and public relations practitioners who say they believe in the intelligence of the average consumer try so hard to cloud their messages? Could it be that, like Plato, they really believe that the masses are easily deceived by the "shadows on the cave wall"?

Think of the huge numbers of infomercials airing on television these days. A great many of them are "performed" before a live audience as if the "guest" were appearing on a talk show. Does the average consumer know that these audiences are paid to be there? Can viewers tell that the "programs" are really commercials posing as talk shows? Why do you suppose the FCC requires these lengthy commercials to carry the disclaimer that they are paid advertising? Why do terms such as "dramatization" have to appear on commercials in which actors pose as real people? Because some believe that average consumers just might be duped by such tactics as fake talk shows and dramatic recreations. This also accounts for the labeling of news images not actually taken during the unfolding of the story being discussed but at some time earlier, as "library footage," or "file footage."

As the line between entertainment and information becomes increasingly blurred, catch phrases such as caveat emptor may no longer provide sufficient warning. Additionally, such techniques as the QER test have to be based on a pragmatic assessment of the abilities of consumers to discern what is real from what is not, especially in instances in which they are expecting reality. Whether you agree with Plato or with Milton, placing the onus of recognition of reality solely on the receiver of your message is failing to live up to your own moral obligations. Intent is still the ultimate measure of truth telling. If, as a media practitioner, you intend to deceive, then you are acting unethically; however, if someone is misled by a message you never expected would be misleading, then your actions may be excused. Likewise, we don't tend to criticize advertising that is clearly fictional. (We don't really believe that frogs and lizards talk—do we?) But, if we are led to believe that someone stands for something she does not, or that a product performs in a way it ultimately does not, or that something fake is something real, then we have been deceived—and deception is unethical.

THE CASE FOR WITHHOLDING INFORMATION

When is withholding information unethical? As discussed earlier, journalists who do not present clear context may, unintentionally, be omitting information vital to understanding. Certainly, if this omission is unintentional, then the outcome can be said to be potentially harmful although the action is not necessarily unethical. Remember, as many philosophers have pointed out, intent is vital to determining the ethicality of an act. Thus, when information is withheld we need to determine the reason before we can condemn the act as unethical.

Advertisers and public relations professionals have long been accused of presenting information that is incomplete; and, as we have already discussed, that is not necessarily unethical because, by nature, both of these professions are supposed to be biased in favor of the client. No one expects an advertisement, for example, to include every detail of a product or its potential uses, although multiplying the uses of a product is usually a good thing. (Think of Arm & Hammer Baking Soda. Who knew you could put it in your refrigerator to dispel odors?) However, the recent laws regarding the advertising of pharmaceuticals reflect the growing concern with advertisers leaving out information vital to understanding the whole range of a product's potential affects. No prescription pharmaceutical may be advertised as having a specific positive effect unless it is accompanied by information concerning its negative side effects. The result has been commercials that are sometimes ludicrous in their happy-voiced disclaimers: Although the product may relieve your allergy symptoms, it may also cause nausea and vomiting!

Think of the countless times a political candidate's previously undisclosed wrongdoings have been "found out" by the press despite an army of news secretaries painting an opposite image, or the corporate PR people who routinely cover for mistakes and misdeeds. What were the PR people at Enron thinking while their company was going to pieces before their eyes? Did the public relations agencies for such companies as Firestone and Enron simply buy into their clients' lines of a solid investment or a safe product? When we think of company executives lying about their products or the value of their stock, where do we place their spokespeople in the hierarchy of deception? Surely, there has to be some culpability on the part of their media representatives. However, as stated throughout this book, it is not always easy to know every detail about a client or that client's product or company, and those gaps in knowledge may, ultimately, have disastrous consequences. At the very least, a PR firm's reputation may suffer during and following such disclosures.

There are times, however, when withholding information may be thought of as not unethical. As discussed in chapter 3, consulting professionals generally maintain client confidentiality in order to defend them from competitors. Not everything needs to be made public. A company's research and development projects are clearly in this category, as are their plans to go public with their stock offerings (a position dictated by the Securities and Exchange Commission), potential expansion projects, or a myriad other "secrets" that ensure the privacy so needed in industries in which competition is high. Where, however, do we draw the line? When does discretion need to become disclosure?

Ethicist Michael Bayles delineates instances when breaching confidentiality (disclosing rather than withholding information) is usually thought to be ethical. He lists three kinds of reasons that can be given for a consulting professional and/or media professional violating confidentiality: the best interests of (1) the client, (2) the professional, or (3) other persons.[16] Bayles considers disclosure in the best interest of the client to be rare and inadvisable, because this could lead to a paternalistic stance rather than the ideal fiduciary position between client and professional.

Confidence can be breached, however, in the best interest of the professional under two kinds of situations: "when it is necessary for professionals (1) to collect a just fee or (2) to defend themselves against a charge of wrongdoing."[17] For our purposes, the second is the more important. Bayles suggests that clients will typically not wish to have information disclosed

---

[16]Michael D. Bayles, *Professional Ethics*, 2nd ed. (Belmont: Wadsworth Publishing Company, 1989), p. 97.

[17]Bayles, *Professional Ethics*, p. 98.

that might show they have done something wrong. The onus of correcting the wrongdoing is, then, placed squarely on the consulting professional in order to prevent harm to innocent third parties, which, concomitantly, injures the professional's reputation and credibility. For this reason, many in both advertising and public relations require disclaimers in their contracts that absolve them of blame should a client lie about a wrongdoing, causing that lie to be passed along by the professional representative.

In the third instance, Bayles suggests identifying and weighing the values and interests of the client against those of affected third parties to arrive at a rule that can, then, be used in similar circumstances in the future. Further, all professionals may disclose confidential information to prevent illegal conduct.[18]

The somewhat tricky relationship between client and consulting professional makes the decision to violate confidentiality a serious one. This step should only be taken when it is clear that (1) the client has violated the law, (2) the client has done something that would harm the reputation and credibility of the professional, or (3) the client has done or plans to do something that will harm innocent third parties. As we discuss in the next chapter, avoiding harm is one of the primary obligations of the media professional. This is equally true of the news media, and especially true of advertising and public relations because of their tendency toward client loyalty.

THE ULTIMATE TRUTH

It must be remembered that advertising and public relations are not, by nature, unethical. Neither is the act of persuasion. The ultimate determinant of the ethicality of a persuasive technique is the degree to which the practitioner intends to deceive in order to manipulate an audience. Manipulation is the same as coercion—the result of telling an outright lie. In both cases the communicator is intentionally altering reality in order to force another person into believing or acting in a way she would not have but for the deception or the lie.

To fail to respect the autonomy of another person goes against most of the principles on which American democracy is founded. It violates the Kantian imperative to treat all human beings with respect; it ignores Mill's caution against bullying the minority; it runs counter to the liberty theory of free speech; and it violates the natural rights of individuals that Locke

---

[18]Bayles, *Professional Ethics*, pp. 111–129.

was so set on protecting. Even the Greek philosophers, who recognized that rhetoric implied persuasion, held that to lie or to mislead by false logic was inherently wrong. Both Plato and Aristotle had little use for Sophists, the group of professional philosophers who specialized in dialectic, argumentation, and rhetoric and who were often known for their elaborate and specious arguments. In fact, the word *sophistry* has come to mean, "a plausible but misleading or fallacious argument." In the final analysis, it is best to remember that persuasion is ethical, manipulation is not.

The same is ultimately true for journalism. Although journalists continually hold up the truth as an icon, they also stoop to consistently newer lows each time they use deception to gather news without first considering alternative methods. At first blush, it may seem that using deceptive techniques in advertising and public relations is so obviously self-serving as to be undeniably unethical. At the same time, deception used in the name of the public's right to know appears to carry a sense of higher purpose. However, if we realize that the news "business" actually is a business, then it is less clear whether deception is being used on behalf of the public or merely to stimulate consumption of the news product.

The growth spurt in television news magazine shows is proof enough that investigative reporting draws viewership. When all the major networks are competing head-to-head on weeknights with amazingly similar products, the push to go for the spectacular is great indeed. And with this rise in competition comes a parallel rise in the temptation to use deceptive techniques to gather the story. Nothing condemns quite like a hidden camera or an ambush interview. As in any war, in this battle to achieve the highest ratings truth is usually the first casualty.

How can we avoid this trap? For all of the media, truth has to become the paramount concern. Deception must not be used in advertising and public relations at all. And in investigative reporting, deceptive news-gathering techniques must be limited to instances in which a vitally important story cannot be gathered in any other way. In the final analysis, the media cannot afford to lie—in any way, for any reason. If we cannot be assured that the default position is always the truth, then the media will continue to slide in esteem, along with their ability to affect lives in positive ways.

We have seen in this chapter that the road to truth is filled with obstacles. Most of these can be avoided easily; some take more effort. Ultimately, the result is worth the effort, for the media are known by the truth they tell—whether it is about a product, a political candidate, or a school shooting. We rely on the media for practically everything we know about the world that we haven't experienced firsthand. It is vitally important that the truth be the rule and not the exception.

EXERCISES

1. Define “truth” in your own words. Define “lying.”
2. Do you believe that a person should always tell the truth? Why or why not? If not, under what circumstances would you excuse a lie?
3. Cite an instance in which you feel you were lied to by any medium. Was the “lie” through deception, incomplete information, distortion, or what?
4. Do you think that speeches should be ghostwritten? Why or why not?
5. How do you stand on the intelligence of media publics? Can we let them decide for themselves whether something is “real,” or should we assume there are those who might be fooled, at least some of the time? What position do you think most advertisers take? Public relations people? Journalists?
6. How do you feel, personally, about the use of undercover reporting techniques on most television news magazine programs? Explain why you either support or don’t support their approach.
7. Most of us understand the persuasive nature of advertising and public relations; however, the news media can be persuasive as well. Cite an instance of persuasion by the news media.
8. Under what circumstances do you think persuasion should not be used by the media? Under what circumstances is persuasion legitimate?
9. Find a photograph from a magazine or newspaper that you think might have been altered in any way, especially digitally. Answer the following questions concerning the photo and its effects:
    - What is the publication in which you found the photo? What kind of audience does this publication appeal to?
    - Does the photo in question pass the “Qualified Expectation of Reality” (QER) test? If not, do you consider the photo unethical? Why or why not?
    - Who are affected by the photo and how are they affected?

HYPOTHETICAL: DECEPTIVE ADVERTISING

A large manufacturer of distilled liquor has recently developed a series of television and print advertisements it has called “public service announcements" (PSAs). These PSAs demonstrate graphically* that the alcohol content of a single beer, a glass of wine, and a mixed drink containing 1.5 ounces of distilled liquor is essentially the same. Their purpose, stated within the PSAs, is to make the public aware that a person consumes the same amount of alcohol in each of these drinks and thus is just as likely to become intoxicated from one as from the others. The name of the company is given in the PSAs as the sponsoring organization.

It is also widely known among marketing experts and others that sales of distilled liquor have suffered at the same time that sales of wine and beer have risen. This may be due in part to the fact that advertisement of distilled spirits is not currently being done in the broadcast media (although it is widely used in print media). This is not an actual law, but an informal and longstanding agreement among advertisers, manufacturers, and broadcasters. The president of the liquor company has denied any relationship between declining sales and the PSAs; however, the word within the company is that the two are, in fact, related. In addition, the three major television networks have refused to run the PSAs calling them an advertisement for distilled spirits; however, the PSAs have subsequently been run in *TV Guide* under the headline "Why are ABC, CBS and NBC afraid to run this message?"

QUESTIONS ON HYPOTHETICAL

1. Are these true public service announcements?
2. Are these messages in the public interest?
3. Are these advertisements? If so, for what exactly?
4. What ethical theories justify either running or not running the spots on television?
5. What ethical justification, if any, can you cite for running beer and wine ads but not ads for hard liquor? If there is no ethical justification for this, what (ethically) is wrong with this differentiation?

HYPOTHETICAL: PR AND THE GUN LOBBY

Because you won a local Public Relations Society of America chapter award for your successful effort at organizing a statewide coalition of interest

*The ads show a picture of a shot glass, followed by an equals sign, followed by a glass of beer, an equals sign, and a glass of wine.

groups to deal with the AIDS threat, you have been approached by a small-arms industry association to organize and serve as executive director for a new group to promote the claimed "constitutional right to bear arms" of nonmilitia citizens, as well as to counter the growing threat of "gun control legislation."

They have in mind a national membership organization that would eventually draw a large proportion of needed revenues from member dues; but in the meantime the industry association will provide generously for the financial needs of the organization, including your salary in excess of $100,000.

They also suggest a name for the organization, giving prominence to the constitutional right to bear arms theme, and they further specify that in order to avoid negative connotations, any connection with the small-arms industry not be divulged.

QUESTIONS ON HYPOTHETICAL

1. Would you take this job? Why or why not?
2. Does this situation violate any professional codes?
3. Justify taking this job. Now, justify not taking the job. Which would you do and why?

CASE STUDY: TO AIR OR NOT TO ERR

The Voice of America (VOA) is an international multimedia broadcasting service funded by the U.S. government that broadcasts over 1,000 hours of news, informational, educational, and cultural programs every week to an audience of some 94 million worldwide. VOA programs are produced and broadcast in English and 52 other languages through radio, satellite television, and the Internet.

The first VOA broadcast originated from New York City on February 24, 1942, just 79 days after the United States entered World War II. It was established to bring uncensored news to countries closed to the free flow of information by the war. Speaking in German, announcer William Harlan Hale told his listeners: "Here speaks a voice from America. Every day at this time we will bring you the news of the war. The news may be good. The news may be bad. We shall tell you the truth."

Originally under the jurisdiction of the U.S. State Department, the VOA got its own charter from Congress in 1976 and is now overseen by an appointed board of governors with State Department representation.

On September 25, 2001, just two weeks after the September 11th attacks in New York City, Pennsylvania, and Washington, D.C., the VOA aired an exclusive interview with Mullah Mohammed Omar, the head of the Taliban and the protector of Osama bin Laden.

The decision of VOA's then acting director, Myrna Whitworth, and André de Nesnera, news director, to broadcast this interview was stridently opposed by the National Security Council and senior State Department officials, including Deputy Secretary of State Richard Armitage. State Department spokesman Richard Boucher denounced VOA and defended the department's position in a briefing on September 24th.

Shortly after the Omar interview was aired, Whitworth was replaced by a new VOA director named by the Bush administration. William Safire, the noted *New York Times* columnist, devoted several derisive op-ed pieces to the VOA, referring to Whitworth as a "seat-warming bureaucrat" unable to control de Nesnera, her news director. An earlier Safire column concerning a related, but different, story involving the VOA's coverage of post–September 11th terrorism was scornfully entitled "Equal Time for Hitler."

According to de Nesnera,

> As veteran VOA journalists, it has always been our mission to follow VOA's charter: that our news be "accurate, objective and comprehensive." As Edward R. Murrow, head of our then parent organization USIA [United States Information Agency] once said: "The measure of our success will be the degree to which we are believed." It was, and remains, our conviction that in order to be credible, VOA must report all news objectively and fairly or we risk becoming merely a propaganda tool of the State Department. More importantly, we fail our worldwide audience of more than 90 million listeners, many of whom rely on us as their sole source of objective news.[19]

In a September 24th memo—excerpts of which were subsequently reprinted in numerous news articles in the United States and abroad—de Nesnera wrote to his staff that "it takes a long time to build up credibility and an instant to lose it."

On Thursday, September 20, 2001, Taliban officials contacted Spozmai Maiwandi, then chief of the VOA's Pashto service, informing her that Mullah Omar was willing to talk to the Voice of America. She conducted the interview along with Ed Warner, a senior news division correspondent. This was a worldwide exclusive, even more remarkable because of the Taliban's persecution of women in Afghanistan. Given the political significance of the interview, Acting Director Whitworth followed protocol and, as a courtesy, informed the National Security Council and the State Department of its

[19]André de Nesnera, letter to Payne Awards Committee, School of Journalism and Communication, University of Oregon, Feb. 8, 2002.

existence. She was subsequently told, on Friday, September 21st, that the VOA could not use it.

Whitworth and de Nesnera decided that the interview would be used, but should be balanced with an interview with the exiled king of Afghanistan, living in Rome. A correspondent was dispatched to the Italian capital to pursue this over the weekend. On Monday, September 24th, following an unsuccessful attempt to speak with the king, Whitworth and de Nesnera decided to use portions of the Mullah Omar interview along with excerpts of President Bush's address to Congress, excerpts from an interview with Georgetown University Islamic expert John Esposito, and remarks by a spokesman for the Northern Alliance opposing the Taliban. Warner wrote the final piece, which was aired on Tuesday, September 25th.

CASE STUDY QUESTIONS

1. What are the arguments you see in favor of running the Mullah Omar piece? What are the arguments against running it?
2. How does the running of the interview contribute or not contribute to exploring the "truth"?
3. Given that the VOA is a government organization and is paid for with taxes, do you see its obligation as a news service being the same as that of privately funded media? Why?
4. Who are the moral claimants in this situation and why are you obligated to them?
5. Discuss the issue of balance in reporting and explain whether you think the interview either added balance or was needed at all.
6. What do you think the role of the media should be during a national crisis? Do you think limitations should be put on the media during times of war? If so, what types and why?

CHAPTER

6

Avoiding Harm

As far back as Hippocrates we have been advised to avoid harming other human beings. However, to what extent, if any, is harm an allowable by-product of communication? As individuals, we probably consider harm to others high on our list of proscriptions; but a great deal hangs on our definition of harm. Do we harm a friend by not telling her the truth about her partner's infidelity? Do we harm ourselves by overeating or drinking too much? Do we harm our children by allowing them to watch television? Do we harm our employers by taking sick leave when we're not really sick? These, and a thousand other questions concerning potential harms, are not as easily answered as we might suppose. And when the harm is potentially great or affects the lives or attitudes of large numbers of people, the answers are even more difficult to obtain.

Communication-caused harm has the potential to affect both individuals and multitudes. The harm caused by the publication of Arthur Ashe's condition was restricted to Ashe, his family, and his friends. Yet all of us are harmed, in a way, when a single person's privacy is violated on our behalf. Remember: The rationale for the news media exposing another's private life is generally the public's right to know. When Princess Diana died in an automobile accident in France in 1998, the blame quickly fell on the media "vultures" who were constantly following her around. Little was said, however, about her courtship of that same media when she sought the spotlight for her own personal messages. And little was mentioned about the seemingly voracious appetite of a celebrity-hungry public that keeps both the tabloids and the "legitimate" media in business.

Can the media operate under a proscription of do no harm? Probably not. Stephen Carter points out that although John Milton "argued that truth would win out, he did not contend that nobody would get hurt in the process."[1] Advertisers regularly harm their competition every time a successful ad results in increased sales for the product being advertised. Public relations practitioners certainly harm competing political candidates' chances each time their own candidate moves higher in the polls because of their aggressive campaigning. It may very well be that, as some scholars propose, the persuasive act naturally causes harm to someone every time it is practiced. And yet we accept these "harms" as a necessary by-product of a democratically sanctioned competition. The nature of both democracy and capitalism is competitive, and competition almost always implies a winner and a loser—with some degree of harm visited on the loser. The question then becomes, How much of that harm is avoidable rather than necessary?

"If . . . harm is done in the service of a greater good, . . . then it is an acceptable side effect." Thus say ethicists Stephen Klaidman and Tom Beauchamp in their book, *The Virtuous Journalist.*[2] However, they warn that, unlike medicine—in which the patient is consulted before any harm is committed (such as a leg amputation to save a life)—in journalism the subject of a story is rarely, if ever, consulted. In addition, "the risk of harm to a person or institution being reported on is rarely disclosed, not always evident, and virtually never refusable." And the potential beneficiary is not the subject of the story who will suffer the harm, it is generally the public.[3]

Klaidman and Beauchamp rely on a definition of harm borrowed from ethicist Joel Feinberg. "Harm involves thwarting, defeating or setting back an interest including: property, privacy, confidentiality, friendship, reputation, health and career."[4] The strength of this definition lies in its breadth. According to this approach, a person may be harmed in a number of ways, not just physically or psychologically—the most commonly assumed types of harm. Under this construction, *USA Today* could be held accountable for its unwarranted disclosure in the Arthur Ashe case because it did not honor his privacy. However, if journalists were to avoid any story in which some form of harm might be visited on the subject, very little news would be forthcoming to the public whom they serve. It is very clear that some type of harm follows from much of what journalists produce as news, and that, in many cases, that harm is either a necessary by-product or literally unavoidable.

---

[1]Stephen Carter, *Integrity* (New York: Basic Books {Harper Collins}, 1996), p. 94.

[2]Stephen Klaidman and Tom L. Beauchamp, *The Virtuous Journalist* (Oxford: Oxford University Press, 1987), p. 93.

[3]Klaidman and Beauchamp, *The Virtuous Journalist*, p. 94.

[4]Joel Feinberg, *Harm to Others* (New York: Oxford University Press, 1984), pp. 34–35.

CAUSAL HARM

For the journalist, then, harm may very well be a necessary concomitant of gathering and disseminating the news. However, are journalists absolved of any blame for causing harm? Before answering that question, we need to differentiate between causal and moral responsibility. In chapter 1, we discussed the difference between responsibility and accountability. Recall that not every act can be blamed on the person directly responsible for the act. A bank teller robbed at gunpoint is not accountable for the money he hands over. In the same sense, a manufacturer of toasters is not accountable if someone uses the appliance cord to hang himself. In the first case, the teller is being forced to hand over the money. In the second, the manufacturer could not reasonably have anticipated the misuse of that particular product. In the same way, journalists, and advertising and public relations practitioners cannot be held accountable for every potential harm they may cause through their communications.

Part of the reason for this is the difference between causal and moral responsibility. *Moral responsibility* refers to being held accountable for an action. So, if an advertiser develops an ad campaign for a liquor manufacturer that deliberately targets a minority population known for its misuse of alcohol, she is complicit in any harm that might be caused by that campaign. She cannot simply declare, "Caveat emptor!" Conversely, if a journalist reports on a story about a public official arrested for drunken driving, he is not causing the harm—the official brought it on herself. This is called *causal harm*. All media practitioners must ask themselves this vital question: Does the action being taken actually cause the harm or does it merely augment an already present harm?

That question was probably asked over and over again during the yearlong media frenzy over the Clinton–Lewinsky affair in 1998–1999. Did the president of the United States deserve to have his private life dragged before the public over and over again? Part of the answer to that question can be answered by asking another: Did he in any way bring this upon himself? The answer to that question is decidedly yes. The harm had already been done. The president had violated a private and public trust by abusing his position, and the story was already known in some circles. Did that give the press free rein to report anything they wanted? Possibly not.

The usual test in cases such as this is whether the private information being reported affects the public figure's public performance. Every journalist has to ask this simplest of questions in advance of releasing any privately held information. However, if the answer is no, does that automatically mean that the information will remain private? It probably should, but it often does not. And when the media decided to go against this most basic of guidelines, did they end up contributing to the very problem they were reporting on? Yes, because the release of that information, in and of itself, probably affected the president's public performance–in this case especially so (at least according to opinion polls taken at the time). So, in some cases, such as this one, the harm that results from covering a story can both add to existing harm (causally related to the subject's actions) and create additional harm due to, among other things, extended coverage. In the latter instance, some blame must fall on the press.

On the other hand, the concept of causal harm coincides nicely with that of distributive justice. You'll recall that distributive justice rests on giving to those who deserve, and withholding from those who do not. In this light, exposing the ineptitude or moral failings of public officials could be seen as a form of justice. Despite the fact that most media practitioners don't see themselves as judges, the result of exposing corruption through media coverage can be ethically justified through both causal harm and distributive justice concepts.

PROFESSIONAL RESPONSIBILITY

According to Klaidman and Beauchamp, "To be morally blameworthy, . . . a harm must be caused by carelessness resulting from failure to discharge a socially, legally, or morally imposed duty to take care or to behave reasonably toward others."[5] As noted in chapter 3, professionals incur a number of obligations by the very fact of having taken on professional roles. As professionals, media practitioners must conform to the minimal expectations of the profession of which they are a part. Failure to do so could result in accusations of professional negligence, or malpractice. Malpractice is most often associated with the legal and medical professions; however, every professional is expected to operate within certain ethical parameters. For journalists as well as advertising and public relations practitioners, these parameters should include avoiding unnecessary harm.

Professional negligence can be charged in instances in which the professional has not exercised "due care" in carrying out her responsibilities. Negligence or "careless" action can be analyzed in terms of the following essential elements:

- an established duty to the affected party must exist;
- someone must breach that duty;
- the affected party must experience a harm; and
- this harm must be caused by the breach of duty.[6]

---

[5]Klaidman and Beauchamp, *The Virtuous Journalist*, p. 99.
[6]Klaidman and Beauchamp, *The Virtuous Journalist*, p. 99.

As we have seen, duty (or obligation) is a natural consequent of social relationships. And as Kant stated, discharge of duty is of paramount importance if we are to maintain moral standing. Breach of duty almost always indicates a lack of integrity and results, at the very least, in lack of trust between the harmed party and the instigator of the harm. When this occurs in a professional–client relationship, the client is far less likely to respect the professional's autonomy and more likely to question his motives. If the professional continues to violate this trust, the client is very likely to call for restrictions on professional autonomy. Censorship is one such threat that is nearly always the result of perceived overzealousness on the part of the media.

LIBERTY-LIMITING PRINCIPLES

Most media practitioners assume that First Amendment protections are inviolable. As we know, such is not the case. Most of the restrictions on speech that exist today have to do with preventing speech-caused harms. Child pornography, cigarette advertising, and libel are all forms of speech restricted because of potential harm to someone. We accept these restrictions, in part, because of an inherent belief in some of the following liberty-limiting principles.

The Harm Principle

In 1859, John Stuart Mill wrote *On Liberty*. In it, he laid out the ethical foundation of democratic individualism. At the same time, Mill considered the circumstances under which individual liberty might be justifiably restricted. Under what has come to be known as the *harm principle*, he stated that a person's liberty may justifiably be restricted only in order to prevent harm that the person's actions would cause to others.

> Acts of whatever kind, which, without justifiable cause, do harm to others, may be, and in the more important cases absolutely require to be, controlled by the unfavorable sentiments, and, when needful, by the active interference of mankind. The liberty of the individual must be thus far limited; he must not make himself a nuisance to other people.

Following on this principle, the government may limit the freedom of any individual or group if their actions are likely to harm any other part of society. Government prohibitions against murder, theft, rape, and speeding are all examples of this principle. The harm principle is probably the only liberty-limiting principle that is noncontroversial and widely accepted.

Under this principle, journalists would have to consider the degree of harm their work causes and then weigh the costs against the benefits of publishing. The same would be true of both advertising and public relations. Ads that had adverse effects on any segment of society could be called into question, as could any public relations communication that might cause undue harm. Of course, defining undue harm is at the heart of the entire debate over harm-causing communication. Part of the problem lies in the inability to draw a correlation between speech and any harm that may have been caused by the speech. For example, a correlation between media violence and social violence has yet to be proved conclusively; however, most of us suspect that there is some link between the two. The most difficult aspect of correlation is that it is easy to ignore or miss altogether variables that might either be the true cause of the harm or, at least, a major contributor to it. In the case of media violence, for instance, a change in societal mores and the easy availability of guns and other weapons are variables that are very likely affecting the level of violence. As Sissela Bok points out, however, just because there may be multiple variables affecting violence in America, that does not absolve the media from their responsibility to do something about it.[7]

The Offense Principle

The *offense principle* states that an act that offends another person may be prohibited. This principle may account for such laws as those against public nudity, or restricting the sale of pornography to those over 18. This principle is often used to justify complaints about tasteless advertising or offensive photographs in newspapers or on television. The movie industry, a number of years ago, adopted a rating system in order that children not be surprised by explicit scenes of sexuality or violence. Recently, The Brooklyn Museum of Art lifted its under-17 prohibition, which it had enforced for years to protect the sensitivity of children to some kinds of art. Ironically, a painting many found sacrilegious drew much media and legal attention almost immediately following this lifting of the under-17 ban.

Although the offense principle does have its advocates, it is easy to argue the difficulty of determining exactly what is offensive. We may agree with Supreme Court Justice Potter Stewart who stated that "I cannot define obscenity, but I know it when I see it"; nevertheless, defining harm-causing communication is still at the heart of determining its ethicality. The pure fact is that what offends one person may not offend another. That is primarily why the offense principle is controversial.

---

[7]Sissela Bok, *Mayhem: Violence as Public Entertainment* (Reading: Addison-Wesley, 1998).

The Principle of Legal Paternalism

The *principle of legal paternalism* asserts that we have the obligation to protect others from harm. All governments are paternal to some degree. Laws requiring helmets for motorcyclists or prohibiting suicide are based on legal paternalism. Unlike William Ross's obligation of noninjury (discussed in chap. 2), paternalism requires us to prevent foreseeable harm, not just to refrain from injuring someone. Under this principle, a newspaper would think twice before running a story about a teen suicide that might cause further attempts within the community.

To an extent, all journalists are paternalistic. Every time an editor or publisher decides to "give us what we need," she is acting paternalistically. Each time a news director decides the order of a newscast, he is acting paternalistically in deciding which is the most important story. Legal scholar Stephen Carter points out that news judgment can involve either telling the public what they need to know or telling them what they want to know, but that the two cannot be pursued simultaneously. In fact, Carter points out that "making judgements about what is useful and useless, what it is good to report and what should be ignored, is a central part of the free speech mission."[8] In this sense, paternalism is a positive element of the news business.

However, paternalism also infers that there are those who cannot or will not act on their own behalves. In fact, the American press is premised on the belief that it is the job of the news media to look out for the best interests of the public. This is a somewhat Platonic concept (recall Plato's view of the common people discussed in chap. 4), and one that clearly considers the public to be either unwilling or unable to look out after itself. In a country in which individualism is so highly prized, you can imagine how popular paternalism is as a concept for protecting the citizenry from harm. Strangely enough, the press often gets faulted for not being paternalistic enough and for pandering to audience wants rather than needs.

The Principle of Legal Moralism

The *principle of legal moralism* holds that something may be prohibited because it is simply immoral. Of all the liberty-limiting principles, this is the only one based almost entirely on a theological definition of morality. The shortcomings of this principle are immediately apparent: Not all religions agree on what is moral and what is not. Even if they could, the question of whether any religious group should be the arbiter of public morals is a large one.

---

[8]Carter, *Integrity*, p. 96.

Most people agree that not only religious groups but also the government should stay out of legislating morality. Such regulations as those prohibiting certain sexual acts between consenting adults are examples of this principle. We have seen repeatedly how difficult it is to define these situations to everyone's satisfaction. Imagine a newspaper not being able to run a story about prostitution because the practice itself might be viewed as immoral, or an advertiser of perfume not being able to suggest that her product induces sexual arousal. The principle of legal moralism is probably the least defensible of the liberty-limiting principles.

MITIGATING HARM IN JOURNALISM

"Act so that you treat humanity, whether in your own person or in the person of any other, always as an end and never as a means only." With this prescription, Immanuel Kant set the stage for the championing of individual autonomy and integrity. He specifically meant that we should avoid, as much as possible, harming other human beings. However, even Kant realized that total avoidance of harm is probably impossible. The question then becomes, If we cannot avoid harm altogether, can we at least mitigate its effects?

Writing in *Brill's Content*, newspaper editor Mike Pride of the *Concord Monitor* in Concord, New Hampshire, cited an instance in which he was getting ready to publish a story concerning the suicide of a local teenager. The victim's family appealed to him personally not to publish the story because of the emotional harm and public embarrassment it would cause them. At their request, and completely against journalistic character, he let them read the story prior to publication. They asked for a single change in copy: omitting an opening paragraph detailing the method of death. Pride realized how little the story would be affected by the deletion of this information and how much pain could be avoided by censoring his own story. The story ran, but without the detailed first paragraph.[9] Was harm avoided altogether? No. Was it mitigated or lessened without a loss of journalistic integrity? Yes.

In the inevitable clash between personal and professional ethics, the weight is usually on the professional side. The reason is that a person takes on the role of a professional willingly, with eyes supposedly open to the potential conflicts inherent in the work itself. For example, a person enlisting in the army who is not aware that part of the commitment of military service is a possible battlefield assignment is basically self-delusional. By the

---

[9]Mike Price, "Out There: Hardball with a Heart," Brill's Content, Volume 1, Number 4, November, 1998, pp. 83–85.

same token, any journalist who does not acknowledge the likelihood that personal standards concerning privacy, for instance, will come into conflict with the professional obligation of news gathering is likewise fooling herself. It is wise to remember that, for journalists, the duty to serve the public usually overrides any duty to observe the individual rights of the subjects of their stories. This does not mean that all compassion and civility should be thrown out the window, however.

Editor/publisher and media critic Steven Brill worries that journalists are so insulated from the rest of society that their decisions are made from within a "cocooned" environment resulting in a "warped sense of their own conduct that renders them unaware of the consequences . . . of what they do."[10] In a recent survey profiled in *Brill's Content*, editor Eric Effron observes that the media's reluctance even to consider self-regulation in problem areas such as invasion of privacy renders them at great odds with the public they purport to serve—a public that has indicated an "overwhelming support for some simple common courtesies on the part of the media."[11] The power of the press likewise results in what Stephen Carter calls "a special First Amendment arrogance." As he states, "The First Amendment, in its current guise as an excuse for everything, makes decisions on what to publish or broadcast virtually risk-free, and thus, almost inevitably, corrupting as well."[12] Carter also warns against the kind of "emotional pornography" that many in journalism indulge in every time they conduct an ambush interview or confront a grieving family member. He points out that the media understand completely that this is "where the money is," and calls for "genuine moral reflection before making a difficult decision."[13]

Others believe that the only answer to media abuses is written guidelines. In addressing the privacy debate, Steven Brill strongly suggests such guidelines.

> The real point is having *some* guidelines, something that gives the public a benchmark from which to hold media organizations accountable—not legally, but in a way that compels them to put their decisions to the test of explaining them when asked.[14]

In fact, guidelines do exist at most news organizations and in several professional codes. As noted earlier, however, codes are often vague when it

---

[10]Steven Brill, "Curiosity vs. Privacy," Brill's Content, Volume 2, Number 8, October, 1999, pp. 98–129.

[11]Eric Effron, "Letter From the Editor," Brill's Content, Volume 2, Number 8, October, 1999, p. 7.

[12]Carter, *Integrity*, pp. 85, 94.

[13]Carter, *Integrity*, pp. 92, 95.

[14]Brill, "Curiosity vs. Privacy," p. 129.

comes to dealing with day-to-day ethical issues, and tend to speak only to the generalities of professional conduct. As Brill suggests, the best use of such policies might be to give the public recourse to an ethical benchmark from which to ask informed questions concerning media activities they consider questionable. As he points out, however, the existence of such guidelines has never prevented the media from violating them.

A central question in any process of making a decision about whether to withhold publication will continue to be: How much does the public need the information, and how successfully does that need compete with the principle that we should avoid the harm that would result from its publication?[15] For journalists, this simple test must be performed whenever release of information has the potential to cause someone harm. By the same token, it would be impossible for editors to perform this balancing act for every story being considered. However, it is not too much to expect that the most obvious cases should require such a weighing of interests. Too much is rationalized on the basis of the public's right to know. As we have seen, that rubric, like caveat emptor, is a poor excuse at best. Again, Steven Brill writes that ". . . the privacy of those who are entitled to it is best protected by editors who understand the fine line between individual rights and the public's right to know, between fairness and decency on one hand and the commercial impulse on the other."

MITIGATING HARM IN ADVERTISING AND PUBLIC RELATIONS

For those in advertising and public relations, the task of mitigating harm is even more demanding. In chapter 3, we discussed the concept of public service as it relates to professional obligation. You'll recall that the fiduciary model best epitomizes the proper balance of client/professional control over decision making. When the professional is allowed to exercise his decision-making authority (based on education, training, and experience) within a framework of professional standards, he cannot easily ignore third-party obligations. However, the fiduciary model assumes a good deal of professional autonomy. By contrast, the advocacy model allows minimal autonomy to the professional who works almost exclusively at the behest of the client. Advocates are at a distinct disadvantage because of the necessary subordination of their standards to their client's wishes. Given that advertising and public relations, alike, work from within both fiduciary and advocacy models, how can harm to third parties be avoided or, at least, mitigated?

---

[15]Klaidman and Beauchamp, *The Virtuous Journalist*, p. 105.

What is needed is a process that allows the function of advocacy to remain a professional role obligated to client interests, professional interests, and personal ethics. Although the role of autonomous professional assumes objectivity, the role of advocate assumes a certain amount (if not a great amount) of subjectivity. The terms, although often mutually exclusive, are not necessarily at odds; and the professional advertising or public relations practitioner may, in fact, be both objective and subjective. The key is the order of approach. Certainly, consulting professionals objectively evaluate potential clients before taking them on. This earliest stage of the consulting process is also the first line of defense against possible ethical conflicts. Objectivity should also be brought to bear in the early stages of campaign development—the period in which a thorough understanding of the issue is obtained. It is during this stage that the professional will determine the ramifications of the proposed actions and its effect on all parties.

During this objective stage, the communications professional may apply any of several applicable ethical theories to the proposed act in order to determine if the act itself (means) and the outcome (ends) are morally responsible. Several standards may be applied, including a determination of the legality of the act (whether it violates existing laws or applicable regulations), company procedures and policies or organizational codes, and any codes or standards existing for the profession (relevant advertising and/or public relations codes). Although this procedure will merely provide guidelines, assuming that all that is legally or professionally permissible may not be ethically permissible, these will allow the professional to advance to succeeding evaluative stages.

The communications professional may also apply standard cost-benefit analysis to the issue, determining the potential financial consequences of the act to the client and the affected third parties. Beyond these monetary considerations, he may attempt to determine societal effects. If, after such applications, the professional determines that the act itself and the intent of the act are morally acceptable, then he may proceed to the succeeding subjective stages of advocacy.

Even after the professional has decided to move on to the role of advocate, that role does not absolve the advertising or public relations practitioner from moral culpability. As has been suggested, the moral guidelines under which the advocate operates presuppose loyalty to one's client or employer; however, the obligation of noninjury is still in effect based on nonconsequential moral duties. The same rules used prior to the decision to become an advocate may be used at this stage to determine individual actions.

According to nonconsequential ethical theory, the obligations assumed as part of a role are of prime importance in making moral decisions. If there are rules governing decision making within an organization, for instance, and those rules say that one should not dispense false information, then an advocate who has been ordered to falsify information can and should refuse to do so based on existing rules. No consideration need be given to the consequences of the act itself. It is sufficient that the rule exists prohibiting it. For the advocate, nonconsequential considerations might include whether an act is illegal or not. Certainly, refusing to perform an illegal act is within the moral scope of even the most loyal advocate.

The existence of a set of guidelines in the form of a code of conduct or ethics is imperative at this stage as well. For the practitioner lacking a formal code within the organization for which she works, an outside, professional code might be cited as legitimization for refusal to carry out an immoral act. An advocate lacking recourse to a professional code might appeal to consequential ethical theory. Lacking any clear-cut guidelines in the form of rules, she may precipitate a complex analysis of both short- and long-term consequences.

In summary, the advocate generally assumes a primary responsibility to the client and to the client's purpose because of the nature of the role of advocacy. However, as precursor to that role, the professional retains his objectivity throughout the exploratory stage in which the issue is defined and the claimants are identified. It is in this early stage that communications professionals must become aware of the effects of their potential actions on all third parties. At both this stage and in the latter stages of advocacy itself, advertising and public relations professionals must continue their vigilance by constant referral to written codes within their own companies and the professions they are a part of. Lacking any clear written guidelines, the advocate may undertake to stand behind the moral shield of protecting the greater good. Ultimately, the major determinant may be the personal morals of the advocate and his willingness to stand up for or forgo them under certain conditions. The approach proposed here suggests that the advocate, like his journalistic counterpart, resort to the traditional use of objectivity in order to determine, without bias, who the moral claimants are in any given situation.

Although using objectivity in this way has helped sort through the biases often inherent in moral decision making, a nagging question remains as to the universal appropriateness of treating affected "others" as objects. As part of the Enlightenment focus on reason, objectivity became a sort of an assumed tool in the conduct of moral decision making. This traditional use of objectivity has received a good deal of criticism recently. There are those today who have suggested that there might be an alternative view of moral decision making by which affected "others" are treated not objectively, but subjectively.

CARING AND HARM

Earlier, we introduced the concept of due care, in terms of which a media professional must discharge some discretion in his actions affecting other people. A total lack of regard, or even a lack of recognition of the obligation of due care, can result in charges of professional negligence. For consulting professionals, such as those in advertising and public relations, due care can mean their paying close attention to their clients' needs and performing only work they are competent to perform. It can also mean taking care not to unduly harm third parties affected by the client's (and the representing professional's) actions. For journalists, due care most often refers to the weighing of harm against benefits prior to running a story. Failure to consider harm to third parties can result in libel suits at worst or in unnecessary injury to an innocent party at the very least.

We have seen that respect for other people is at the heart of a number of philosophies—most notably, Immanuel Kant's. In this sense, *respect* refers to a feeling of deference toward someone and a willingness to show consideration or appreciation to them. Respect itself is related to a number of other concepts, including sympathy, the ability to empathize with others, compassion, and caring for others. These words are all closely related and often interchangeable. "Sympathy," for example, refers to the act or power of sharing the feelings of another; "empathy" means to identify with and understand another's situation, feelings, and motives. Compassion and caring are likewise closely related. "Compassion" refers to a deep awareness of the suffering of another coupled with the wish to relieve it. "Caring" means to feel and exhibit concern for others, and can include empathy. No one would disagree that these are major determinants of moral action; however, to what degree they can or should be incorporated into a system of media ethics is debatable.

We have seen that professional obligations to truth telling, dissemination of important information to the public, loyalty to legitimate client interests, and other such duties often clash with personal convictions of compassion and care for others. We have also considered whether personal ethics can or should override professional ethics in circumstances in which the role of a professional is operational. To some extent, these considerations and assumptions are based on the degree of importance attached to certain professional undertakings. We assume that some harm is a necessary by-product of many media activities, and that our primary responsibility is to do our jobs while mitigating as much harm as we can. However, is it possible, or even conceivable, that we could carry out our functions as media practitioners while working in a situation in which the default would be "no harm to anyone"?

In her seminal work, *In a Different Voice*, developmental psychologist Carol Gilligan proposes what she calls an "ethic of care." According to Gilligan, most of our moral concepts have developed from a particularly male perspective. The major approach to moral philosophy over the past several hundred years has been what might be called an "ethic of justice," which is deeply rooted in a desire for individual autonomy and independence. The focus of this ethic is the balancing of competing interests among individuals. It is easy to see this model at work in the philosophies of Hobbes, Locke, Kant, and scores of other Enlightenment thinkers. In fact, individualism and sanctioned competition are at the heart of the American system of government and economics. And although Gilligan doesn't necessarily take umbrage with this result, she does point out the troubling consequences of an ethic of justice untempered by an ethic of care.[16] The formality of such concepts as duty and justice often results in objectification of human beings, or, at least, a distancing of the parties involved in and affected by moral decision making. Caring, on the other hand, requires a closer relationship between parties and recognition of the other as a subjective being.

Gilligan proposes that the female moral voice is characterized by caring. It considers the needs of both the self and of others, and is not just interested in the survival of the self. There is also more to this approach than simply the avoidance of harm. Ideally, no one should be hurt in interchanges among human beings. Although not dismissing the importance of justice and fairness, Gilligan points out that moral decisions should also make allowances for differences in needs. In other words, *need may dictate an obligation to care*. However, feminist author Joan Tronto points out that a more appropriate term for obligation would be *responsibility*. She holds that obligation implies formal relationships and agreements, and refers to explicit promises and duties. Responsibility allows that we may have played a part in bringing about the circumstances that give rise to the need being expressed. In addition, responsibility requires that we ask ourselves whether we are the ones best suited to give the care requested.[17]

Unlike Kant's imperfect duties, which were to be followed only if nothing else prohibited the action, the ethic of care requires, at minimum, that need be recognized as an important component of human interaction. Gilligan, and others using her approach as a basis for their own systems of care, point out that although an ethic of care may be a predominantly female

---

[16]Carol Gilligan, *In a Different Voice: Psychological Theory and Women's Development* (Cambridge: Harvard University Press, 1982), pp. 19, 73–74, 127, 143, 156–65, 174.

[17]Joan Tronto, *Moral boundaries: A Political Argument for an Ethics of Care* (New York: Routledge, 1993), pp. 12, 102–160.

construction, it is not limited to the female perspective and can (and should) be used by male and female alike.

Based on an "obligation to care," this approach would have us view ourselves as part of a network of individuals whose needs (when they become clear) create a duty in us to respond. In responding, we must pay attention to the details of the need and to the effects of our response on others potentially influenced by our actions.[18] This does not mean that every need requires a response. The seriousness of the need, the likely benefit derived from our response, our ability to respond to this particular need, and the competing needs of others in our network must also be weighed. Like most ethical decisions, responding to need requires a weighing of interests; however, relating to the need on an emotional level is a vital consideration absent from many other such formulas.

Individual autonomy, a mainstay of most Enlightenment philosophy, is not entirely absent from the concept of care. Julia Wood, in *Who Cares? Women, Care, and Culture*, suggests that a flexible sense of autonomy would allow us to value both the needs and interests of others, at the same time not neglecting our own needs. This flexibility would recognize the primary qualities our culture seems to value in caregivers: *partiality* (the ability to focus with feeling on the needs of others), *empathy* (having insight into others' needs), and *willingness to serve others*. Wood proposes a concept of *dynamic autonomy* that involves an awareness of our individuality coupled with an ability to choose when to accentuate our own desires and points of view and when to emphasize and cooperate with those of others.[19]

Confucian philosophy agrees with much of the ethic of care, and disagrees with Western liberal thought that individual autonomy is the most important consideration of human interaction. For a Confucian, human interaction is an indispensable part of life—an essential component necessary to achieving self-realization. As Confucian philosopher Henry Rosemont Jr. states, "It is not merely that we are obliged, of necessity, to interact with others, we must care about them as well. . . ." Confucians are defined by their interactions with others. They are not autonomous; rather, they are "relational," leading morally integrated lives in a human community. As Confucius points out, "[I]f I am not to be a person in the midst of others, what am I to be."[20]

---

[18]Rita C. Manning, *Speaking from the Heart: A Feminist Perspective on Ethics* (Lanham, MD: Rowman & Littlefield, 1992), pp. 49, 56, 65–69, 139, 152.

[19]Julia T. Wood, *Who Cares? Women, Care, and Culture* (Carbondale: Southern Illinois University Press, 1994), pp. 41–49, 106–10.

[20]Henry Rosemont, Jr., "Whose Democracy? Which Rights?: A Confucian Critique of Modern Western Liberalism," Unpublished paper (St. Mary's College of Maryland).

Can the Media Care?

The question remains whether the media can consider an ethic of care as a realistic component of their moral curriculum. As we've seen, the media, especially journalists, value autonomy above almost all else. Caring and care giving imply a subjective viewpoint. We have also seen that the notion of objectivity itself can be viewed as a flawed concept. For example, feminist theorist Linda Steiner holds that

> a feminist ethic challenges the treatment of mass media subjects as objects—challenges the objectification of both mass media sources as well as their audiences. "The goal would be to respect others' dignity and integrity, to make the process more collaborative and egalitarian, less authoritarian and coercive."[21]

Not only feminist authors, but many others also point out that honoring the ideal of objectivity establishes an us–them relationship between the media and virtually everyone else. Although journalism seems to be the focus of much of the public's concern over the caring versus harm debate, advertising and public relations are merely assumed to be logically without care for anyone except the client. This difference in public attitude stems as much from a misunderstanding of the nature of the information media versus the persuasive media as it does from any lack of expectation that the latter will ever change. As we shall see, all of the media currently have in place ethical models that reflect, to some degree, a consideration of care.

Public Journalism Again. Part of the response to a distancing of the media both from their sources and their publics has been *public journalism*, an approach that considers the news media as both responsible and responsive to the community. As we discussed in chapter 3, a news outlet practicing public journalism would be community oriented by design. In fact, we are seeing more of this reflected both in the type of coverage and in the ambience of local television news. Many bemoan the smiling faces and happy talk of much of this type of broadcasting, but the approach is decidedly community centered. Even local newspapers are experimenting with community-oriented approaches, such as the creation of voter forums during elections and Web sites that invite reader involvement in deciding the content of news.

Some worry that any public involvement in deciding what is news is dangerous; others point out that the economic necessity of providing consum-

---

[21]Linda Steiner, "Feminist Theorizing and Communication Ethics," *Communication*, 12 (1989): 157–173, as cited in Richard L. Johannesen, *Ethics in Human Communication*, 4th ed. (Prospect Heights: Waveland Press, 1996), p. 236.

ers with what they want as much as with what they need is already a move in that direction. Quoted in Louis Day's *Ethics in Media Communications*, ABC's Ted Koppel apparently sees the fact that business decisions drive news decisions as a virtue, "because it gives the public a significant voice in shaping the news agenda. In short, the application of marketing principles to journalism has helped to 'democratize' the profession."[22] Although the economic necessity of giving the public what they want may be driving some movement toward a more participatory form of journalism, we cannot place a moral value on such motives because the intent, as Kant would say, is not to do good but to remain economically viable. On the other hand, the move toward public journalism is, by and large, an authentic attempt to bring the news media and the public closer together—clearly indicating a change in the level of care with which the media may be dealing with their constituents.

Persuasive Models and Care

Journalism may be reluctant to inject an ethic of care into its discipline, but public relations has a long history of trying to show that it's doing just that. And although many would argue that public relations is biased by nature in favor of the client, we have seen that an adherence to professional standards should disallow such total obeisance to any one party—especially the client. The fiduciary model of the professional–client relationship (covered in chap. 3) assumes that both the professional public relations practitioner and her client will work together to effect the most beneficial solution to the client's problems. However, the balanced relationship between the two primary parties exists only insofar as it does not ignore relevant third parties. The professional is under a special obligation not to harm others in the pursuit of his client's interests.

The ideal of advocacy, as it is construed in the legal profession, relies on total client loyalty; neither public relations nor advertising, however, can claim the same status as that profession. Third parties must be considered. The clients of public relations have no constitutionally guaranteed right to representation by a PR agency, nor do the clients of advertising agents. Professionals in both of these fields not only can, but also should turn down client requests that would unduly harm third-party claimants. Professional codes in both advertising and public relations call for a balancing of interests in favor of noninjury to third parties. Articles of those codes that address not lying to the media or to consumers (theoretically on behalf of clients) are examples of the recognition of third-party concerns. However, simply recognizing third-party concerns doesn't

[22]Louis Day, *Ethics in Media Communications: Cases and Controversies*, p. 218.

imply a caring attitude in the sense of an ethic of care. As we discussed earlier in this chapter, even advocates can, and should, reject client aims that unnecessarily harm third parties.

Educator and theorist James Grunig proposes four models for the practice of public relations: press agentry/publicity, public information, two-way asymmetric, and two-way symmetric. In the *press agentry/publicity* model, the practitioner's role might be that of a press agent, functioning as a one-sided propaganda specialist. The *public information* model presents the practitioner as journalist, carefully disseminating balanced information to the public. Practitioners in a *two-way asymmetric* model are seen as "scientific persuaders," using social science techniques to gather information on attitude and behavior characteristics of their publics, then adjusting their messages accordingly in order to influence those publics. And, finally, the *two-way symmetric* model uses practitioners as mediators between organizations and their publics. One of the key differences among these models is the emphasis placed on either persuasion or mutual understanding as an end.[23]

Grunig proposes the two-way symmetric model as an ideal for public relations. Although he recognizes persuasion as a legitimate function of the public relations role, he posits that mutual understanding ultimately leads to a more beneficial relationship between the public relations practitioner's client and that client's constituencies. More profound associations are built on understanding gained, most often, through communication, negotiation, and compromise. It can be inferred from this model and its goal that care must, at least, be a part of the process leading to compromise (although compromise itself is viewed by some feminist scholars as a by-product of competition and, therefore, a negative outcome). Regardless, some care (perhaps in the form of respect) for the position and views of the "other" is required in this model.

The two-way asymmetric (persuasive) model may also operate under an assumption of respect for both the integrity and the intelligence of the parties being persuaded (as Aristotle's *Rhetoric* suggests). However, as we saw in chapter 5, the techniques of persuasion can, and often are, used unethically. And any technique that has persuasion as its intended outcome is far more easily open to abuse than a technique having mutual understanding as it goal. The reality of public relations, however, is that persuasion is a recognized and respected communication technique. If we are to accept the traditional ideal of persuasion as a process necessary to the successful application of democracy as a form of government, then we must accept that

[23]James Grunig and Todd Hunt, *Managing Public Relations* (New York: Holt, Rinehart and Winston, 1984), pp. 21–25.

ethical persuasion is a legitimate approach to coming to grips with different points of view.

This does not invalidate the possibility of incorporating an ethic of care into the persuasive process itself. All that is needed, as Linda Steiner points out, is respect for the dignity and integrity of the receivers of your message. As we have noted throughout this book, coercion and manipulation through communication are decidedly unethical and are actions for which there can be no excuses. Remember that respect, as Kant pointed out, is the least we owe to other human beings; and respect is very definitely a form of caring.

Does this mean that persuasion done in order to sell something other than a political point of view is less than ethical or cannot take advantage of an ethic of care? Ideally, this "respectful" approach to persuasive communication should apply equally to public relations and advertising. A goal of mutual understanding is probably not as appropriate for most advertising as it is for some public relations. Even advertising whose primary purpose is to inform doesn't usually seek or need mutual understanding. It requires only a fairly complete understanding of the needs of the receivers of the information, and that can be gained through audience analysis. Grunig's press agentry/publicity and two-way asymmetric models (although not intended for advertising) are certainly the most appropriate. However, even these models, if practiced conscientiously, can be respectful of audience dignity and integrity. You'll recall from chapter 5 that audiences are often viewed by advertising practitioners as gullible, else why would so many ads seek to obfuscate reality? How the advertising professional views the audience dictates the level of respect reflected in the advertisement. The intelligence of a targeted audience is not denigrated by serious advertisers with ethical intent. On the other hand, the harder an ad tries to misrepresent reality for the purpose of deception, the less respect it shows for the audience. Of course, part of the analysis has to be the audience's QER (qualified expectation of reality). If audiences expect the information—or the form of its presentation—to be real and it isn't, they have been intentionally duped.

In the final analysis, media communicators cannot afford to ignore such characteristics as empathy and caring. You'll recall that Confucius didn't even have a word for *reason* or *rational* separate from his concept of *emotion*. Or, as Steiner contends, "virtues" such as empathy and caring can and should function alongside concepts like integrity, fairness, and respect for others. Journalists and advertising and public relations practitioners alike may need to adjust their traditional conceptions of such time-honored practices as near total objectivity in both informing and persuading in order that some indication that "we are all in this together" be admitted to themselves and to those they affect so profoundly.

THE RIGHT THING TO DO

No mass medium is free from the obligations of truth telling and noninjury, and no mass medium should be purposely devoid of care and respect for those it affects with its words and pictures. Telling the truth and avoiding harm are often one and the same thing; however, the delicate balance involved in telling the truth while avoiding harm requires, at times, the equilibrium of a high-wire walker.

Can we expect that no one will ever be harmed by a media act? Probably not. But we should expect that the media will do no unnecessary harm and that, as far as possible, they will respect the dignity and integrity of everyone whose lives they touch. It really isn't impossible to believe that those who choose to become media professionals do so because they care. They care about letting us know what is going on in our lives and how to deal with it. They care that we think about and understand the world we live in. And they care about whether we're using a bath soap that makes us feel clean and fresh (not a bad thing, really).

However, the perceived value of autonomy, as Steven Brill has pointed out, tends to hobble the media through fear of interference in their discharge of a constitutionally guaranteed right of expression—even if that "interference" is self-imposed. As professionals, media practitioners expect to be free to choose their own ends, without having them dictated or altered by others. As we have seen, however, we are not necessarily locked into a moral system devoid of care for others. As philosopher Michael Sandel has argued,

> By insisting that we are bound only by ends and roles we choose for ourselves, [modern Western liberalism] denies that we can ever be claimed by ends we have not chosen—ends given by nature or God, for example, or by our identities as members of families, peoples, cultures, or traditions.[24]

If we accept, even tacitly, the tenets of communitarianism, we must allow obligation to others a higher priority than either a strict adherence to personal autonomy or blind allegiance to professional duty. Even the consideration of this point of view during the deliberative process is a step in the right direction.

The point is, if the mass media really care about doing their jobs well, shouldn't they automatically worry about telling the truth and avoiding harm? As media legend Fred Friendly once said to a panel of journalists and public relations practitioners, "Stop thinking about what you have the right to do, and start thinking about what is the right thing to do." The two shouldn't be mutually exclusive, and, with some concentrated effort on the part of media practitioners, they won't be.

---

[24]Michael J. Sandel, *Democracy's discontent: America in search of a public philosophy* (Cambridge, MA: Belknap Press of Harvard University Press, 1996), p. 70.

EXERCISES

1. Discuss whether you agree or disagree with using each of the four liberty-limiting principles cited in this chapter. Cite situations in which each might be appropriately used.
2. How may a public relations advocate ensure that third-party interests are being considered?
3. As individuals, we are all obligated to avoid harming others. Most such "private" harms (trespass, battery, robbery, murder, assault, property damage, and so on) are also governed by laws. As media professionals, especially journalists, our leeway to cause harm in pursuit of a "greater good" is much greater. What is your opinion as to how harm-causing media actions should or shouldn't be limited?
4. Discuss how an "ethic of care" might be incorporated into journalistic practice, advertising, and public relations. Are there any drawbacks to using a care-driven approach in media practice?
5. Do you think news journalists can become more responsive to community needs without losing objectivity? If not, why not? If so, how?
6. Find a print advertisement from a magazine or newspaper that you think might have ethical implications. Answer the following questions concerning the ad and its effects.

   - What is the publication in which you found the ad? What kind of audience does this publication appeal to?
   - What is the ethical issue surrounding the ad?
   - Who are affected by the ad and how are they affected?
   - What ideals/values do you think would be espoused by the various parties involved with or affected by this ad? How do they conflict?
   - Are there any laws, rules, or codes that would prevent you from playing a part in the development or running of an ad like this?
   - Which of the ethical theories we have discussed have a direct bearing on your assessment of this ad? In what way?
   - Would you run this ad as it is?
   - If not, what would you do differently to sell this product (if you'd sell it at all)?

   Try to come up with complex ads, not easy, simple to analyze ads. Also, look at the information in the text on the effects of advertising and use it in your argument.

CASE STUDY: ARTHUR ASHE AND INVASION OF PRIVACY

Tennis legend Arthur Ashe was the first black man to win Wimbledon and the U.S. Open. After his retirement from tennis, Ashe joined the struggle for human rights in the United States and emerged as a leading critic of apartheid in South Africa. He wrote a highly regarded three-volume history of black athletes in America. By all accounts, he was generous with his time and gracious when dealing with the public.

On April 8, 1992, however, Arthur Ashe was faced with one of the most difficult decisions of his life. Unknown to all but a few, he had contracted HIV, probably from a blood transfusion during a heart bypass operation in 1983. Ashe, an intensely private man, had managed to keep his condition a secret from everyone except his family and close friends. However, all that changed when a reporter from *USA Today* contacted him in early April of 1992.

The reporter, acting on a tip from an anonymous source, called to confirm whether Ashe had AIDS or not. Realizing that his secret would now, very probably, become public knowledge, Ashe was faced with the dilemma of letting the media expose his private life, or taking the initiative and releasing the information himself. He asked *USA Today*'s sports editor to allow him 36 hours before the paper ran the story so that he could prepare a statement. The editor, Gene Polincinski, replied that, "as a journalist, it was not my role to help him plan a press conference—and . . . it was inappropriate for me to withhold a news story that I could confirm."[25]

During the subsequent press conference, put together literally on the spur of the moment in order to preempt the *USA Today* scoop, Ashe displayed both anger and dismay at the actions of the media. He chastised them for forcing him into "the unenviable position of having to lie" in order to protect his family's privacy or to go public with what he considered to be private information. In a *Washington Post* article written by Ashe, he discussed how he felt about the media's intrusion into his private affairs. "I wasn't then, and I am not now, comfortable with being sacrificed for the sake of the 'public's right to know.' "[26]

Although *USA Today* held the story in the United States pending Ashe's confirmation, it released the story to its overseas edition after a talk with the former tennis star just prior to his press conference in which he admitted to being HIV positive.

After going public, Ashe became active in the fight against AIDS, forming a fund-raising foundation and joining the boards of the Harvard AIDS Insti-

---

[25]Debra Gersh, "Unclear boundaries: was it news that former tennis pro Arthur Ashe has AIDS?", *Editor and Publisher* 18 April 1992: 7–10.

[26]Howard G. Chua-Eoan, "The burden of truth," *People Weekly*, 20 April 1992: 50–51.

tute and the UCLA AIDS Institute. He died of pneumonia 10 months after his public announcement. Just four days before he died, he had given a speech on AIDS, and was scheduled to appear at an AIDS forum in Hartford, Connecticut, the day he died. He was forced to cancel at the last minute, but sent a videotaped message instead.

CASE STUDY QUESTIONS

Read the following statements made by media people following the Arthur Ashe press conference. Try to figure out what theories they are basing their opinions on. Do you think their reasoning is sound? Why or why not?

[Ashe] is exactly correct. Keeping quiet made sense. Privacy is precious, and once lost, may never be retrieved. So Arthur Ashe was careful to protect his terrible secret. Whose life was this, anyway? (Fred Bruning, *Maclean's*)[27]

Of course the fellow has a right to act in what he considers his own best interests. But no reporter or editor should feel obligated to assist in the suppression of what Ashe, or anyone else, views as confidential or inappropriate. Cruel as it may seem, the wishes of a stricken man cannot substitute for editorial judgment. The process is imperfect, and its justice notoriously rough, but the objective is clear. Personal concerns are secondary to the principles of a free press. (Fred Bruning, *Maclean's*)

We can lament the terrible turn of events that threaten the life of so fine a man as Arthur Ashe but we do not honor him—or the freedom he championed—by confusing sympathy with self-censorship. (Fred Bruning, *Maclean's*)

[T]he Press (in this case a reporter and an editor from *USA Today*) reached into the most private precinct of [Ashe's] life (inside his body itself) and forced him to reveal his disease to millions of strangers. Ashe and his wife, Jeanne, have a five-year-old daughter. The girl was entitled to privacy and to tenderness in how she would be told, and when. (Lance Morrow, *Time*)[28]

There was no public need to know, or right to know. Everyone is not fair game to be dragged onstage for involuntary exposure. Does AIDS make Ashe, or anyone, public property? As Ashe said, he is neither a political candidate nor a businessman beholden to stockholders. That Arthur Ashe is a "public figure" whom people recognize as he walks down the street is precisely the best argument for any decent human being's not informing the whole world that the man has AIDS. (Lance Morrow, *Time*)

---

[27]Fred Bruning, "How a private citizen lost his privacy rights," *Maclean's*, May 4, 1992 v105 n18 p13(1).

[28]Lance Morrow, "Fair game?," *Time*, April 20, 1992 v139 n16 p74(2).

If Ashe had had leukemia, would reporter and editor have published the story? Maybe, in one paragraph. But not if Ashe had asked them not to. AIDS made it different. Irresistible. Juicy gossip. (Lance Morrow, *Time*)

If a star volunteers, out of vanity or some other need, to tell all, the story may be interesting, even helpful to others. Arthur Ashe did not volunteer. He did not invite the world in. A pattern of revelation that routinely puts the most intimate details on public display has nearly obliterated an appreciation of both the right of privacy and the obligations of kindness. (Lance Morrow, *Time*)

"It is a news story, absolutely. Unfortunately it is a story that's bigger than the individual, even when the person is as great a person as Arthur Ashe. AIDS itself is a story. The reaction to this whole thing is the best proof possible. The fact that Arthur Ashe is stricken with AIDS is a tragedy. The fact that he lost a measure of his privacy is a tragedy." (Paul McMasters, executive director of the Freedom Forum First Amendment Center at Vanderbilt University, quoted in an article by Debra Gersh, *Editor & Publisher*)[29]

"[Ashe] deserves the same privacy considerations this newspaper routinely gives rape victims. Like them he, too, should not be twice victimized by being made to suffer the harsh glare of the public spotlight. To say he is a public figure and thus fair game for such intrusive news coverage ignores the fact that even celebrity rape victims are afforded a cloak of anonymity by this and most other newspapers." (*USA Today* and Gannett News Service columnist DeWayne Wickham, quoted in an article by Debra Gersh, *Editor & Publisher*)

"This is a tough one. Ashe is no longer a performer. Had he chosen to keep his heart surgery secret, he deserved to have his request honored. He did elect to keep his present condition a secret. Somebody betrayed him. News of an ex-athlete's fatal disease can't simply be cataloged under the 'public's right to know.' " (*Boston Globe* columnist Dan Shaughnessy, quoted in an article by Debra Gersh, *Editor & Publisher*)

"When the news arrived at *USA Today*, the newspaper had no choice. The silent and generous conspiracy was a noble act of some loyal people, but there is no room for a newspaper in a conspiracy, generous or otherwise. The controversy itself makes you wonder how many other generous conspiracies are out there and how many newspapers are involved."

"The public may not have a right to know, but it sure does want to know. It was a hell of a story. As insensitive as it sounds, that is what this game is all about." (The *Boston Herald*'s Gerry Callahan, quoted in an article by Debra Gersh, *Editor & Publisher*)

"This story makes me queasy. Perhaps it is the disparity between the value of information conveyed and the magnitude of the pain inflicted." (*New York*

---

[29]Debra Gersh, "Unclear boundaries: was it news that former tennis pro Arthur Ashe has AIDS?", *Editor & Publisher*, April 18, 1992 v125 n16 p7(3).

Times columnist Anna Quindlen, quoted in an article by Debra Gersh, *Editor & Publisher*)

"In recent years, mass media have been sliding down a slippery slope in pursuit of the private lives of celebrities. These stories sell newspapers and pump up tv ratings, but they do little for public discourse."

"Instead of investigating the private sphere regarding this or that celebrity with AIDS, mass media could be deploying investigative resources aimed at the public arena—the AIDS research effort, inadequacies in the health care system, the success of needle exchange programs, how homophobia has slowed the effort, etc." (Jeff Cohen, executive director of the New York-based Fairness & Accuracy in Reporting (FAIR), quoted in an article by Debra Gersh, *Editor & Publisher*)

"We tell ourselves that we are serving the public; but the bloodthirstiness and competitiveness with which we pursue our quarries are evidence enough that we are in search of nothing more noble than headlines."

"Unlike those among my colleagues and competitors who say that they have had difficulty forming clear conclusions about the treatment of Ashe, I have had no difficulty at all: Ashe was absolutely right to insist on his privacy and *USA Today* was absolutely wrong to violate it. No public issues were at stake. No journalistic 'rights' were threatened." (Jonathan Yardley of the *Washington Post*, quoted in an article by Debra Gersh, *Editor & Publisher*)

"No journalist likes to inflict pain. We do so from time to time, but we like to think that we have no choice. We balance the pain we inflict against the certainty that the public has a stake and has to be informed. When Arthur Ashe appeared before the cameras and announced he was HIV positive, anyone could see the pain. What was not so clear is why we had to know." (The *Washington Post*'s Richard Cohen, quoted in an article by Debra Gersh, *Editor & Publisher*)

CHAPTER

7

A Checklist for Ethical Decision Making

Throughout the preceding chapters we have seen how ethical behavior on the part of the mass media might be governed. We have looked at a great many theories proposed by some of the finest minds in philosophy. We have seen how the opposing ideals of professional autonomy and societal obligation can, and frequently do, clash during the process of moral decision making. What we haven't seen is a synthesis of these ideas and philosophies into a working model for decision making. That's what this chapter is all about.

Without a method whereby moral decision making becomes routine—so ingrained in our thought processes that we cannot separate it from our other decision-making tools—we will continue to flounder in the waters of inconsistency. Mass media practitioners must learn to approach decisions with ethical ramifications in the same, sensible way they do other choices. They must avoid the temptation to answer with pat aphorisms such as "buyer beware," or "the public's right to know." They must resist the urge to hide behind the protection of the First Amendment, for that law protects only legally, not ethically—and it typically protects only the perpetrator, not the victim.

In short, the mass media must consider their actions, and they must show their constituencies that they have done so with the best interests of everyone at heart. Ultimately, the media show that they care by their actions, not their justifications for those actions; however, in the rarified air of the mass communication industries, legitimate justification is often as hard to come by as pirate's gold and equally as valuable. The polls show that the public doesn't respect the media—any part of it. It has been the contention of this book that that lack of respect is often deserved but certainly avoidable.

Any moral decision-making process worth its salt must allow for three things: reflection, justification, and consistency. In order to rationalize our reasons to ourselves, we must reflect on all of the facets of the dilemma we are facing. We must do so without presumption that any particular course of action is automatically appropriate. An honest assessment will provide the only means to an equitable solution. We may be called upon to justify our decisions to others. We must be prepared to do so with the expectation that we will never satisfy everyone, but with the determination to try. Finally, we must be consistent, for moral consistency is one of the hallmarks of integrity, and integrity may be the most valuable coin of the moral realm.

The following checklist approach to moral decision making has been developed over years of experimenting with both students and professionals. It grew out of the work of others, most notably former *Washington Post* ombudsperson Joann Byrd. It is somewhat involved, but with value to each of its steps, none of which is sufficient without the others. The ultimate goal of this checklist is to allow for the formulation of principles and guidelines by which to make future decisions. At the very least, its consistent use should so educate the user that future moral decisions might become more second nature.

The approach used in this checklist tends to stress the commonalties of the mass media rather than their differences. In fact, this worksheet approach is based on the notion of developing common ground for discussion. For example, although a lie in advertising may bring legal penalties, its moral standing is not far different from a lie in public relations. A free speech issue having to do with protesters pulling books from a school library has a lot in common with a demand to stifle tabloid journalism. The point is that when discussing a case of whether to fire a perfectly qualified news anchor simply because she is over 40, the theories outlined earlier and the use of this checklist will invariably lead to a resounding no.

As has already been stated, blind obedience to any one philosophy is not sufficient for an educated analysis of a moral issue. Therefore, the checklist seeks to pull together the best that these philosophies have to offer. At the same time, the weaknesses we have discussed throughout this book should be recognized and avoided. Blind adherence to any rule, no matter how well intentioned, can lead to callousness. By the same token, service always to the greater good can result in tyrannizing a deserving minority. We cannot let our emotions rule our decisions any more than we can let our reason (often cold and calculating) do so. And we must remember that service to our professions and service to society are not always one and the same thing. There are times when each of these may fairly overrule the other. Although it is probably true that we can justify almost any decision using an approach such as the one suggested here, it must be borne in mind that we will be judged not solely by our own principles but, to a greater degree, by the principles of those we most affect. As media representatives, it is in our best interest to admit to those principles in order that we may function as a benefit to society and not a burden.

A CHECKLIST FOR MORAL DECISION MAKING

Each of the following points is followed by commentary on its meaning and importance to the overall outcome of the moral decision-making process.

1. What is the ethical issue/problem? (Define in one or two sentences.)

It is important to recognize that every problem has more than one component, and that not every component involves an ethical decision. Therefore, the ethical issue involved in the case must be stated succinctly, and it must be made clear that other elements of the problem have not been confused with the ethical component. For example, in a case involving a decision to advertise a product in a certain way, the client's right to advertise must be separated from any ethical question involved in the planned advertisement, and the issue must be stated in such a way that the ethical component is clear. The question, or issue, may not be whether the client should advertise, but whether the client should advertise in a particular manner that might have ethical ramifications.

2. What immediate facts have the most bearing on the ethical decision you must render in this case? Include in this list any potential economic, social, or political pressures.

Only the facts that bear on the ethical decision need be listed. For instance, although it may certainly be a fact that a given newspaper employs 500 people, it may have no bearing on its decision to run a story that potentially violates someone's privacy.

The realities of the two most important factors of any decision made within the mass media industry must also be recognized. Very often, economic or political factors are present that, although typically nonmoral in nature, will probably have a direct effect on the ethical decision-making process. In the world of media industries, "doing the right thing" may very well lead to severe economic consequences, and those consequences must be seriously weighed. This weighing most often leads to compromise. The same is true for political forces affecting a decision. Most people may not admit to political pressure, but its almost constant presence should be noted; decision makers must be prepared to deal with it and to recognize how it will affect their decisions.

3. Who are the claimants in this issue and in what way are you obligated to each of them? (List all affected by your decision.) Define your claimants based on the following obligations:

- a promise/contract you made (implied or express)? (Fidelity)
- a wrong you committed that you now have to make up? (Reparation)
- gratitude for something one of the claimants did for you? (Gratitude)
- the merit of the claimants when compared with each other? (Justice)
- your ability to help someone out who needs and deserves help? (Beneficence)
- your ability to avoid harming anyone unnecessarily? (Noninjury)

This is the first point at which ethical theory is applied. The notion of moral claimants is tied both to consequential and nonconsequential theory. From a utilitarian perspective, for example, majority interests must be considered; thus the majority claimants must be recognized as a group. As John Stuart Mill would have us consider the rights of the minority also—because he would limit that liberty which severely affects the rights of others under his "harm principle"—that minority must also be recognized. Duty-based theories (nonconsequential) such as William Ross's also require us to be aware of all claimants potentially affected by our decisions. His six prima facie duties allow not only for a listing of claimants, but also how to decide on who they are by applying these categories of obligation: fidelity/reparation, gratitude, justice, beneficence, self-improvement, and noninjury. For example, if, as a reporter, you are obligated by the duty of fidelity to honor your implied contract with the public to give them the news they want to read, that reading public must be listed as a claimant on your decision. Likewise, if you are obligated by the duty of noninjury to refrain from violating a person's privacy, that person (perhaps the subject of your story) must be listed as a claimant. At this point, conflicts will begin to show up among various claimants and the obligations to them.

At this stage the decision maker (moral agent) should try to step into the shoes of the various claimants and try to determine, honestly, what their perspective is. This is one of the hardest tasks in ethical decision making. Many philosophers say that to be able to see a problem from another's perspective is a great gift. Philosophers such as John Rawls suggest we step behind a "veil of ignorance" from whence we become free of the encumbrances of our existence (social status, education, ethnic/cultural heritage, etc.). It is only from there as "original" people that we can make moral decisions free from the affecting variables of our lives. Although this may seem a bit extreme, the key here is to try to see the problem from as many perspectives as possible.

4. List at least three alternative courses of action. For each alternative, ask the following questions:

- What are the best- and worse-case scenarios if you choose this alternative?
- Will anyone be harmed if this alternative is chosen, and how will they be harmed?
- Would honoring any ideal/value (personal, professional, religious, or other) invalidate the chosen alternative or call it into question?
- Are there any rules or principles (legal, professional, organizational, or other) that automatically invalidate this alternative?

It is extremely important to list at least three alternatives. As Aristotle noted, there are always at least two, and these two often represent the extremes. Nothing is ever either black or white, and we must be forced to think in terms of compromise, even if that compromise doesn't exactly conform with our personal notion of what is the right thing to do. A true golden mean is not simply a watered-down decision. It bears the marks of that internal struggle already begun above, and is the result of hard thinking. We must also be prepared to state where we would go if such a compromise fails. It is not sufficient to state that we would go to a source and ask permission before revealing that person's name to a court of law. We must be prepared to drop back to another option if the compromise option fails. It is also important to realize which options may be most favored by which parties. Although it is probably apparent by this time, putting it down in writing serves to clarify the decision maker's position and shows exactly where it conflicts with the preferences of others involved in or affected by the decision.

Best- and worst-case scenarios—This is a great exercise for discovering whether or not we can live with our decisions. By visualizing the absolute best and worst outcomes for each alternative, the potential effects that decision may have on others may then be assessed. It is important to deal with the probable (not necessarily possible) extremes here, because anything may be possible. For example, although it is possible that any person having his or her privacy invaded may be so distraught as to commit suicide, it isn't very probable.

Harm—Likewise, it is vital to recognize what options will harm which claimants. It is the rare case in which no harm will be done by the carrying out of any option. By listing the options and the concomitant harms, we are made to weigh the amount of potential harm involved with each alternative, and to understand that avoiding harm is practically impossible. This might lead, as utilitarians suggest, to choosing the option that will produce the least amount of harm. It might also lead to a closer examination of our values according to, for instance, the ethic of care.

Ideals versus options—The term ideals, as defined by ethicist Vincent Ryan Ruggiero, refers to "a notion of excellence, a goal that is thought to bring about greater harmony to ourselves and to others."[1] For example, our culture respects ideals such as tolerance, compassion, loyalty, forgiveness, peace, justice, fairness, and respect for persons. In addition to these human ideals are institutional or organizational ideals, such as profit, efficiency, productivity, quality, and stability. So, at this point, we are required to list those ideals that apply to the various claimants.

Ideals often come in conflict with each other, much the same way that the obligations already listed will conflict. We must recognize these conflicts and be prepared to list ideals in the order in which they should be honored. This calls for a serious bout of internal struggling and may be the first time we are forced to consider the ultimate direction our decision will take. For example, if we choose to place the journalistic ideal of providing information our audience wants over the societal ideal of honoring privacy, we are well on the way to deciding to run a story that may, in fact, violate someone's privacy.

Beginning here and continuing through the process, we must winnow our options. The first step is to compare the options with the ideals of all concerned parties. For example, if we have chosen to honor the journalistic obligation of providing the kind of news our readers demand, then an option to withhold a story that would be of vital interest to readers would be invalidated. Again, we are not asked to make a decision yet, only to see how our options stack up against the various criteria.

Rules—The winnowing process continues here by applying what D. J. Fritzsche refers to as *conjunctive rules*, specifying a minimal cutoff point for a decision.[2] Principles, defined above, are simply the step preceding rules and can be viewed as roughly analogous to the rules derived from them. An example of an ethical conjunctive rule derived from a principle might be: "Any action that would involve lying will not be considered." An example of

---

[1]Vincent Ryan Ruggiero, *The Moral Imperative* (Port Washington: Alfred Publishers, 1973).

[2]D. J. Fritzsche, A Model of Decision-Making Incorporating Ethical Values. *Journal of Business Ethics*, *10*, 1991, pp. 841–852.

an actual rule might be the SPJ code's admonition to "Test the accuracy of information from all sources and exercise care to avoid inadvertent error." Application of such a "rule" would clearly invalidate using quotes out of context, for example.

5. Consider the following ethical guidelines and ask yourself whether they either support or reject any of your alternatives.

Guidelines based on consequences: Weighing benefits and harms

- Is the "good" brought about by your action outweighed by the potential harm that might be done to anyone? (Mill's *Harm Principle*)
- Is any of the harm brought about by anyone other than the moral agent? (Causal Harm)
- Will anyone be harmed who could be said to be defenseless? (Paternalism)
- To what degree is your choice of alternatives based on your own or your organization's best interests? (Ethical Egoism)
- Which of the alternatives will generate the greatest benefit (or the least amount of harm) for the greatest number of people? (Utilitarianism)
- Does this alternative recognize the interrelationships of the parties involved? Does it help anyone by recognizing legitimate needs? (*Ethic of Care*)

Guidelines based on the action itself: Honoring integrity

- Are you willing to make your decision a rule or policy that you and others in your situation can follow in similar situations in the future? (Kant)
- Does the alternative show a basic respect for the integrity and dignity of those affected by your actions? (*Ethic of Care*) Have you or will you be using any person as a means to an end without consideration for his/her basic integrity? (Kant)
- Is the intent of this action free from vested interested interest or ulterior motive? (Kant's "good will")
- Describe the character of a person adopting this alternative, if possible by attributing a positive virtue juxtaposed with its negative counterpart. For example, can an "efficient" character also be viewed by some as an "emotionless" character? How would you reconcile any conflicts in perception?

This is the final winnowing stage, the point at which the ethical theories come into play. This final stage prior to an actual decision completes the complex reasoning process we have been forced into. We will discover here, as previously, that there is much conflict among these theories. There will be no easy solutions. One person may use utilitarian theory to support running a story in the interest of the "greater good"; another person may cite Kant's proscription against using a person as a means to an end as reason for not running the same story. What is most important is to use only those theories that apply directly to a given decision. The best way to accomplish this is simply to answer the questions honestly while considering all sides of the issue. A particular theory may not seem to apply from one perspective, but it very well may from another.

It is important to note that just because a particular theory seems to justify a certain action doesn't mean that the action is the right one to take. Remember the weaknesses of the various theories discussed in chapter 4. For example, utilitarianism allows for otherwise egregious actions to be taken in the interest of the majority. Justifying a questionable act simply because it benefits a designated majority will not wash in the minds of most people. We cannot ignore these problems and must counterbalance them with other theories—in this example, perhaps, the theory of distributive justice or the harm principle.

In other words, we must not fall into the trap of choosing theoretical justification only because it bolsters an already held position. We must choose it because we have arrived at an option through the "agony of decision making," and the theoretical support we have chosen truly reflects our belief in the rightness of our decision.

6. Determine a course of action based on your analysis.

People often begin the entire decision-making process by coming into a case with a decision already in mind. However, as we proceed through this worksheet, we are forced to look at each case from too many angles to have a fixed position. Remember, the decision itself is not as important as the process. The goal is to provide the tools needed to assess ethical dilemmas and to reason through them. There are no right answers, only well-reasoned answers, which leads us to the final point.

7. Defend your decision in the form of a letter addressed to your most adamant detractor.

As Stephen Carter has pointed out, a person of integrity will be willing and able to justify her actions to others. If we have truly thought through the process and made a decision based on sound reasoning, then we should be able to defend that decision. The most appropriate person to defend it to is that claimant who has lost the most or been harmed the most. The very least the people out there can ask for is that we, as a media representatives, have actually considered our decisions.

AN EXAMPLE

The following case was completed by a college student. Although the case is a fairly typical journalistic problem, it should be stressed again that the worksheet has broad application and is not limited to a single type of ethical issue. The facts of the case will become clear through the explication.

1. Issue:

An activist group composed of concerned parents and several leading citizens has found a local paper's series coverage of high school sex and the transmittal of sexually transmitted diseases (STDs) offensive. The group members argue that such coverage affects the moral character of the high school and other students and does not belong in so public a forum as the local paper. They are also concerned that the identities of the students used as "case studies" in the series might be discovered, and that the reputation of the entire school district might be harmed.

2. Relevant facts include:

- Several leading citizens (including two school board members) have signed a letter to the editor asking that the series be terminated.
- Their concern is over the "delicate" nature of the topic in so public a forum.
- Some state that the names of the "sources" should be made known so that they can seek medical treatment and not be allowed to "spread the disease."
- The paper is the only one in town.
- The series is also slated to cover the danger of AIDS and other STDs.
- The paper has taken care to conceal the names of actual students it has interviewed.
- Readership has dropped with the advent of "soft" news on local TV, especially the tabloid type syndicated programs airing just before prime time.

- As editor and primary decision maker in this case, I am aware that my own high school-age children face the same problems my paper is portraying.
- Special considerations include the need for confidentiality of sources, the general moral tenor of the community (it is fairly conservative), and whether the newspaper is using the series simply to boost circulation.

3. Claimants:

- ***Parents:*** Parents seek some measure of control over their children's behavior, especially in the area of sex education. Many would prefer the subject be confined to their households for discussion. Parents of students featured in series are especially vulnerable, even if the students' names are withheld. (Duty of noninjury.)
- ***Students:*** They are not naive, but some of them, like their parents, might prefer the topic be discussed in a less open forum, although they might see this as a useful service to their peer group. Students used as sources for the story need to protect their identities and are relying on the paper to maintain their confidentiality. Also, they would probably want their "lessons" to be of some use to others. (Duties of noninjury and fidelity to sources not to reveal names.)
- ***Reporters:*** Need to protect their right to gather and print information they feel is important to the public interest, often despite public opinion to the contrary. (Duty of self-improvement; duty of fidelity to the profession and the community.)
- ***The paper itself:*** Must maintain its viability by producing stories that not only inform the community but compete well in the marketplace. (Duty of fidelity to the paper and to the community.)
- ***School officials:*** Might feel they are being put in a bad light because students under their supervision are the ones being featured in this series. (Duty of noninjury; duty of justice.)
- ***Community members*** (Those who do not fit into above categories): They have a right to be kept aware of topics of concern/importance to the community. Despite the letter to the editor, many community members may, in fact, support the story being run. (Duty of fidelity, possibly gratitude.)

4. The options, as I see them, are:

a. Continue with the series as is;
b. discontinue the series;

c. continue with the series, but offer to reduce offensive language or incidents pictured in the stories to an acceptable level; or
d. continue with the series, and work with student and parent groups toward some resolutions to the problems portrayed in the stories. This way, we are a part of the solution, and do not just recount the problem.

Favored options:

- Activist parents and citizens clearly would favor option *b*, and wouldn't view option *c* as complete enough a measure.
- The paper would favor *a*, but would probably view *c* as censorship. It might consider *d*.
- Students could go either way, but would probably favor *a*.
- Community would probably favor *d*.

Best- & worst-case scenarios:

- *Continuing the series as is* Best case—no one gets hurt. The series is respected by community as good journalism. Lives are affected in a positive way. Worst case—could alienate more of my target audience. The paper could lose readership. I could lose my job.
- *Discontinue the series* Best case—our support among those protesting the series grows. Worst case—some in the community would be pleased if we don't continue the series; however, the paper would lose its journalistic integrity and will have violated its mandate to give the people what they need, not just what they want. We might also be violating the students' trust, since they probably want the story told.
- *Continue the series but with editing for language and graphic content* Best case—no one is concerned about the editing. The story remains effective despite the editing. Worst case—the editing softens the story to the point that it is ineffective. Editing under community pressure is a bad precedent to set.
- *Continue the series and work with the community toward a solution* Best case—the series brings the problem to the community's attention. The paper is recognized as a good citizen. Worst case—people are still angry. The paper shifts its focus to public journalism and away from objective journalism.

Harm

Any action would likely cause harm (or perceived harm) to some party, but in differing degrees.

Ideals

Ideals include: freedom of choice (for readers); freedom of speech (for the paper and its journalists); freedom from harm (for students, the schools and parents); respect for minority opinion; freedom from censorship (for the paper and for the community members who might wish to see the stories).

Conflicting ideals:

- Evidently, some parents and influential citizens favor stopping the series, thus upholding the principles of majority rule (to the extent that it is or may become a majority) and the right to protect their community from what they see as unnecessary exposure.
- The paper's obligation to present information of concern and interest to the community and its right to be free from censorship obviously will conflict at times with some community opinions or ideals.
- Students, parents, and schools who might be harmed from this would complain that their rights to protection from this kind of story are being violated by the paper. After all, isn't it up to the community to say what is best for it?
- The community is likely to favor overall freedom of the press, despite disparate elements within the community who might feel otherwise. The decision may turn on how loudly the activist group protests.
- My tendency, at this point, is to honor freedom of the press as an ideal, trying to keep in mind that I must limit, to the best of my ability, the harm that could come from my publishing the series in question. I must also make sure that increased readership is not the sole reason for my position.
- No ideal, viewed in context, invalidates any option. Viewed singularly, any ideal will rule out certain options.

RULES

The code of the Society of Professional Journalists, Article I, states that it is the responsibility of journalists to provide news of public importance and interest. In fact, the code states that this is the "overriding mission" of the mass media. I think that this series could be said to be in the interest of the public. Some would question the subject, and Article V of the SPJ code states that the news media should not pander to morbid curiosity about details of vice and crime. However, I don't believe this series panders to public curiosity in any way. As to naming the sources of the stories, Article III of the code strictly forbids this. I would say that the SPJ code is on the side of the media in this case.[3]

5. Ethical theories:

Consequential:

- John Stuart Mill's harm principle allows restraints on liberty only if there is harm (or violation of another's liberty). The harm in this case has not been demonstrated. Indeed, there is a strong argument that this series will be beneficial because it will help make the community more aware of the problem of STDs.
- Egoism could be driving the paper to run the stories because it may help stimulate sales; however, given the SPJ code and the importance of the subject to the community, I think that the paper is not acting in an egoistic manner here.
- An argument could be made on utilitarian grounds that the objecting citizens represent a majority of citizens in the community. However, continuing to publish the series is more in line with First Amendments intent, which is also utilitarian by nature and speaks to a greater societal good.

Nonconsequential:

- There is a clear Kantian rule embodied in the First Amendment: "Don't censor." In fact, and despite the obvious court-sanctioned exceptions, the First Amendment is couched in pretty clear "perfect duty" language.
- William Ross's prima facie duties apply in a number of ways. The newspaper owes a duty of fidelity to the citizens of the community. A newspaper operates to bring news to the community that it wants and needs to remain an informed citizenry. If the paper were to publish only that news which the community wanted, it would not be doing its civic duty. Noninjury, on the other hand, would have us consider the potential harmful effects of the stories on students. However, I would argue that we do greater harm covering up this sort of epidemic. Beneficence is also applicable, because by printing the series of stories we are helping society come to grips with this problem.
- Aristotle's golden mean is not especially applicable here because the middle ground would have us partially censor the stories, which goes against our First Amendment position of noncensorship. Plus, I believe that the stories would lose some of their impact if censored.

---

[3]This reference is to an earlier version of the SPJ code.

6. Decision:

I would continue to publish the series, making sure that no sensationalism creeps into the stories in any way. They will be factual and truthful. I will personally respond to the upset citizens of the community via an editorial that will contain much of my defense, as follows:

7. Defense:

The position of those seeking to prevent publication is that citizens, and especially parents, should have some say in the degree to which their children are exposed to unsettling (and possibly sensational) information. This seems reasonable. However, as the only newspaper in town, we are obligated to present the community not just with news it wants, but also with news it needs. In an open, democratic society this means exposing the community to a variety of issues, some which potentially conflict with some individuals' standards. In every controversial story there will be something that someone finds objectionable. Although you may disagree that some of the issues we choose to bring to your attention are worthy, we reserve the right, as citizens ourselves, to work on your behalf in presenting the news. We admit the paternalistic nature of this arrangement; however, we will continue to listen to you and to try to respond to your complaints, at the same time reserving the right to make the kind of judgments our training has prepared us to make. In short, we wouldn't print a story we thought was not in the best interest of the community of which we are an integral part. Most importantly, we believe that any limitation on the freedom of expression in this country is counterproductive and can only lead to further restrictions of our most valued liberty.

SUMMARY

Applying ethical thought to the mass media decision-making process requires two vital components: a rudimentary grounding in the relevant ethical theories, and a structured approach to analyzing the issues on a case-by-case basis. It is clearly impossible to bring every relevant theory to bear on every case; however, there are certain thinkers whose theories have contributed immensely to the ethical foundations of modern American mass media. The common ground is the democratic system in which the media professions operate. Therefore, the primary theorists are those who have proposed ethical guidelines based on the sanctity of the individual as an active citizen in a society in which he or she may exert some control. However, other theorists went beyond these considerations to reflect on the nature of virtue and good will that ultimately guides our decisions, adds so much to our deliberations, and limits our blind obedience to the greater good. We must also not forget that community plays an increasingly vital role in our lives; and there are those who deem community the most important consideration, not necessarily subservient to individual will. Taken as a whole, these theorists and others contribute but the building blocks for a more complete understanding of the role of ethics in our decision-making processes.

We are not an either-or society when it comes to ethics. We staunchly defend individual rights, yet complain that any sense of community is vanishing in these hectic and often confusing times. It is clear that we should value both individual autonomy and community interests. Ethical decisions need not ignore individuality in order to recognize community, or favor community over personal autonomy. We simply must realize that both can often be served simultaneously if we are simply willing to communicate and compromise. We should also recognize that there will be times when one need will override the other. In these instances, we must exercise special caution that those affected by our decisions are not unduly injured. The only way to accomplish this is to hold both individual rights and community needs as valid media concerns. And the only way to do this (to paraphrase Fred Friendly) is to make the agony of decision making so intense that we can only escape by thinking.

Decision making can more easily become a part of our lives if it is the product of a structured method of analysis focusing on the things we all have in common and viewed in the light of the relevant ethical theories. We can be taught to think in a logical fashion by forcing ourselves, at least initially, to conform to this step-by-step analysis. It is to be hoped that this will lead to an ability to do the same in the day-to-day routine of deadline-based decision making. Previously considered cases can then be used as reference points for future decisions. And those issues that do not follow from previous exposure to similar circumstances can be analyzed on their particular merits based on familiarity with this decision-making model. The lessons learned in every decision-making situation should serve not only to better our ethical skills but also to better our professions, and, by extension, all of society.

HYPOTHETICAL: SPORTS TEAM NAMES

You are the marketing director for the Watertown, New York, Mohawks, a minor-league baseball team. Watertown is a midsize community of about 200,000 people. It has two city colleges and a dozen high schools. The Mohawks have been around for nearly 50 years and have been a source of much pride to the growing community. Last year, especially, the community got behind the team when it took a run at the state championship against a traditionally stronger rival from downstate. The Mohawks won and eventually went all the way to the regional level before being defeated by a much tougher team from Albany.

The Mohawks have been a popular attraction for summer visitors to Watertown. Recently, however, there have been rumblings of discontent from the head of the history department at Watertown City College. In a letter to the editor of the *Watertown Daily News*, the professor criticized the team and the city for allowing the name of a distinct group of Native Americans to be trivialized by its use as a sports team designation. Both the editor of the paper and the citizens of Watertown are familiar with the growing controversy over using Native American tribal names and generic references to American Indians in general for sports teams. The ongoing brouhaha over the Washington Redskins, Atlanta Braves, and Cleveland Indians is still fresh in most people's minds. However, this was hitting too close to home for many in Watertown.

The battle lines have already been drawn, and the arguments are familiar to you, as the marketing director, and to most of the people in a position to affect your decision in some way. Basically, the arguments in favor of keeping names such as Redskins and Braves cite other ethnic sports team designations that don't seem to garner controversy: the Fighting Irish of Notre Dame and the Minnesota Vikings, for instance. Some cite fan loyalty, tradition, and shared history as reasons for not abandoning traditional team names. Others say that naming a team after a Native American tribe is a sign of respect for the bravery of the American Indian in general. The other side of the argument cites the ongoing oppression of the Native American cultures by the now-dominant Anglo culture of this country. Native Americans resent the use of logos depicting them as mascots, and call it racism pure and simple. They feel that the continuing use of American Indian names for sports teams accomplishes nothing positive in the continuing struggle of Native Americans to regain their place in our society.

The newspaper hasn't taken a position on the name controversy yet, and the community hasn't had time to coalesce into camps over the issue. However, as marketing director for the team, it's your job to consider the ramifications of all potential consequences to your client before they happen—if possible.

Analyze this situation using the moral checklist in this chapter.

FURTHER ANALYSIS

Now that you have reached the end of this book, try using the moral checklist presented in this chapter on the case studies and hypotheticals in previous chapters to obtain a more detailed analysis of those problems.

APPENDIX: Media Codes of Ethics

Professional codes of ethics are generally guidelines for those working in a particular occupation considered by its members or by others to be a profession. Remember from chapters 1 and 3 that there are often differences among professional ethics and personal or societal ethics, and these differences need to be not only recognized but also understood. No one can perform a job without an understanding of how that job affects others. We also need to understand how others will view us if we seem to violate the codes of our society, codes by which everyone else lives.

It is, therefore, important for us to explore exactly what the various professional codes say and to try to understand why they say it. Keep in mind, while you read through these codes, the various purposes codes can be put to. Also remember that codes can often be self-serving. Try to recognize those instances in which they are, and ask yourself why you think this is so. If it is not for the good of all of society, then your action is usually for the good of only a few and that may or may not be sufficient rationale for ethical decision making.

Following are a number of codes developed for various media industries or specific portions of those industries. Note the differences. Like all professional codes, these reflect the intricacies of the professions they represent and should respond to the specific ethical needs of those professions.

Keep in mind, also, that for every industry-wide code there will be dozens, maybe hundreds, of individual codes that are drafted by individual advertising agencies, PR firms, and news-gathering operations around the country. They will sometimes differ from industry-wide codes, but more often than not they will simply amplify or clarify issues addressed more generally in the umbrella codes. Included here is the code of ethics for the Seattle *Times* so that you may see some of those clarifications. Compare it with the first code here from the Society of Professional Journalists to see the differences.

Whether a code is industry-wide or outlet-specific, it should be relevant and useful. Remember, however, that it is only a first step in ethical decision making. The bulk of the workload is still on you, the decision maker. If you don't think for yourself, no code in the world will be of any use to you.

* * *

THE SOCIETY OF PROFESSIONAL JOURNALISTS' CODE OF ETHICS*

PREAMBLE

Members of the Society of Professional Journalists believe that public enlightenment is the forerunner of justice and the foundation of democracy. The duty of the journalist is to further those ends by seeking truth and providing a fair and comprehensive account of events and issues. Conscientious journalists from all media and specialties strive to serve the public with thoroughness and honesty. Professional integrity is the cornerstone of a journalist's credibility. Members of the Society share a dedication to ethical behavior and adopt this code to declare the Society's principles and standards of practice.

SEEK TRUTH AND REPORT IT

Journalists should be honest, fair and courageous in gathering, reporting and interpreting information.

Journalists should:

- Test the accuracy of information from all sources and exercise care to avoid inadvertent error. Deliberate distortion is never permissible.
- Diligently seek out subjects of news stories to give them the opportunity to respond to allegations of wrongdoing.

---

*transcription

- Identify sources whenever feasible. The public is entitled to as much information as possible on sources' reliability.
- Always question sources' motives before promising anonymity.
- Clarify conditions attached to any promise made in exchange for information. Keep promises.
- Make certain that headlines, news teases and promotional material, photos, video, audio, graphics, sound bites and quotations do not misrepresent. They should not oversimplify or highlight incidents out of context.
- Never distort the content of news photos or video. Image enhancement for technical clarity is always permissible. Label montages and photo illustrations.
- Avoid misleading re-enactments or staged news events. If re-enactment is necessary to tell a story, label it.
- Avoid undercover or other surreptitious methods of gathering information except when traditional open methods will not yield information vital to the public. Use of such methods should be explained as part of the story.
- Never plagiarize.
- Tell the story of the diversity and magnitude of the human experience boldly, even when it is unpopular to do so. Examine their own cultural values and avoid imposing those values on others.
- Avoid stereotyping by race, gender, age, religion, ethnicity, geography, sexual orientation, disability, physical appearance or social status.
- Support the open exchange of views, even views they find repugnant.
- Give voice to the voiceless; official and unofficial sources of information can be equally valid.
- Distinguish between advocacy and news reporting. Analysis and commentary should be labeled and not misrepresent fact or context.
- Distinguish news from advertising and shun hybrids that blur the lines between the two.
- Recognize a special obligation to ensure that the public's business is conducted in the open and that government records are open to inspection.

MINIMIZE HARM

Ethical journalists treat sources, subjects and colleagues as human beings deserving of respect.

Journalists should:

- Show compassion for those who may be affected adversely by news coverage. Use special sensitivity when dealing with children and inexperienced sources or subjects.
- Be sensitive when seeking or using interviews or photographs of those affected by tragedy or grief.
- Recognize that gathering and reporting information may cause harm or discomfort. Pursuit of the news is not a license for arrogance.
- Recognize that private people have a greater right to control information about themselves than do public officials and others who seek power, influence or attention. Only an overriding public need can justify intrusion into anyone's privacy.
- Show good taste. Avoid pandering to lurid curiosity.
- Be cautious about identifying juvenile suspects or victims of sex crimes.
- Be judicious about naming criminal suspects before the formal filing of charges.
- Balance a criminal suspect's fair trial rights with the public's right to be informed.

ACT INDEPENDENTLY

Journalists should be free of obligation to any interest other than the public's right to know.

Journalists should:

- Avoid conflicts of interest, real or perceived.
- Remain free of associations and activities that may compromise integrity or damage credibility.
- Refuse gifts, favors, fees, free travel and special treatment, and shun secondary employment, political involvement, public office and service in community organizations if they compromise journalistic integrity.
- Disclose unavoidable conflicts.
- Be vigilant and courageous about holding those with power accountable.
- Deny favored treatment to advertisers and special interests and resist their pressure to influence news coverage.
- Be wary of sources offering information for favors or money; avoid bidding for news.

BE ACCOUNTABLE

Journalists are accountable to their readers, listeners, viewers and each other.

Journalists should:

- Clarify and explain news coverage and invite dialogue with the public over journalistic conduct.
- Encourage the public to voice grievances against the news media.
- Admit mistakes and correct them promptly.
- Expose unethical practices of journalists and the news media.
- Abide by the same high standards to which they hold others.

Sigma Delta Chi's first Code of Ethics was borrowed from the American Society of Newspaper Editors in 1926. In 1973, Sigma Delta Chi wrote its own code, which was revised in 1984 and 1987. The present version of the Society of Professional Journalists' Code of Ethics was adopted in September 1996.

* * *

AMERICAN SOCIETY OF NEWSPAPER EDITORS ASNE STATEMENT OF PRINCIPLES

ASNE's Statement of Principles was originally adopted in 1922 as the "Canons of Journalism." The document was revised and renamed "Statement of Principles" in 1975.

PREAMBLE. The First Amendment, protecting freedom of expression from abridgment by any law, guarantees to the people through their press a constitutional right, and thereby places on newspaper people a particular responsibility. Thus journalism demands of its practitioners not only industry and knowledge but also the pursuit of a standard of integrity proportionate to the journalist's singular obligation. To this end the American Society of Newspaper Editors sets forth this Statement of Principles as a standard encouraging the highest ethical and professional performance.

ARTICLE I—Responsibility. The primary purpose of gathering and distributing news and opinion is to serve the general welfare by informing the people and enabling them to make judgments on the issues of the time. Newspapermen and women who abuse the power of their professional role for selfish motives or unworthy purposes are faithless to that public trust. The

American press was made free not just to inform or just to serve as a forum for debate but also to bring an independent scrutiny to bear on the forces of power in the society, including the conduct of official power at all levels of government.

ARTICLE II—Freedom of the Press. Freedom of the press belongs to the people. It must be defended against encroachment or assault from any quarter, public or private. Journalists must be constantly alert to see that the public's business is conducted in public. They must be vigilant against all who would exploit the press for selfish purposes.

ARTICLE III—Independence. Journalists must avoid impropriety and the appearance of impropriety as well as any conflict of interest or the appearance of conflict. They should neither accept anything nor pursue any activity that might compromise or seem to compromise their integrity.

ARTICLE IV—Truth and Accuracy. Good faith with the reader is the foundation of good journalism. Every effort must be made to assure that the news content is accurate, free from bias and in context, and that all sides are presented fairly. Editorials, analytical articles and commentary should be held to the same standards of accuracy with respect to facts as news reports. Significant errors of fact, as well as errors of omission, should be corrected promptly and prominently.

ARTICLE V—Impartiality. To be impartial does not require the press to be unquestioning or to refrain from editorial expression. Sound practice, however, demands a clear distinction for the reader between news reports and opinion. Articles that contain opinion or personal interpretation should be clearly identified.

ARTICLE VI—Fair Play. Journalists should respect the rights of people involved in the news, observe the common standards of decency and stand accountable to the public for the fairness and accuracy of their news reports. Persons publicly accused should be given the earliest opportunity to respond. Pledges of confidentiality to news sources must be honored at all costs, and therefore should not be given lightly. Unless there is clear and pressing need to maintain confidences, sources of information should be identified.

These principles are intended to preserve, protect and strengthen the bond of trust and respect between American journalists and the American people, a bond that is essential to sustain the grant of freedom entrusted to both by the nation's founders.

* * *

RADIO-TELEVISION NEWS DIRECTORS ASSOCIATION [RTNDA]: CODE OF ETHICS AND PROFESSIONAL CONDUCT

The Radio-Television News Directors Association, wishing to foster the highest professional standards of electronic journalism, promote public understanding of and confidence in electronic journalism, and strengthen principles of journalistic freedom to gather and disseminate information, establishes this Code of Ethics and Professional Conduct.

PREAMBLE

Professional electronic journalists should operate as trustees of the public, seek the truth, report it fairly and with integrity and independence, and stand accountable for their actions.

PUBLIC TRUST: Professional electronic journalists should recognize that their first obligation is to the public.

Professional electronic journalists should:

Understand that any commitment other than service to the public undermines trust and credibility. Recognize that service in the public interest creates an obligation to reflect the diversity of the community and guard against oversimplification of issues or events. Provide a full range of information to enable the public to make enlightened decisions. Fight to ensure that the public's business is conducted in public.

TRUTH: Professional electronic journalists should pursue truth aggressively and present the news accurately, in context, and as completely as possible.

Professional electronic journalists should:

- Continuously seek the truth. Resist distortions that obscure the importance of events.
- Clearly disclose the origin of information and label all material provided by outsiders.

Professional electronic journalists should not:

- Report anything known to be false.
- Manipulate images or sounds in any way that is misleading.

- Plagiarize.
- Present images or sounds that are reenacted without informing the public.

FAIRNESS: Professional electronic journalists should present the news fairly and impartially, placing primary value on significance and relevance.

Professional electronic journalists should:

- Treat all subjects of news coverage with respect and dignity, showing particular compassion to victims of crime or tragedy.
- Exercise special care when children are involved in a story and give children greater privacy protection than adults.
- Seek to understand the diversity of their community and inform the public without bias or stereotype.
- Present a diversity of expressions, opinions, and ideas in context.
- Present analytical reporting based on professional perspective, not personal bias.
- Respect the right to a fair trial.

INTEGRITY: Professional electronic journalists should present the news with integrity and decency, avoiding real or perceived conflicts of interest, and respect the dignity and intelligence of the audience as well as the subjects of news.

Professional electronic journalists should:

- Identify sources whenever possible. Confidential sources should be used only when it is clearly in the public interest to gather or convey important information or when a person providing information might be harmed. Journalists should keep all commitments to protect a confidential source.
- Clearly label opinion and commentary.
- Guard against extended coverage of events or individuals that fails to significantly advance a story, place the event in context, or add to the public knowledge.
- Refrain from contacting participants in violent situations while the situation is in progress. Use technological tools with skill and thoughtfulness, avoiding techniques that skew facts, distort reality, or sensationalize events.
- Use surreptitious newsgathering techniques, including hidden cameras or microphones, only if there is no other way to obtain stories of signifi-

cant public importance and only if the technique is explained to the audience.

- Disseminate the private transmissions of other news organizations only with permission.

Professional electronic journalists should not:

- Pay news sources who have a vested interest in a story.
- Accept gifts, favors, or compensation from those who might seek to influence coverage.
- Engage in activities that may compromise their integrity or independence.

INDEPENDENCE: Professional electronic journalists should defend the independence of all journalists from those seeking influence or control over news content.

Professional electronic journalists should:

- Gather and report news without fear or favor, and vigorously resist undue influence from any outside forces, including advertisers, sources, story subjects, powerful individuals, and special interest groups.
- Resist those who would seek to buy or politically influence news content or who would seek to intimidate those who gather and disseminate the news.
- Determine news content solely through editorial judgment and not as the result of outside influence.
- Resist any self-interest or peer pressure that might erode journalistic duty and service to the public. Recognize that sponsorship of the news will not be used in any way to determine, restrict, or manipulate content.
- Refuse to allow the interests of ownership or management to influence news judgment and content inappropriately.
- Defend the rights of the free press for all journalists, recognizing that any professional or government licensing of journalists is a violation of that freedom.

ACCOUNTABILITY: Professional electronic journalists should recognize that they are accountable for their actions to the public, the profession, and themselves.

Professional electronic journalists should:

- Actively encourage adherence to these standards by all journalists and their employers. Respond to public concerns. Investigate complaints and correct errors promptly and with as much prominence as the original report.
- Explain journalistic processes to the public, especially when practices spark questions or controversy.
- Recognize that professional electronic journalists are duty-bound to conduct themselves ethically. Refrain from ordering or encouraging courses of action that would force employees to commit an unethical act.
- Carefully listen to employees who raise ethical objections and create environments in which such objections and discussions are encouraged.
- Seek support for and provide opportunities to train employees in ethical decision-making.

In meeting its responsibility to the profession of electronic journalism, RTNDA has created this code to identify important issues, to serve as a guide for its members, to facilitate self-scrutiny, and to shape future debate.

Adopted at RTNDA 2000 in Minneapolis September 14, 2000.

* * *

AMERICAN ADVERTISING FEDERATION THE ADVERTISING PRINCIPLES OF AMERICAN BUSINESS*

TRUTH

Advertising shall tell the truth, and shall reveal significant facts, the omission of which would mislead the public.

SUBSTANTIATION

Advertising claims shall be substantiated by evidence in possession of the advertiser and advertising agency, prior to making such claims.

---

*Adopted by the American Advertising Federation Board of Directors, March 2, 1984, San Antonio, Texas.

COMPARISONS

Advertising shall refrain from making false, misleading, or unsubstantiated statements or claims about a competitor or his products or services.

BAIT ADVERTISING

Advertising shall not offer products or services for sale unless such offer constitutes a bona fide effort to sell the advertised products or services and is not a device to switch consumers to other goods or services, usually higher priced.

GUARANTEES AND WARRANTIES

Advertising of guarantees and warranties shall be explicit, with sufficient information to apprise consumers of their principal terms and limitations or, when space or time restrictions preclude such disclosures, the advertisement should clearly reveal where the full text of the guarantee or warranty can be examined before purchase.

PRICE CLAIMS

Advertising shall avoid price claims which are false or misleading, or savings claims which do not offer provable savings.

TESTIMONIALS

Advertising containing testimonials shall be limited to those of competent witnesses who are reflecting a real and honest opinion or experience.

TASTE AND DECENCY

Advertising shall be free of statements, illustrations or implications which are offensive to good taste or public decency.

* * *

AMERICAN SOCIETY OF MAGAZINE EDITORS [ASME]: GUIDELINES FOR EDITORS AND PUBLISHERS

ELEVENTH EDITION JANUARY 2002

Magazines are successful only if readers trust the information and advice given. This trust can be broken all too easily—by either perception or reality. ASME has created these guidelines to ensure that the clear distinction between advertising and editorial content is never blurred.

In October 1996, ASME announced the following standard for editorial independence, in an effort to affirm the highest standards in magazine journalism, and to underscore magazine editors' traditional independence from untoward commercial or other extra-journalistic pressures.

The chief editor of any magazine must have final authority over the editorial content, words and pictures that appear in the publication.

Editors and their publishers have an obligation to enforce and maintain the best journalistic practices. If, for example, a reader gets the impression that an article was created or altered to satisfy an advertiser or special interest group, that reader is likely to discount the content of the article and distrust the publication—and the brand.

In September 1997, Magazine Publishers of America [MPA] and ASME issued a joint statement about notifying advertisers of editorial content prior to publication.

As editors and publishers, we strongly believe that editorial integrity and credibility are the magazine industry's most important assets. As a result, we believe that magazines should not submit table of contents, text or photos from upcoming issues to advertisers for prior review. We are confident that editors and publishers can inform advertisers about a publication's editorial environment or direction without engaging in practices that may at the very least create the appearance of censorship and ultimately could undermine editorial independence.

Since the guidelines that follow cannot possibly cover every situation that arises, we hope that all magazine editors and publishers will respect ASME's guidelines in spirit and in practice. Due to the volume of inquiries in recent years, ASME cannot pass judgment or grant approval on proposed content before publication. If an editor or publisher is not sure whether an ad or article complies with these guidelines, ASME suggests proceeding with caution—when in doubt, slug it "advertisement" or "promotion," as detailed in the guidelines. Make sure it is easy for readers to tell what kind of content it is.

In order to ensure that online entities with an editorial component also maintain the highest standards, ASME and Magazine Publishers of America jointly issued "Best Practices for Digital Media" in August 2000.

Please note: Any magazine that willfully or repeatedly violates these guidelines will be declared ineligible for National Magazine Awards, and the editor ultimately responsible for the violations (if a member of ASME) may be expelled from the organization.

GUIDELINES FOR EDITORIAL AND ADVERTISING PAGES

1. Layout and Design

The layout, design and typeface of advertising pages should be distinctly different from the publication's normal layout, design and typefaces. Any page of advertising that contains text or design elements that have an editorial appearance must be clearly and conspicuously identified with the words "advertising," "advertisement" or "promotion" horizontally at or near the center of the top of the page in type at least equal in size and weight to the publication's normal editorial body typeface.

2. Use of the Magazine's Logo, etc.

At no time should a magazine's name, logo or editorial staff be used in a way that suggests editorial endorsement of any advertiser. Specifically:

- (a) No advertisement or purely promotional contest may be promoted on the cover of the magazine or included in the editorial table of contents. This includes cover stickers and other inserts.
- (b) In general, the publication's name or logo should not appear on any advertising pages except when advertising the magazine's own products and services. The magazine's name or logo may be used to label its own multi-advertiser sections (e.g., classified ad pages, seasonal gift guides), merchandising joint promotions, and contests conceived or controlled by the publisher, but those pages must carry the

words "advertising," "advertisement" or "promotion," as detailed in Guideline No. 1.

3. Adjacency and Sponsorships

Advertising pages should not be placed adjacent to related editorial material in a manner that implies editorial endorsement of the advertised product or services. No advertising copy should state or imply advertiser control or improper involvement in the preparation of editorial materials in an issue. Similarly, an advertiser's name or logo may not be used on any editorial pages to suggest advertising sponsorship of those pages, nor should any editorial page be labelled as "sponsored" or "brought to you" by an advertiser.

4. Editorial Contests

If an advertiser or outside organization provides the prize or prizes for an editorial contest, sweepstakes or free offer featured on editorial pages, the editorial copy must not suggest an endorsement of that advertiser's products or services and must not feature the advertiser's or product's logo in connection with the magazine's logo. The contest must remain under the editors' sole control, and the participating advertiser may not be involved in the contest judging or any aspect of the editorial presentation.

5. Editorial Review of Ad Pages

In order for the publication's chief editor to have the opportunity to monitor compliance with the guidelines, advertising pages should be made available to the editor in ample time for review and to recommend any necessary changes.

GUIDELINES FOR SPECIAL ADVERTISING SECTIONS, SINGLE-SPONSOR ISSUES, AND CUSTOM PUBLISHING

Definitions

A special advertising section is a set of advertising pages unified by a theme, accompanied by editorial-like text or by editorial material from another magazine that supports the theme. Such a section consists of two or more pages, often including a cover, that is paid for by one or more advertisers.

A single-sponsor issue is underwritten by a sole advertiser.

A single-sponsor issue that is created especially for an advertiser without editorial input is considered custom publishing.

1. Content

The content of special advertising sections should be sufficiently distinct from the magazine's editorial material, so readers will not confuse editorial pages with sponsored content. The size and number of special advertising sections within a single issue should not be out of balance with the size and nature of the magazine.

2. Sponsorship Declaration

Each text page of a special advertising section must be clearly and conspicuously identified as a message paid for by advertisers. If an entire issue is underwritten by a single advertiser, this should be disclosed to readers in a publisher's or editor's letter, explaining that the advertiser had no influence over the editorial content.

3. Labelling, Layout and Design

In order to identify special advertising sections clearly and conspicuously:

- (a) The words "advertising," "advertisement," "special advertising section" or "special advertising supplement" should appear horizontally at or near the center of the top of every page of such sections containing text, in type at least equal in size and weight to the publication's normal editorial body typeface.
- (b) The layout, design, typeface, and literary style of special advertising sections or custom-publishing products should be distinctly different from the publication's normal layout, design, typefaces and literary style.

4. Use of the Magazine's Name/Logo, etc.

Special advertising sections should not be slugged on the publication's cover or included in the editorial table of contents. In general, the publication's name or logo should not appear as any part of the headlines or text of such sections, except in connection with the magazine's own products or services. Exception: The magazine's name or logo may be used to label its own multi-advertiser sections (e.g., classified ad pages, seasonal gift guides), merchandising joint promotions and advertiser contests, but those pages must carry the words "advertising," "advertisement" or "advertising promotion," as detailed in Guideline 3(a).

5. Adjacency

Advertising sections should not be placed adjacent to editorial material in a manner that implies editorial endorsement of the advertised product or services. Similarly, an advertiser's name or logo may not be used on any editorial pages to suggest advertising sponsorship of those pages, nor should any editorial page be labelled as "sponsored" or "brought to you" by an advertiser.

6. No Editorial Involvement

The names and titles of editors, editorial staff members and regular editorial contributors should not appear on, or be associated with, special advertising sections for their own publication, for other publications in their field, or for advertisers in the fields they cover. Nor should editorial staff members work on projects prepared by the publisher for one or more advertisers.

7. Editorial Review of Ad Pages

In order for the publication's chief editor to have the opportunity to monitor compliance with these guidelines, material for special advertising sections should be made available to the editor before publication, in ample time for review and to recommend necessary changes. In order to avoid potential conflicts or overlaps with editorial content, publishers should notify editors well in advance of their plans to run special advertising sections.

ASME/MPA BEST PRACTICES FOR DIGITAL MEDIA

Credibility is key to the success of all digital-media businesses with an editorial component. Users must trust the advice and information given, just as they do that of offline brands. While linking and other technologies can greatly enhance the user experience, the distinction between independent editorial content and paid promotional information should remain clear.

Thus we recommend the following standards (subject to change as the medium evolves):

1. The home page and all subsequent pages of a publication's website should display the publication's name and logo prominently, in order to clarify who controls the content of the site.
2. All online pages should clearly distinguish between editorial and advertising or sponsored content. If any content comes from a source other than the editors, it should be clearly labelled. A magazine's name or logo

should not be used in a way that suggests editorial endorsement of an advertiser. The site's sponsorship policies should be clearly noted, either in text accompanying the article or on a disclosure page (see item 8), to clarify that the sponsor had no input regarding the content.

3. Hypertext links that appear within the editorial content of a site, including those within graphics, should be at the discretion of the editors. If links are paid for by advertisers, that should be disclosed to users.
4. Special advertising or "advertorial" features should be labelled as such.
5. To protect the brand, editors/producers should not permit their content to be used on an advertiser's site without an explanation of the relationship (e.g., "Reprinted with permission").
6. E-commerce commissions and other affiliate fees should be reported on a disclosure page, so users can see that the content is credible and free of commercial influence. Exact fees need not be mentioned, of course, but users who are concerned about underlying business relationships can be thus reassured. (See Condé Nast's statement at the bottom of the *Epicurious* home page regarding its relationship with its featured merchants.)
7. Advertisers or e-commerce partners should not receive preferential treatment in search engines, price comparisons and other applications presented under the content provider's brand. An editorial site should not try to vouch for others' tools that it may offer.
8. A website should respect the privacy of its users. If a site intends to collect information about its visitors–whether the data will be disseminated to third parties or not–it must offer users a chance to decline if they choose, through an "opt-out" option. As part of its privacy policy, the site should explain its use of cookies and other data collection methods and tell what it intends to do with the information it gleans. Potential benefits to the user–broader site access, better personalization features, etc.–should be presented as well.

* * *

PUBLIC RELATIONS SOCIETY OF AMERICA [PRSA] MEMBER CODE OF ETHICS 2000

PREAMBLE

This Code applies to PRSA members. The Code is designed to be a useful guide for PRSA members as they carry out their ethical responsibilities. This document is designed to anticipate and accommodate, by precedent, ethical challenges that may arise. The scenarios outlined in the Code provision are actual examples of misconduct. More will be added as experience with the Code occurs.

The Public Relations Society of America (PRSA) is committed to ethical practices. The level of public trust PRSA members seek, as we serve the public good, means we have taken on a special obligation to operate ethically.

The value of member reputation depends upon the ethical conduct of everyone affiliated with the Public Relations Society of America. Each of us sets an example for each other—as well as other professionals—by our pursuit of excellence with powerful standards of performance, professionalism, and ethical conduct.

Emphasis on enforcement of the Code has been eliminated. But, the PRSA Board of Directors retains the right to bar from membership or expel from the Society any individual who has been or is sanctioned by a government agency or convicted in a court of law of an action that is in violation of this Code.

Ethical practice is the most important obligation of a PRSA member. We view the Member Code of Ethics as a model for other professions, organizations, and professionals.

PRSA MEMBER STATEMENT OF PROFESSIONAL VALUES

This statement presents the core values of PRSA members and, more broadly, of the public relations profession. These values provide the foundation for the Member Code of Ethics and set the industry standard for the professional practice of public relations. These values are the fundamental beliefs that guide our behaviors and decision-making process. We believe our professional values are vital to the integrity of the profession as a whole.

ADVOCACY

- We serve the public interest by acting as responsible advocates for those we represent.
- We provide a voice in the marketplace of ideas, facts, and viewpoints to aid informed public debate.

HONESTY

- We adhere to the highest standards of accuracy and truth in advancing the interests of those we represent and in communicating with the public.

EXPERTISE

- We acquire and responsibly use specialized knowledge and experience.
- We advance the profession through continued professional development, research, and education.
- We build mutual understanding, credibility, and relationships among a wide array of institutions and audiences.

INDEPENDENCE

- We provide objective counsel to those we represent.
- We are accountable for our actions.

LOYALTY

- We are faithful to those we represent, while honoring our obligation to serve the public interest.

FAIRNESS

- We deal fairly with clients, employers, competitors, peers, vendors, the media, and the general public.
- We respect all opinions and support the right of free expression.

PRSA CODE PROVISIONS

FREE FLOW OF INFORMATION

Core Principle

Protecting and advancing the free flow of accurate and truthful information is essential to serving the public interest and contributing to informed decision making in a democratic society.

Intent

- To maintain the integrity of relationships with the media, government officials, and the public.
- To aid informed decision making.

Guidelines

A member shall:

- Preserve the integrity of the process of communication.
- Be honest and accurate in all communications.
- Act promptly to correct erroneous communications for which the practitioner is responsible.
- Preserve the free flow of unprejudiced information when giving or receiving gifts by ensuring that gifts are nominal, legal, and infrequent.

Examples of Improper Conduct Under This Provision:

- A member representing a ski manufacturer gives a pair of expensive racing skis to a sports magazine columnist, to influence the columnist to write favorable articles about the product.
- A member entertains a government official beyond legal limits and/or in violation of government reporting requirements.

COMPETITION

Core Principle

Promoting healthy and fair competition among professionals preserves an ethical climate while fostering a robust business environment.

Intent

- To promote respect and fair competition among public relations professionals.
- To serve the public interest by providing the widest choice of practitioner options.

Guidelines

A member shall:

- Follow ethical hiring practices designed to respect free and open competition without deliberately undermining a competitor.
- Preserve intellectual property rights in the marketplace.

Examples of Improper Conduct Under This Provision:

- A member employed by a "client organization" shares helpful information with a counseling firm that is competing with others for the organization's business.
- A member spreads malicious and unfounded rumors about a competitor in order to alienate the competitor's clients and employees in a ploy to recruit people and business.

DISCLOSURE OF INFORMATION

Core Principle

Open communication fosters informed decision making in a democratic society.

Intent

To build trust with the public by revealing all information needed for responsible decision making.

Guidelines

A member shall:

- Be honest and accurate in all communications.
- Act promptly to correct erroneous communications for which the member is responsible.
- Investigate the truthfulness and accuracy of information released on behalf of those represented.
- Reveal the sponsors for causes and interests represented.
- Disclose financial interest (such as stock ownership) in a client's organization.
- Avoid deceptive practices.

Examples of Improper Conduct Under This Provision:

- Front groups: A member implements "grass roots" campaigns or letter-writing campaigns to legislators on behalf of undisclosed interest groups.
- Lying by omission: A practitioner for a corporation knowingly fails to release financial information, giving a misleading impression of the corporation's performance.
- A member discovers inaccurate information disseminated via a Web site or media kit and does not correct the information.

- A member deceives the public by employing people to pose as volunteers to speak at public hearings and participate in "grass roots" campaigns.

SAFEGUARDING CONFIDENCES

Core Principle

Client trust requires appropriate protection of confidential and private information.

Intent

To protect the privacy rights of clients, organizations, and individuals by safeguarding confidential information.

Guidelines

A member shall:

- Safeguard the confidences and privacy rights of present, former, and prospective clients and employees.
- Protect privileged, confidential, or insider information gained from a client or organization.
- Immediately advise an appropriate authority if a member discovers that confidential information is being divulged by an employee of a client company or organization.

Examples of Improper Conduct Under This Provision:

- A member changes jobs, takes confidential information, and uses that information in the new position to the detriment of the former employer.
- A member intentionally leaks proprietary information to the detriment of some other party.

CONFLICTS OF INTEREST

Core Principle

Avoiding real, potential or perceived conflicts of interest builds the trust of clients, employers, and the publics.

Intent

- To earn trust and mutual respect with clients or employers.
- To build trust with the public by avoiding or ending situations that put one's personal or professional interests in conflict with society's interests.

Guidelines

A member shall:

- Act in the best interests of the client or employer, even subordinating the member's personal interests.
- Avoid actions and circumstances that may appear to compromise good business judgment or create a conflict between personal and professional interests.
- Disclose promptly any existing or potential conflict of interest to affected clients or organizations.
- Encourage clients and customers to determine if a conflict exists after notifying all affected parties.

Examples of Improper Conduct Under This Provision:

- The member fails to disclose that he or she has a strong financial interest in a client's chief competitor.
- The member represents a "competitor company" or a "conflicting interest" without informing a prospective client.

ENHANCING THE PROFESSION

Core Principle

Public relations professionals work constantly to strengthen the public's trust in the profession.

Intent

- To build respect and credibility with the public for the profession of public relations.
- To improve, adapt and expand professional practices.

Guidelines

A member shall:

- Acknowledge that there is an obligation to protect and enhance the profession.
- Keep informed and educated about practices in the profession to ensure ethical conduct.
- Actively pursue personal professional development.
- Decline representation of clients or organizations that urge or require actions contrary to this Code.
- Accurately define what public relations activities can accomplish.
- Counsel subordinates in proper ethical decision making.
- Require that subordinates adhere to the ethical requirements of the Code.
- Report ethical violations, whether committed by PRSA members or not, to the appropriate authority.

Examples of Improper Conduct Under This Provision:

- A PRSA member declares publicly that a product the client sells is safe, without disclosing evidence to the contrary.
- A member initially assigns some questionable client work to a non-member practitioner to avoid the ethical obligation of PRSA membership.

* * *

INTERNATIONAL ASSOCIATION OF BUSINESS COMMUNICATORS [IABC] CODE OF ETHICS FOR PROFESSIONAL COMMUNICATORS

Preface

Because hundreds of thousands of business communicators worldwide engage in activities that affect the lives of millions of people, and because this power carries with it significant social responsibilities, the International Association of Business Communicators developed the Code of Ethics for Professional Communicators.

The Code is based on three different yet interrelated principles of professional communication that apply throughout the world.

These principles assume that just societies are governed by a profound respect for human rights and the rule of law; that ethics, the criteria for determining what is right and wrong, can be agreed upon by members of an organization; and, that understanding matters of taste requires sensitivity to cultural norms.

These principles are essential:

- Professional communication is legal.
- Professional communication is ethical.
- Professional communication is in good taste.

Recognizing these principles, members of IABC will:

engage in communication that is not only legal but also ethical and sensitive to cultural values and beliefs; engage in truthful, accurate and fair communication that facilitates respect and mutual understanding; and, adhere to the following articles of the IABC Code of Ethics for Professional Communicators.

Because conditions in the world are constantly changing, members of IABC will work to improve their individual competence and to increase the body of knowledge in the field with research and education.

Articles

1. Professional communicators uphold the credibility and dignity of their profession by practicing honest, candid and timely communication and by fostering the free flow of essential information in accord with the public interest.
2. Professional communicators disseminate accurate information and promptly correct any erroneous communication for which they may be responsible.
3. Professional communicators understand and support the principles of free speech, freedom of assembly, and access to an open marketplace of ideas; and, act accordingly.
4. Professional communicators are sensitive to cultural values and beliefs and engage in fair and balanced communication activities that foster and encourage mutual understanding.
5. Professional communicators refrain from taking part in any undertaking which the communicator considers to be unethical.
6. Professional communicators obey laws and public policies governing their professional activities and are sensitive to the spirit of all laws and regulations and, should any law or public policy be violated, for whatever reason, act promptly to correct the situation.

7. Professional communicators give credit for unique expressions borrowed from others and identify the sources and purposes of all information disseminated to the public.
8. Professional communicators protect confidential information and, at the same time, comply with all legal requirements for the disclosure of information affecting the welfare of others.
9. Professional communicators do not use confidential information gained as a result of professional activities for personal benefit and do not represent conflicting or competing interests without written consent of those involved.
10. Professional communicators do not accept undisclosed gifts or payments for professional services from anyone other than a client or employer.
11. Professional communicators do not guarantee results that are beyond the power of the practitioner to deliver.
12. Professional communicators are honest not only with others but also, and most importantly, with themselves as individuals; for a professional communicator seeks the truth and speaks that truth first to the self.

Enforcement and Communication of the IABC Code for Professional Communicators

IABC fosters compliance with its Code by engaging in global communication campaigns rather than through negative sanctions. However, in keeping with the sixth article of the IABC Code, members of IABC who are found guilty by an appropriate governmental agency or judicial body of violating laws and public policies governing their professional activities may have their membership terminated by the IABC executive board following procedures set forth in the association's bylaws.

IABC encourages the widest possible communication about its Code.

The IABC Code of Ethics for Professional Communicators is published in several languages and is freely available to all: Permission is hereby granted to any individual or organization wishing to copy and incorporate all or part of the IABC Code into personal and corporate codes, with the understanding that appropriate credit be given to IABC in any publication of such codes.

The IABC Code is published in the association's annual directory, The WorldBook of IABC Communicators. The association's monthly magazine, *Communication World*, publishes periodic articles dealing with ethical issues. At least one session at the association's annual conference is devoted to ethics. The international headquarters of IABC, through its professional development activities, encourages and supports efforts by IABC student chapters, professional chapters, and districts/regions to conduct meetings and workshops devoted to the topic of ethics and the IABC Code. New and renewing members of IABC sign the following statement as part of their application: "I have reviewed and understand the IABC Code of Ethics for Professional Communicators."

As a service to communicators worldwide, inquiries about ethics and questions or comments about the IABC Code may be addressed to members of the IABC Ethics Committee. The IABC Ethics Committee is composed of at least three accredited members of IABC who serve staggered three-year terms. Other IABC members may serve on the committee with the approval of the IABC executive committee. The functions of the Ethics Committee are to assist with professional development activities dealing with ethics and to offer advice and assistance to individual communicators regarding specific ethical situations.

While discretion will be used in handling all inquiries about ethics, absolute confidentiality cannot be guaranteed. Those wishing more information about the IABC Code or specific advice about ethics are encouraged to contact IABC World Headquarters (One Hallidie Plaza, Suite 600, San Francisco, CA 94102 USA; phone, 415-544-4700; fax, 415-544-4747).

THE SEATTLE TIMES: NEWSROOM POLICIES AND GUIDELINES

January 29, 1999

The following are standards of professional conduct for a Seattle Times staff that already conforms to high standards of journalistic integrity.

These standards set forth guidelines of honorable conduct. They cannot cover every circumstance or answer every question involving professional conduct. But the guidelines set the tone for what's expected of everyone in the News and Editorial Departments. Editors should make sure that freelancers whose work appears in The Times are not in violation of our policies.

Staff members covered by the Guild Agreement are not to engage in outside activities which (1) consist of or include services performed for any medium in competition with The Times, (2) exploit their connection with The Times, or (3) are performed for any noncompetitive employer to the embarrassment of The Times businesswise. These guidelines are intended to clarify the provisions of that Agreement. Should there be any conflict between application of these guidelines and the Guild Agreement, the Guild Agreement shall prevail. Any dispute as to application of these guidelines to staff members covered by that Agreement shall be resolved pursuant to the Guild Agreement.

General standards

Fundamental for staff members of The Times is the obligation to perform their duties as the professionals they are. Interpretation of what conduct is appropriate in any particular situation is based upon professional responsibility. In no instance shall individual interests conflict with or appear to conflict with staff members' professional duties at The Times. The integrity of this newspaper evolves from the integrity of each member of the staff.

Each of us is to avoid impropriety, conflicts of interest or the appearance of impropriety or conflicts of interest.

Misuse of employee status

Staff members should not use their connections with The Times to receive any benefit or advantage in commercial transactions or for other personal gain.

Example: It is improper to use The Times stationery to write a personal complaint to a merchant or public agency. In a personal complaint situation or business transaction, avoid any implication that you are acting for The Times or threatening to use your newspaper connections for personal gain.

Employment and outside interests

The first obligation of staff members is to perform the duties for which they are employed by The Times.

Any outside employment should not put the staff member in a possible conflict of interest. In any such other employment, a staff member's title or assignment at The Times is not to be exploited.

There is a risk of conflict of interest or the appearance of such conflict of interest in work in publicity or public relations, whether paid or unpaid, in involvement in boards of directors, committees, etc., even of charitable and/ or social-welfare organizations, or in accepting appointments to boards and commissions having to do with public policy. Therefore, staff members should advise an editor of any involvement or affiliation which might result in a conflict of interests. Staff members should not serve as official scorers or contest judges or have other official involvement in an event the newspaper is covering. Staff members faced with such invitations or personal interests should advise, as appropriate, the editor, managing editor or editorial-page editor.

Free-lancing

Free-lancing for publications not in direct competition with The Times usually is permissible. Staff members writing or photographing on a continuing basis for a noncompetitive newspaper or magazine should advise the editor or managing editor for the News Department staff and the editorial-page editor for the Editorial Department staff of such continuing relationships.

Contests

Staff members may not enter articles or photographs published in The Times in contests that are not sponsored by professional journalistic organizations. An exception would be a contest of journalistic excellence sponsored by a foundation deemed by the appropriate editors previously listed to be free of commercial or self-serving interests. No awards of significant value may be accepted from any organizations other than those just described.

Investment

A staff member could embarrass The Times businesswise and exploit his or her connection with The Times by having a business relationship with a news source or by making news decisions that involve businesses in which he or she has a personal investment. Staff members with investments or stock holdings in corporations should avoid making news decisions that involve those corporations.

Staff members should advise an editor if they are uncertain about the possibility of conflict of interest or the appearance of conflict of interest in business relations or personal investments.

Example: If a reporter were assigned to cover a Utility Commission hearing on an electric company's rate increase and that reporter owned stock in the utility, the reporter should let his or her editor know of the investment.

Political activity

Our profession demands impartiality. If a staff member is a candidate for public office, whether the office is nonpartisan or unpaid, or is working, for pay or as a volunteer, in a political campaign or organization or has a close relative (spouse, parent, child, brother or sister) in a political campaign or organization, the staff member should not report on or make news judgments about such a campaign or organization. A staff member should advise his or her editor before reporting on or making news judgments about campaigns or organizations if there is a possibility of a conflict of interest or the appearance of a conflict of interest.

A staff member should not display in the News or Editorial Departments candidate posters or placards supporting or denouncing a candidate, political party or public issue. To do so could give the impression, intended or not, of partiality.

Relationships

A member of The Times staff should not write or photograph or make news judgment about any individual related to him or her (spouse, parent, child, sibling or in-laws), or with whom the staff member has a close personal relationship.

Travel

Free trips are prohibited except in the rarest of circumstances, and then only with the approval, as appropriate, of the editor, managing editor or editorial-page editor. All expenses—transportation, lodging, meals and incidentals—involved in travel for news coverage or background information will be paid by The Times.

If airlines or cruise firms won't accept payment for inaugural flights or maiden voyages, such trips will not be taken.

Staff members may not use their Times connections to solicit trips or special press rates or press fares from airlines or other transport or from travel organizations, hotels, agencies and domestic or foreign governments.

Some possible exceptions that would require the approval, as appropriate, of the editor, managing editor or editorial-page editor:

- If an airline or cruise firm is under the control of a totalitarian government or any other government which refuses to allow payment and if the inaugural flight or maiden voyage is of compelling news value, the appropriate editor previously mentioned would waive the rule.
- Either of the three editors may, as appropriate, approve a reduced-fare trip or special travel arrangement if it is the only way to complete an assignment, such as when military transport is involved or when a staff member needs to be aboard a press plane of an athletic team or political candidate.

- In case of the team or candidate plane, the newspaper would ask to be billed for the shared cost involved.

Staff members are to use common sense and discretion in emergency situations.

Example: If there is a shipping disaster off the Coast and a military helicopter is the only transportation available, the staff members covering the story could accept the ride if there's no time to communicate for approval from an editor. However, an editor should be informed of the circumstances as soon as possible after return to the office.

Another example: If a Boeing plane is on its first flight and a Times reporter and photographer are offered places on a chase plane—the only plane allowed in the area by the Federal Aviation Administration—we could accept the invitation with the approval of the editor or managing editor. This is another example of altering the rule when the news value is of compelling significance.

Tickets

We pay our own expenses to cover the news.

Reporters, photographers and editors assigned to cover sports, other spectator events or political events for spot news or future use of information may use press boxes, review seats, press rooms and other special facilities. However, The Times wants to pay for its share of such accommodations and will wherever possible.

When possible, staff members should pay for tickets and food and refreshments served at such events.

It is improper for staff members who are not on assignment to attend events as nonpaying spectators or to accept free meals provided by sports, political or other newssource organizations.

Free tickets or passes to sports events, movies, theatrical productions, fairs, circuses, ice shows and other events for which the public pays shall not be accepted by staff members and their families. When tickets to such events are delivered to a Times editor, the tickets should be returned with a letter courteously declining them and with an explanation of our policy.

Staff members who attend the events for professional reasons will pay for tickets and will be reimbursed by The Times.

Nightclub admission or cover charges and costs of meals and other refreshments incurred in professional work will be paid by The Times.

When it is socially awkward or even impossible to pay for a meal, refreshments or entertainment, a staff member should use good judgment in how far to go in insisting on paying. When someone insists on buying a staff member a meal or a drink, the staff member should try to reciprocate at a later date.

Gifts

We accept no work-connected gifts or gratuities of significant value. We don't accept free lodging, sample merchandise, special press rates or any other reduced rate or no-pay arrangements not available to the general public.

Gifts of insignificant value—key chain, pencil holder, calendar, etc.—may be kept if it's awkward to return them.

Gifts of significant value will be returned to the donor with an explanation of our policy. Where it is impractical to return a gift, it will be given to a charity.

Gifts of liquor, wine and beer are considered of more than token value and may not be kept.

Books and records

Books and records sent to The Times for review are considered to be news handouts or releases. They are not to be sold.

A book, a record or a tape may be kept by the person to whom it is assigned for review. Books and recordings not reviewed are to go to departmental editors, then to the editor's secretary. Staff members may then check out the material from the newsroom lending library. Periodically, the accumulated books and recordings will be sent to charity organizations.

Books of reference value (arts, sciences, architecture, medicine, etc.) that would be helpful to a reporter or editor dealing with such subjects may be kept in such specialists' files at The Times.

Memberships

Staff members may not accept free or reduced-rate memberships in private clubs or other organizations when such memberships involve or appear to involve a staff member's position at The Times. The Times will pay the costs when such memberships are considered by The Times to be necessary for news or editorial purposes.

Use of products

Because of their Times status, staff members sometimes are offered free or reduced-rate purchase of products, merchandise or services not available to the general public. Staff members should not take advantage of such offers. If there is felt to be a need for clarification, staff members should review the policy with an appropriate editor. Examples of such products include cameras or other photographic equipment and supplies, automobiles, boats, furniture, sporting goods, appliances and clothing. With the permission, as appropriate, of the editor, managing editor, or editorial-page editor, a staff member may use for a short time a product to test or evaluate it for news or feature articles or for photography.

Performing services for competing medium

1. No staff member, except when acting in the capacity of a member or officer of the Guild. may appear on a competing broadcasting medium or supply material to a competing print medium without prior approval from his or her department head. Approval normally will not be given if the appearance or material constitutes performing services for the competing medium unless it serves the interests of The Seattle Times.
2. Examples of such normally prohibited work include:
   a) Performing services as a panelist on a television or radio program.
   b) Performing services as a professional specialist (e.g., politics, religion, science, medicine, drama, visual arts, films, sports, etc.), including interviews before, during, or after sporting events.
3. Approval normally will be given for:
   a) Appearance on any broadcast medium which would, in the opinion of the management, serve or promote the interests of The Seattle Times. If approval is given, time spent on such appearances shall be considered working time and The Seattle Times will compensate staff members accordingly. Any compensation received by staff members from outside sources for such appearances will normally be deducted from, and offset against, any compensation payable by The Seattle Times for such appearances.
   b) Appearances on any broadcasting medium to respond to questions involving newsworthy events involving The Seattle Times, such as a labor dispute, demonstration, lawsuit, award, comic selection, circulation growth, new technology, etc.

c) Appearing on any public-broadcasting medium or submitting material to nonadvertising publications such as church periodicals, university publications, and scholarly journals.

Ownership of work product

Under the federal Copyright Act, any material produced by a Seattle Times employee that is within the scope of his or her employment is considered "work for hire," whether or not published in The Seattle Times, and copyright belongs to The Seattle Times. Such material may not be sold, licensed, or otherwise authorized for republication except by permission of The Seattle Times and on such terms as it may specify as copyright owner.

References

Alter, J. (1996, May 27). Beneath the waves. *Newsweek, 127.*

Baker, C. E. (1992). *Human Liberty and Freedom of Speech.* New York: Oxford University Press.

Bayles, M. D. (1989). *Professional ethics* (2nd ed.). Belmont, CA: Wadsworth Publishing Company.

Bok, S. (1982). *Secrets: On the ethics of concealment and revelation.* New York: Pantheon Books.

Bok, S. (1994). *Violence, children, and the press: Eight rationales inhibiting public policy debates* (Discussion Paper D-16). Cambridge, MA: The Joan Shorenstein Barone Center for Press, Politics and Public Policy, Harvard University, John F. Kennedy School of Government.

Bok, S. (1998). *Mayhem: Violence as public entertainment.* Reading, MA: Addison-Wesley.

Brill, S. (1999, October). Curiosity vs. privacy. *Brill's Content, 2,* 98–129.

Bruning, F. (1992, May 4). How a private citizen lost his privacy rights. *Maclean's, 105,* 13.

Byrd, J. (1993). *Let's stop abusing the First Amendment.* Ruhl Lecture. Eugene, OR: University of Oregon School of Journalism and Communication.

Carter, S. (1996). *Integrity.* New York: Basic Books (Harper Collins).

Christians, C. G., Rotzoll, K. B., & Fackler, M. (1997). *Media Ethics* (5th ed.). New York: Longman.

Chua-Eoan, H. G. (1992, April 20). The burden of truth. *People Weekly,* 50–51.

Cunningham, S. (1999). Getting it right: Aristotle's 'golden mean' as theory deterioration. *Journal of Mass Media Ethics, 14*(1).

Davis, K., & Blomstrom, R. L. (1975). *Business and society* (3rd ed.). New York: McGraw Hill.

Day, L. (1997). *Ethics in media communications: Cases and controversies* (2nd ed.). Belmont, CA: Wadsworth Publishing Company.

De Nesnera, A. (2002). *Payne Awards Nomination Letter.* University of Oregon School of Journalism and Communication, Eugene, OR.

Effron, E. (1999, October). Letter from the editor. *Brill's Content, 2,* 7.

Entman, R. (1989). *Democracy without citizens: Media and the decay of American politics.* New York: Oxford University Press.

Feinberg, J. (1984). *Harm to others.* New York: Oxford University Press.

Foss, S. K., & Griffin, C. L. (1995). Beyond persuasion: A proposal for an invitational rhetoric. *Communication Monographs, 2,* 2–18.

Freedman, M. (1988). Social responsibility and compensatory justice. In J. Callahan (Ed.), *Ethical issues in professional life* (pp. 349–354). New York: Oxford University Press.

Fritzsche, D. J. (1991). A model of decision-making incorporating ethical values. *Journal of Business Ethics, 10*, 841–852.
Gearhart, S. M. (1979). The womanization of rhetoric. *Women's Studies International Quarterly, 2*, 195–201.
Gersh, D. (1992, April 18). Unclear boundaries: Was it news that former tennis pro Arthur Ashe has AIDS? *Editor and Publisher*, 7–10.
Gert, B. (1988). *Morality: A new justification for the moral rules*. New York: Oxford University Press.
Gilligan, C. (1982). *In a different voice*. Cambridge, MA: Harvard University Press.
Grunig, J., & Hunt, T. (1984). *Managing public relations*. New York: Holt, Rinehart, and Winston.
Hampton, J. (1997). *Political philosophy*. New York: Westview Press.
Harris, J. (2001). Remarks to the American Society of Newspaper Editors.
Jefferson, T. (1823). *Letter to M. Corey*. Archived at Monticello: Jefferson Digital Archive. Available at http://etext.virginia.edu/jefferson/
Jensen, J. V. (1981). *Argumentation: Reasoning in communication*. New York: Van Nostrand.
Johannesen, R. L. What should we teach about formal codes of communication ethics. *Journal of Mass Media Ethics, 3*(1), 59–64.
Johannesen, R. L. (2002). *Ethics in Human communication* (5th ed.). Prospect Heights, IL: Waveland Press.
Kennedy, G. A. (1991). *Aristotle on rhetoric: A theory of civic discourse*. New York: Oxford University Press.
Klaidman, S., & Beauchamp, T. (1987). *The Virtuous Journalist*. Oxford, UK: Oxford University Press.
Kultgen, J. (1988). *Ethics and professionalism*. Philadelphia: University of Pennsylvania Press.
Lasch, C. (1990). Publicity and the lost art of argument. *Gannett Center Journal*, 1–11.
Lebacqz, K. (1985). *Professional ethics: Power and paradox*. Nashville, TN: Abingdon.
Lippmann, W. (1922). *Public opinion*. New York: Macmillan.
MacIntyre, A. (1981). *After virtue*. Notre Dame, IN: University of Notre Dame Press.
Manning, R. C. (1992). *Speaking from the Heart: A Feminist Perspective on Ethics*. Lanham, MD: Rowman & Littlefield.
McMannus, J. (2002). *Does Wall Street Have to Trump Main Street?* Available at www.gradethenews.org
Merrill, J. C. (1997). *Journalism ethics: Philosophical foundations for news media*. New York: St. Martin's Press.
Meyer, P. (1987). *Ethical journalism*. New York: Longman.
Midgley, M. (1991). *Can't we make moral judgments?* Bristol: Bristol Press.
Midgley, M. (1994). *The ethical primate: Humans, freedom and morality*. London: Routledge.
Midgley, M. (1995). *Beast and man: The roots of human natures*. London: Routledge.
Mill, J. S. (1991). In J. Gray (Ed.), *On liberty and other essays*. New York: Oxford University Press.
Morrow, L. (1992, April 20). Fair game? *Time, 139*, 74.
Postman, N. (1992). *Technopoly: The surrender of culture to technology*. New York: Alfred K. Knopf.
Preston, I. (1975). *The great American blow-up: Puffery in advertising and selling*. Madison, WI: University of Wisconsin Press.
Price, M. (1998, November). Out there: Hardball with a heart. *Brill's Content, 1*, 83–85.
Rachels, J. (1993). *The Elements of Moral Philosophy*. New York: McGraw Hill.
Ridder, T. (2001). Mercury News Will Remain Strong in Hard Times. Available at www.poynter.org
Ridley, M. (1998). *The origins of virtue*. New York: Penguin Books.
Rosemont, H. J. *Whose democracy? Which rights?: A Confucian critique of modern western liberalism*. Unpublished paper, St. Mary's College of Maryland.
Rosen, J. (1993). Beyond objectivity. *Nieman Reports*.
Ross, W. D. (1930). *The right and the good*. Oxford: Clarendon Press.
Ruggiero, V. R. (1973). *The moral imperative*. Port Washington, NY: Alfred Publishing Company.

Ruggiero, V. R. (1975). *Beyond feelings: A guide to critical thinking.* Port Washington, NY: Alfred Publishing Company.

Saltzman, J. (1997). A chill settles over investigative journalism: Food Lion markets' victory over ABC News. *USA Today (magazine), 125,* 29.

Sandel, M. (1982). *Liberalism and the limits of justice.* Cambridge: Cambridge University Press.

Sandel, M. (1996). *Democracy's discontent: America in search of a public philosophy.* Cambridge, MA: The Belknap Press of Harvard University Press.

Scanlon, T. M. (1998). *What we owe each other.* Cambridge, MA: The Belknap Press of Harvard University Press.

Simon, W. H. (1978). The ideology of advocacy: Procedural justice and professional ethics. *Wisconsin Law Review*, 29–144.

Smith, H. (1994). *World's religions: A guide to our wisdom traditions.* San Francisco: Harper.

Sproule, J. M. (1980). *Argument: Language and its influence.* New York: McGraw-Hill.

Steiner, L. (1989). Feminist theorizing and communication ethics. *Communication Monographs, 12,* 157–173.

Stone, I. F. (1988). *The Trial of Socrates.* Boston: Little Brown & Company.

Sullivan, R. J. (1994). *An introduction to Kant's ethics.* Cambridge: Cambridge University Press.

Tronto, J. (1993). *Moral boundaries.* New York: Routledge.

Wagner, D. (1997). Making news, breaking ethics. *Insight on the News, 13*(10), 10.

Wheeler, T., & Gleason, T. (1994, August). *Digital photography and the ethics of photofiction: Four tests for assessing the reader's qualified expectation of reality.* Paper presented at the Association for Education in Journalism and Mass Communication.

Wilson, J. Q. (1993). *The moral sense.* New York: The Free Press.

Wood, J. T. (1994). *Who cares? Women, care, and culture.* Carbondale, IL: Southern Illinois University Press.

Wrighter, C. P. (1972). Weasel words: God's little helpers. In *I Can Sell You Anything.* New York: Ballantine Books.

Author Index

A

Alter, J., 25
Aristotle, 99

B

Baker, C. E., 2, 106, 108
Bayles, M. D., 49, 51, 53, 54, 56, 58, 61, 63, 139, 140
Beauchamp, T. L., 148, 150, 156
Blomstrom, R. L., 42
Bok, S., 124, 152
Brill, S., 155
Brittain Mckee, K., 28
Bruning, F., 169
Byrd, J., 58, 62, 91

C

Carter, S., 91, 102, 148, 153, 155
Christians, C. G., 18, 28
Chua-Eoan, H. G., 168
Cunningham, S., 99
Curley, E., 103

D

Davis, K., 42
Day, L., 33, 125, 163
de Nesnera, A., 146

E

Effron, E., 155
Entman, R., 6, 7

F

Fackler, M., 18, 28
Feinberg, J., 148
Foss, S. K., 130
Fritzsche, D. J., 86, 177
Freedman, M., 41

G

Gearhart, S. M., 130
Gersh, D., 168, 170
Gert, B., 7, 34
Gilligan, C., 160
Gleason, T., 135

Griffin, C. L., 130
Grunig, J. E., 8, 30, 41, 130, 164

H

Hampton, J., 110
Harris, J., 45, 46, 48
Hart, J., 46
Hunt, T., 8, 30, 130, 164

J

Jefferson, T., 5
Jensen, J. V., 134
Johannesen, R. L., 2, 14, 67, 68, 69, 98, 127

K

Kennedy, G. A., 131
Klaidman, S., 148, 150, 156
Kultgen, J., 53, 54

L

Lasch, C., 43, 55
Lebacqz, K., 69
Lippmann, W., 80

M

MacIntyre, A., 111
Manning, R. C., 161
McMannus, J., 47
Merrill, J. C., 81, 110
Meyer, P., 67
Midgley, M., 77, 122
Mill, J. S., 104, 110
Morrow, L., 169

P

Preston, I., 125
Price, M., 154
Postman, N., 105

R

Rachels, J., 33, 75, 76, 83, 98
Ridder, T., 47
Ridley, M., 77
Rosemont Jr., H., 22, 161
Rosen, J., 43
Ross, W. D., 34, 38
Rotzoll, K. B., 18, 28
Ruggiero, V. R., 19, 177

S

Saltzman, J., 124
Sandel, M. J., 111, 166
Scanlon, T. M., 34
Schauer, F., 105
Simon, W. H., 60
Smith, H., 110
Sproule, J. M., 134
Steiner, L., 162
Stone, I. F., 15
Sullivan, R. J., 89

T

Taylor, H., 95
Tronto, J., 160

W

Wagner, D., 124
Wheeler, T., 135
Wilson, J. Q., 77
Wood, J. T., 161
Wrighter, C. P., 126

Subject Index

A

Accountability, 7–9, 10
Advertising, 14–15, 17, 51–53, 57, 125–130, 156–159, 197–198
Advocacy, 60
Agency, 60
Aristotle, 81, 99, 101
Autonomy, ix, 44, 61, 166

C

Care, 162–165
Case studies
  broadcasting, 144–146
  journalist defined, 72–73
  Newsweek, 23–25
  obligation, 46–48
  patriotism, 26–27
  privacy, 168–171
Claimants, 181
Coercion, 2
Communication, 2–3
Communication-caused harm, 147
Communitarianism, 55, 109
Community interest, ix
Consequences, 32–33, 37–40, 42
Consequentialism, 91–97, 184
  Mill, John Stuart, 94–95, 104
Constraint, 9
Credibility, 12
Cultural relativism, 75

D

Defamation, 119–120
Duties, 34–35

E

Egoism, 92–93
Ethical theory, ix, 12–13, 74
  consequentialism, 91–97, 184
  means and ends, 86
  nonconsequentialism, 86–91, 184
Ethics
  decision making, 172–180
  definition, 1
  standards, 17–18
  unethical, 1–2
  virtue, 98–102

F

Fiduciary model, 61–66

Free speech theories, 102, 108–112
  Milton, John, 103–104
  Spinoza, Benedict, 103

H

Harm, 148–151, 154–161, 177, 182, 190–191
Harm principle, 151–152
Hobbes, Thomas, 82–83
Hypothetical, 45–46, 71–72, 115–116, 142–144, 186

I

Ideal, 19, 183
Immorality, 1–2
Instrumental value, 19
Integrity, 3
Intrinsic value, 19

J

Journalism, 43, 51–57, 122–125, 141, 154–156, 191–194, *see also* News media
  paternalism, 58–59

L

Legality, 20–21
Legal moralism, principle of, 153–154
Legal paternalism, principle of, 153
Libertarianism, 40
  and obligation, 40–41
Liberty theory, 106–108
Linkages, 29–32, 38–39
Locke, John, 83
Loyalty, 16–17, 65

M

Marketplace, 4
Marketplace of ideas, 104–105
Mass media, 11–12
  differences, 13–16
  ethical standards, 17–18
Media
  and ethics, 22
  and morality, 3
  democratic foundations, 4–5
  obligations, 42, 44
  professionalism, 49–51
Moral claimant, 28–29
Moral decision making, 2, 172–180
Moral excuses
  constraint, 9
Moral guidelines, 21
Morality
  definition, 1
Moral responsibility, 149–150

N

News media, 4, 13–14, 16–17, *see also* Journalism
Nonconsequentialism, 86–91, 184
  Kant, Immanuel, 87–91

O

Obligation, 32–41, 42, 44
  duties, 34–35
Offense principle, 152
Organizational systems theory, 29

P

Paternalism, 58–59, 153
Persuasion, 129–135, 163–165
  emotional appeal, 133
  reasoned argument, 132
Plato, 79–81
Principle, 19
Privacy, 10–11, 120
Pro bono work, 55–57
Professional–client relationship, 59, 62
Professional codes, 21, 66–70, 188–221
Professionalism, 49–51, 70
  values, 53–54
Professional responsibility, 150–151
Public interest, 5, 53–54, 56
Public journalism, 55–56, 162–163
Public relations, 5, 15–16, 17, 51–53, 57, 125–130, 156–159, 204–211

R

Reason, 76–77
Relativism, 75, 77
  cultural, 75
Responsibility, 7–9, 149–151, 160, *see also* Social responsibility
Rhetoric, 15
Rousseau, Jean-, 84–85

S

Social contract theory, 78–79
Social responsibility, 41–44, *see also* Responsibility
Subjectivism, 75–76

T

Trust, 62
Truth, x, 117–119, 121–123, 125–129, 135–137, 140–141, 166, 189, 194, 197

U

Unethical, 1–2
Utilitarianism, 93–94, 95–97
  distributive justice, 97

V

Values, 18–20, 53–54
Virtue ethics, 98–102